Murder at the Office

NEW★
HORIZON
PRESS

Dear Reader

We proudly present the newest addition to our internationally acclaimed true crime series of *Real People/Incredible Stories*. These riveting thrillers spotlight men and women who perform extraordinary deeds against tremendous odds: to fight for justice, track down elusive killers, protect the innocent or exonerate the wrongly accused. Their stories, told in their own voices, and in their own words, reveal the untold drama and anguish behind the headlines of those who face horrific realities and find the resiliency to fight back...

Murder at the Office: A Survivor's True Story is the incredible true story of what became known as "The Atlanta Massacre," one of the worst acts of workplace violence in America. **Murder at the Office** tells of Brent C. Doonan's heroic escape and survival from mass murderer Mark O. Barton, a killer who left nine dead and many others wounded on a hot day in July, 1999.

The next time you want to read a crackling, suspenseful page-turner, which is also a true account of a real life hero illustrating the resiliency of the human spirit – look for the New Horizon Press logo.

Sincerely,

Dr. Joan S. Dunphy
Publisher & Editor in Chief

Real People/Incredible Stories

Murder at the Office
A Survivor's True Story

by

Brent C. Doonan

New Horizon Press
Far Hills, NJ

New Horizon Press
P.O. Box 669
Far Hills, NJ 07931

Doonan, Brent C.
Murder at the Office: A Survivor's True Story

Cover Design: Robert Aulicino
Interior Design: Susan M. Sanderson

Library of Congress Control Number: 2005924255

ISBN 10: 0-88282-272-1
ISBN 13: 978-088282-272-3

New Horizon Press books may be purchased in bulk quantities for educational, business, or sales promotional use. For information please write to New Horizon Press, Special Sales Department, PO Box 669, Far Hills, NJ 07931 or call 800-533-7978.
email: nhp@newhorizonpressbooks.com

www.newhorizonpressbooks.com

Manufactured in the USA

2010 2009   2008   2007   2006 / 5   4   3   2   1

Dedication

This book is dedicated to all victims of violent crime, especially to those affected by Mark Barton's actions on July 29, 1999. Because of the litigation that immediately followed the shootings, I was forbidden to express my sincere condolences to the families of those who lost loved ones. I continue to keep you and your families in my thoughts and prayers.

This story is also my catharsis. The reliving and writing about the details of that tragic day is my final release.

My goal in sharing this story and those of others who also survived is to remind everyone to believe in the power of hope. Though at times this story may be difficult to read, in the end it is a story of living. For there is no medicine as strong, no inducement as great, nor encouragement so powerful as the answered prayer for life tomorrow. And the reminder that if life comes crashing down, we must pick up the pieces and carry on.

Author's Note

This book is based on the experiences of Brent C. Doonan and reflects his perceptions of the past, present and future. The personalities, events, actions and conversations portrayed within this story have been taken from his memories, interviews, research, court documents, letters, personal papers, press accounts and the memories of some participants.

In an effort to safeguard the privacy of certain people, some individuals' names and identifying characteristics have been altered. Events involving the characters happened as described. Only minor details have been changed.

Table of Contents

Acknowledgements

It has taken me over six years to come to grips with July 29, 1999 and equally as long to organize the details of that day so that I might share this story with others. I would like to express my appreciation to those who have assisted in making this book a reality.

Specifically, I would like to thank the following:

I gratefully acknowledge my friends and family who encouraged and supported me while writing about my experiences. I am especially grateful to my father, Kenny, who convinced me to take the time to share this story with you.

To my literary agents, Ron and Mary Laitsch, thank you for never giving up on this book. I am grateful for your relentless dedication.

To Dr. Joan Dunphy and the staff at New Horizon Press, thank you for believing in this story and your dedication to making it a success. I especially thank Chris Nielsen, Production Manager, for making a first time author feel so comfortable throughout the entire process. A special thank-you also goes to Christina Mucciolo for all her hard work and dedication to this project.

To Robert Woodcox, thank you for your assistance in reorganizing and rewriting portions of this book.

To Phillip Doran of applyingsystems.com for producing the marketing DVD simply because he believed in getting this story out to others. Thank you P.J.

To the doctors and staff at Northside Hospital in Atlanta, thank you for taking such good care of me and my family during our time of need. Your efforts will never be forgotten.

To the thousands of people who prayed for my recovery, many of whom I do not know, I remain most grateful.

Last but certainly not least, I want to thank my wife, Sarah. As you know, it was not easy for me to relive these experiences in such great detail. As a result of this book, I was forced to recover from the traumatic event not once but twice. Thank you for your undying encouragement, loving support and for never giving up on my dream to see this book to completion.

prologue

When Mark Barton strode into the Momentum Securities office, the stock market was down. The day traders were peering intently at their screens and no one looked up at the casually dressed former trader as he pulled out two objects from under his red shirt–a nickel-plated .45 caliber Colt and a black 9mm Glock.

"It's a bad trading day and it's about to get worse!" Barton said loudly.

Barton's first two shots hit Kevin Dial at close range. Dial was so close to the gun when it fired, gunpowder covered and burned into his skin around the wound through his back. The second bullet went straight to his heart killing him instantly.

Then Barton turned his guns on those at the work stations as pandemonium erupted.

"What the hell is going on here?"

Barton stopped this question with a bullet that ripped through Scott Webb's lung and lodged in his chest. Barton began working his way down the rows of work stations as he moved. He took a shot at Andrew Zaprzala and another at James Jordan, hitting him in the side. Jordan tried running towards a hallway door, but before he got there a second bullet struck him in the arm.

Next, two bullets struck Brad Schoemehl. One raced through his back and another through his shoulder. A single bullet hit Edward Quinn in the neck.

Barton wasn't finished. He looked in the direction of the receptionist's desk and shot Marci Brooking. Now he was on the move again. Reaching the front of the office, he fired three shots into Russell Brown, killing him immediately.

With sounds like firecrackers exploding in mid-air, Barton fired one gun then the other at Momentum employees. Bullet casings flew. The smell of death and gunpowder permeated the air. Employees that were hiding or already shot tried not to call attention to themselves. For good measure, Barton shot Webb again at point-blank range and fired a third bullet into Schoemehl.

Then Barton raced out the door to find his next target. He crossed Piedmont Road, a busy six lane road in the Buckhead financial district of Atlanta and approached the All-Tech Investment Group.

No one was aware that Mark Barton had just killed four people across the street when he entered the brokerage offices of All-Tech. Before he started losing big money, he had been a popular trader in the office. He had spent hours at a time sitting at a computer terminal trading stocks using All-Tech's advanced computer network. Clients were able to trade stocks on a second by second basis. Depending how the market was doing at that moment, traders could make large sums of money in minutes. Or as Barton found out, they could also lose it even faster.

Other traders knew him as a funny and outgoing man. He always had a pleasant way about him. Typically thirty to forty people were trading stocks. If his trading day was going well, Barton told everyone about his good fortune and hoped for the best for their days. If things took a decline, then he kept it to himself, not seeming to bother anyone with his problems. When asked, he had a flippant air about his losses; no matter how dramatic they were he simply said, "Ah, that's nothing."

The All-Tech staff hadn't seen Barton since he lost a large sum of money and was five figures in debt to them. Brent Doonan, the office manager of All-Tech, had taken a liking to Barton and was optimistic he would return to pay the money he owed. Brent had gotten nervous, since Barton hadn't contacted him for several weeks. He was relieved when he saw him that day, thinking they could square everything away.

So as Barton walked across the trading room floor, when traders saw him, they greeted him and chatted. Some asked where he had been and others commented about the bad market that day. Soon Barton excused himself after seeing Brent in the glass paneled conference room with a new client. With the same quirky smile he always had, Barton waved to him and motioned for Brent to come out. A short while later, Brent opened the door.

"Hey Brent, I need to talk to you. It's important. Can I have a minute?" Barton asked.

Brent replied, "Yes, Mark. Just a minute."

As he was closing the door, Barton added, "Hurry up Brent. You're really going to love this!"

Barton walked to the main office. He greeted the other office manager, Scott Manspeak,er and his assistant, Kathy Van Camp. They all began to chat. During the conversation, Scott noticed Barton's forearms. They had tiny specks of red all over them. Scott then noticed the specks on Barton's hands and the collar of his shirt. *He must have been painting and splattered himself,* Scott thought to himself.

While talking, Barton casually reached for the control rod to the blinds in the office. He slowly turned it and closed them. The bright windows looking out on the trading floor became sealed to outside observers and the room got significantly darker. He turned about and walked back out the door. Scott and Kathy were left wondering what was happening. Scott jokingly said, "What's he going to do, kill us?" They both laughed and continued their work.

Barton crossed the trading floor and headed back to the conference room. The typical smile he usually had was gone. He had a much more serious expression. He opened the door and said, "Brent, come here quick. Really, you're going to love this!"

Brent excused himself from the new trainee, got up and followed Barton to the conference room.

Walking over to the main office, Brent thought of what the big news Barton had to share could be. Perhaps it was the new product he was working on. A chemist by trade, Barton had often talked about a new soap he was developing. Maybe he finished it and got a large sum of money for it. Brent hoped that today would be the day Barton would repay the debt he owed to All-Tech. Brent hoped he was going to be given a check for $30,000.

As soon as Brent walked into the main office Barton closed the door behind them. Brent immediately noticed that the blinds were closed and suddenly felt cut off not only from the rest of the office, but from the world.

Barton's breathing became labored. He still had the same serious expression on his face. Then he said, "Today is going to be visual."

Brent was confused. He wasn't sure what that meant. Scott and Kathy stared silently, also wondering what Barton was talking about.

Barton pulled up his shirt and took out two handguns that were tucked in the waistband of his shorts. He crossed his arms over each other, pulling them out like a cowboy in a movie.

For a split second, Brent thought it was a joke. They were cap guns. This must be another one of Mark's childish pranks.

Seconds later, two bullets tore through Brent Doonan's body. He didn't feel any pain and it wasn't until he began to feel warm thick blood pooling around him that he realized what had happened. He began to panic. Quickly the searing pain wracked him. The pain was more intense than any he had ever felt in his life.

As Brent lay bleeding profusely, he heard several more gunshots go off over his head. He wasn't sure if he got shot again, but he then remembered there were two more people in the room with them, Brent's business partner, Scott, and their assistant, Kathy. He couldn't see either of them because of the way he had landed. His head was facing away from them. He knew not to turn. If Barton saw any movement he would know Brent was still alive. If he moved, it was very likely Barton would fire another bullet into him and make sure he was dead. He tried to lie still and not give any indication that he was breathing. Hopefully, Barton would leave the office and then when he was gone, Brent could get help.

But Barton stepped through the doorway of the office and began firing more shots. Brent could hear people screaming, running and falling to the floor. More gunshots cracked throughout the entire office. After Brent, Scott and Kathy, Barton turned his attention to the clients on the trading floor.

Brent knew he had to do something. He couldn't allow himself just to lie on the floor staring at the bottom of a computer printer. Scenarios raced through his head. He could try to get out of the building and get help. He could try to subdue Barton, but Brent quickly realized how unlikely it was that that would happen. Barton outweighed him by eighty pounds, was four inches taller and had at least two guns. Brent was badly wounded and continuing to bleed more and more. He wasn't in any condition to take Barton down. Somehow he had to make it out of the room and down a hallway to the nearest stairway so he could get to an exit. It was a long way to go, but better than the alternative, trying to get past Barton.

More gunshots continued to ring out and people fell lifeless to the floor or slumped in their chairs. As Brent struggled to get to his feet, he glimpsed Scott and Kathy, both lying on the floor not moving. Brent felt lightheaded and very weak. The sounds and smell of relentless gunfire from outside of the room made him nauseous. He tried clinging to the wall to steady himself. At each gunshot Brent instinctively wanted to get down on the floor, but in his unsteady condition he thought if he fell down again he would never make it back up.

Still, Brent struggled to pull himself up and saw Barton with his back to the door and still firing shots around the large trading room. Brent watched as Barton took careful aim at people trying to hide and then fired off shots in their direction. Feet, legs, heads, anything Barton could see he made an attempt to hit. Some bullets missed, others did not.

Jamshid Havash was hit in the back by a bullet from Barton's 9mm. He was killed instantly. Yuzef Liberson and Fred Herder tried to take cover, but Barton was faster. Herder was hit in the back and Liberson was struck in the head by a single bullet. Dean Delawalla attempted to race to an exit, but Barton stopped him with shot that struck him in the middle of his back. Barton shot him again as he was falling. Joseph Dessert was hit twice by the .45. One bullet struck his shoulder; the second hit his upper chest, killing him instantly.

Around one table, where a group was trying to hide, Barton shot at four people. Charles Williams was hit in the chest, Harry

Higginbotham in the head and Sang Yoon in the arm. Meredith Winnit, an office assistant, was hit in the back.

If Barton turned around and saw Brent he would surely try to finish him off. Playing dead was no longer an option. As Brent began to make his way out of the doorway, he watched as one trader tried frantically to run. He was making a dash for the door. He looked to Brent as if he was running on ice. The door seemingly never got closer. Obviously, the man was putting all his energy into his escape. Nevertheless, he seemed to be running in slow motion. Barton slowly raised one of his guns, took careful aim and pulled the trigger. The bullet struck the man square in the back. He instantly dropped to the floor. The momentum from running slid him another few feet. Then he stopped, lying face down, not moving.

As Brent tried to focus on getting out of the doorway he saw Barton raise his gun again. This time he was taking aim at a young woman. She was directly in front of Barton and had nowhere to go. The gun was a few feet from her head as Barton was about to squeeze the trigger. Suddenly Brent lunged from inside the doorway. He put all his weight and speed into knocking Barton off balance. The gun went off. The bullet missed the woman and shot out a computer monitor. Brent had hit Barton with his good shoulder and completely surprised him. However, it was only a temporary surprise. Barton quickly spun around and steadied himself. Brent quickly tried to make a dash around a conference table. Barton fired off two more shots at Brent. The first struck his left arm. The second hit him below his left shoulder blade and came out the left side of his chest.

Brent was still running towards the hallway. The pain he felt earlier had doubled. He ran down the hallway, occasionally bouncing into the sides of the walls, like he was a pinball. Everywhere Brent touched blood was left behind. Because of Brent's significant blood loss, the normally bright looking hallway now looked like it was black and gray. Brent didn't know if Barton was behind him or if he thought he was dead.

As he was stumbling down the hallway, Brent saw the service elevator. He had completely forgotten about it. The service room was tucked away in a small room that opened off into the hallway. Immediately he began frantically hitting the button. The motors behind the door began to make a whirring sound, but the doors didn't open. Brent realized that the elevator was on the top floor of the seven story building and would have to make its way all the way down. Panic took over and Brent tried to pry open the doors with his bloody hands. He crawled to the door and opened it slightly to see down the hallway. Suddenly Mark Barton appeared at the other end of the hallway. Brent's only hope was the elevator. He began muttering to himself, "Please God, don't let me die"…

chapter one

Misfit

Truman Barton was stationed in Germany when his and his wife, Gladys's, only son, Mark, was born in 1955. The family stayed in Europe until they were relocated to Sumter, South Carolina, during Mark's childhood.

Located in the heart of South Carolina, the city of Sumter lies within Sumter County in the midlands region of the state. A little under fifty miles from South Carolina's capitol, Columbia, Sumter dates back to 1845. Sumter was named after General Thomas Sumter, also known as the "Fighting Gamecock" during the American Revolution. General Sumter was the basis for Mel Gibson's character in the movie *The Patriot*. Sumter was once a quiet farming community until the arrival of the Shaw Air Force Base in 1941, which boosted the local economy and diversified the area. The Shaw Air Force Base is located ten miles from Sumter and is home to the Ninth Air Force and headquarters for the Twentieth Fighter Wing of the United States Air Force. Today, Sumter, South Carolina is also the home of the University of South Carolina.

The Bartons lived in a red brick house on a street lined with pecan and magnolia trees. Mark's father worked as a civilian contractor at the sprawling Shaw Air Force Base. A strict disciplinarian, Truman Barton was very stern with his son; the harsher the punishment, the better. Mark's father wanted to inflict a lesson that would make an impression, one that was not likely to be forgotten. In contrast, Mark's mother was thought of as a nice, quiet, gentle woman. She worked as a secretary at the local Methodist church.

Throughout school, Barton was very introverted. Most of the other students considered him a loner. Gangly and awkward as a teenager, he had few friends and he wasn't involved in school sports. On occasion, peering out from horn-rimmed glasses, he was called a "nerd" or "geek." He did not have a girlfriend, but was very focused and excelled in his course work, scoring well on standardized tests, particularly in math and chemistry. Needing someone to confide in during his sophomore year in high school, Barton began talking with Harry Taylor, a psychologist. Mark talked with Dr. Taylor about feeling like an outcast at school and the anger of not being able to fit in.

Taylor often asked Barton, "Mark, why don't you try out for one of the sports teams this year? It could be a great opportunity for you."

"I'm an outcast. Why should I try to participate?" Barton replied.

"Well, you wouldn't be an outcast if you got involved. You would feel part of a team. I think it would be a step in the right direction."

Barton just waved his arm and sighed. Though eventually he grew to have an imposing physique at 6'4" and 205 pounds, he never tried out for any of the sports teams.

Instead of playing sports or joining a club, Barton began using his analytical abilities for more than just academics. Taking an interest in petty crimes, it was as if he began to embrace his talent for going undetected. Before, he had hoped to be noticed, but now he began to think of how he could disappear into the shadows.

"Whenever I go anywhere I size up how to break in, where the money is, what I can steal and how I can get away," he confessed to Taylor.

Taylor thought Barton was becoming more and more withdrawn. He again suggested other school activities, but they were quickly refused by Barton.

Over time, Taylor observed that Barton was becoming angrier and angrier and "fancied himself a master criminal."

Soon, simply thinking about his plans was not good enough, so Barton started to test them out. Several of his schemes resulted in success, working exactly the way he had thought they would, but at fourteen he was caught breaking into a drug store.

His parents were very disappointed with him. It didn't look very appropriate that the son of an employee of the United States Air Force and a secretary for a local church was a thief. His father punished him severely and hoped that would set his son on a straight course.

Then at the age of sixteen the long-haired teenager's interest in chemistry heightened when he began taking psychedelic drugs. He had heard about the possible results when morning glory seeds are taken after they have been chemically treated. With patience and the right steps, a powder can be extracted from the seeds. When the powder is mixed with certain chemicals it can have a potent hallucinogenic effect, very similar to LSD. With Barton's knowledge of chemistry it wasn't difficult for him to get the desired effects. Taylor thought after Barton began to take this drug he was never quite the same again.

At one point Barton had such vivid hallucinations that he went to the emergency room. The experience frightened him.

"He ingested a great deal of it and overdosed. He had hallucinations and had to go to the emergency room. It did something very bad to him." Taylor suspected that the toxic effects of the ingestion of the drug might have been exacerbated by the chemicals Barton used for extracting the drug.

Afterwards, Barton's behavior was dramatically different from the quiet student he was known as. He became frightened by visions of demons shooting up through the floor. Barton totally lost the ability to read and had to learn it all over again. He cut off all his hair, which at the time was a counter culture move, and took up the Bible. His new found religious fanaticism and his shaved head further alienated him from his peers. A few years earlier he was hoping to be accepted by his peers, but after his overdose it seemed just the opposite. When he visited Taylor at home for their friendly chess matches, Barton started bringing the Bible with him and jabbered madly about finding "answers to all questions."

Because of Barton's strange behavior, Taylor lost touch with him. "He didn't make any sense. The drugs blew him away."

In 1973, a semi-finalist for the National Merit Scholarship, Barton graduated from Sumter High School. His school yearbook had gotten his name wrong twice. He was "Jack Barton" in 1971 and "Mack Barton" in 1972. His picture was missing in his senior yearbook. He was identified only as a "Merit Scholar Semi-Finalist."

One of Barton's English teachers described his social problems in high school, "If someone didn't fit into a group and find an identity, they could just slide through unnoticed. Mark was one of those."

After high school, Barton drifted briefly through Clemson University for one semester. He had another psychotic episode and was hospitalized. After dropping out of Clemson, he remained on anti-psychotic drug therapy under the treatment of a psychiatrist throughout the rest of the school year.

When his treatments ended he enrolled at the University of South Carolina. While at college he learned how to synthesize methamphetamine. Methamphetamine is an addictive stimulant that strongly activates certain systems in the brain. Immediately after smoking or injecting it, the user experiences an intense sensation. The rush lasts only a few minutes, but can be extremely pleasurable. Users can become addicted quickly, and use it with increasing frequency in increasingly large doses.

Mark Barton was soon making the drug and selling it. He eventually began to use the substance to get high. Once again, at age twenty, he got caught trying to burglarize another drug store and was placed on probation. His drug abuse had caused him to take a year longer than normal to finish college. He graduated in 1979, with a bachelor-of-science degree in chemistry.

After graduating he moved from one dead end job to another. The same year he married Debra Spivey, a fellow student he had met while working as a night auditor at a local hotel. They lived in Atlanta, where Barton got a job testing cleaning compounds and then moved to Texarkana, Texas. There he got a position at TLC Manufacturing, a small company that made janitorial cleaning products. He began as a chemist with the company and within five years was promoted to manager of operations and then general manager. His salary was about $86,000 a year. The Bartons had their first child, a son, in 1988. Now Barton had the appearance of a normal, successful family man. To outsiders he seemed like an average father who wore Dockers and polo shirts and liked to chip golf balls in his front yard. It seemed as if his erratic behavior had subsided.

Barton's secretary of four years later commented that she saw a different side of him. "He thought people were out to get him. When somebody got on his bad side, you stayed there."

Behind closed doors, Barton was quick-tempered, devious and malicious. Barton recorded his telephone conversations with other employees, as he had a deep-seated grudge against one of the company's top salesman. To cause delays in the delivery of products, Barton elusively altered orders the man had placed.

Barton's personality underwent a change from a harmless prankster to someone who would have outbursts of uncontrollable behavior when he was unable to solve business related, chemical problems at work. There were incidents in which Barton threw things in his workplace. Most of his co-workers thought of him as not necessarily mean or rude, but as having an attitude similar to a spoiled child - a person who never could admit to doing wrong.

Barton's paranoia was not limited to the office. His wife could not do anything without his permission. Debra couldn't leave the house without telling him first where she was going, what she was going to do and when she was going to be back. He began to humiliate her, with the two often arguing in public. After Debra suffered a miscarriage, Barton cruelly belittled and mocked her. He referred to her by the depreciating nickname he gave her, "Stupid." At this point, though, neighbors didn't see much of the young family. The Bartons rarely socialized or went out in public, spending most of their evenings alone at home.

The Bartons joined a Baptist congregation with about 3,000 members. The family did little to acquaint themselves with the minister and the other churchgoers. However, they posed for a photo for the church directory, in which Barton is smiling, while a sullen looking Debra is seated next to him holding their one-year-old son.

Finally, Barton's odd behavior became too much of a distraction in the office. On September 13, 1990 he was fired by TLC's board of directors. They cited a deficit in his management capabilities and said they had to let him go. Barton interpreted his firing as a way for the company to save money. Employees later described him as being very upset and angry when he left.

One week later, in the middle of the night, Barton broke into the TLC offices through a loading dock door. Once inside, he strode to the room used for coffee breaks, moved a refrigerator and crawled through a window to get to the computers in the executive offices. After downloading confidential client lists, secret chemical formulas and financial data, he wiped the hard drives clean of information. Then after disabling both computers, he searched through the filing cabinets and stole the hard copies of the records he had downloaded. He also took two folders that contained the formulas for all of the products made by the corporation.

Mark Barton left the same way he got in.

Co-workers knew it had to be Barton. The police report indicated that all locks to the building were changed after he turned in his keys. A co-worker told police Barton had told him, "There are ways to get into the business without using keys."

While talking to co-workers, police quickly learned of Barton's erratic behavior and firing. Swiftly labeling the former employee as the principal suspect, detectives went to talk to Barton at his home.

Sitting in Barton's living room, the police asked him about his whereabouts on the night of the break-in. Barton adamantly denied knowing anything about the burglary. When the detectives suggested he had a motive for wanting to hurt the company that had just fired him, Barton again proclaimed his innocence.

As the questions continued, Barton let a telling piece of information slip, saying, "Anyone could have entered through the loading dock door." The police had not disclosed the point of entry. Immediately the detectives knew that even if he was not the guilty party, he still must know something else. They continued to listen to him when Debra entered the room. Barton turned to her and said, "They think I stole the formulas." Once again, the detectives had not revealed the information that the formulas were missing. Again, Barton implicated himself by knowing details that only the guilty party would know.

When they left the house the detectives looked at each other and nodded, confirming their belief that Barton was guilty.

If they charged him with the crime there was an excellent chance they could get a conviction. Barton clearly had a motive. He had a history with the company and knew how to get in and he also knew where everything was and what he wanted to take. In addition, Barton's history of past attempted burglaries only strengthened the case against him.

The police charged him with felony burglary and Barton briefly went to jail, but surprisingly was released within hours. TLC told police they had settled the matter, withdrawing their complaint.

Company officials decided they did not want to pursue the case. Barton had bargained with his ex-employer for his release from jail. In exchange for his freedom he would return everything that he had stolen and agreed to leave the state of Texas forever, which he did. The company had to spend thousands of dollars to replace the files.

The Bartons left Texas sometime near midnight in a beat up Ford pickup. All their earthly possessions were piled high in the bed and cinched down with twine. They drove for two days until they arrived in Macon, Georgia. The Bartons slept in the truck during the trip.

Soon after arriving, Barton set up a firm he compared with a "paper route." With hopes of starting over, the family began to try to rebuild their life together. Barton and Debra had their second child, a girl, in 1991. They bought a new house in Douglasville, Georgia. Barton found a job as a salesman for a chemical company. However, the relationship between Barton and his wife became rocky when he met a receptionist in her early twenties, Leigh Ann Lang. They entered into an affair just three days after meeting. Barton said, "She liked older guys. She made that known to everybody."

Nevertheless, he tried to keep up the veneer of normalcy at home. On Saturdays, Barton cooked breakfast for his children and joined them watching cartoons. Later he said that whenever Debra wasn't home, he and the kids would "run through the house and beat each other with pillows and just get totally out of hand."

Meanwhile, Barton and Leigh Ann spent most of their time at work flirting with each other. At night they had drinks with co-workers. He bought a new wardrobe and began perfecting a tan. Over time, his wife Debra grew suspicious of him and the two of them began to quarrel more and more. One night Debra wrote in her diary, "We will reap the wrath of Mark tonight." She wrote that she was able to tell something was wrong by the expression on his face while he was cutting the grass.

Each time they argued, Debra accused him of having an affair. He just shrugged and said she was being paranoid. Barton later said about Debra's suspicions, "The key to the whole thing was I started going to the tanning bed, and she didn't like that...all throughout the relationship...because I was in outside sales. She found her own dog's hair on me one time...and she asked me if it was another lady's hair...I just denied it."

At the same time, Barton began to get information on taking out a life insurance policy on Debra. He talked with an insurance agent and explained that he wanted to get a one million dollar life insurance policy on his wife.

The insurance agent read through the papers Barton had filled out. After reviewing them he asked, "Mr. Barton, why is it you want to get this policy?"

Barton said, "It's her idea. I used to be the president of a company and my wife began to enjoy it. She felt as time went on, she became as important as I was. She developed an extreme sense of self-worth."

The agent nodded and explained the premiums he would have to pay for the policy. Barton quickly realized he wouldn't be able to pay the premiums on a one million dollar policy, so he had to settle for $600,000 one.

In June 1993, on a trip to Charlotte, North Carolina, Barton and Leigh Ann had dinner with a few of her friends. They talked about their futures and what would happen to their relationship. Barton said, "I have never loved anyone more than Leigh Ann. By October, I'll be able to marry her."

At the end of August, Leigh Ann was ready to end her own marriage. She packed up all her belongings and moved out. Quickly finding an apartment, she moved in with her sister.

On Labor Day weekend, Debra and her mother drove in Mrs. Spivey's red Thunderbird for a holiday visit to a riverside campground they had just rented in Cherokee County, Alabama. Barton stayed with their children in their home. By the end of the weekend the bodies of Debra Barton and her mother, Eloise Spivey, were found in the rented trailer, bludgeoned to death. Eloise had been hit viciously eight to ten times. Debra's wounds numbered in the teens and all were blows to the head and face. The evidence of depravity inside the trailer was hard to fathom. Two once lovely faces with gentle looks now appeared more like misshapen lumps of raw hamburger. Debra's skull was split in two. Her soft flowing hair was now tangled with what was left of her features, clumped and matted with blood. The two women were brutally murdered and the killings had gone undetected by as many as 600 people vacationing nearby.

Newspaper articles speculated the motive might have been robbery. However, Danny Smith, the first investigator to arrive, said the scene appeared to have been staged. It was a half-hearted attempt to make the crime scene look like a simple robbery that escalated into murder.

He told reporters, "Whoever did this wanted us to think it was motivated by robbery, when in fact the perpetrator came here with only one thought in mind: murder."

Eloise's purse had been dumped out and two rings were missing. But six $100 bills, credit cards and other valuable jewelry were left unmoved. Her .32 caliber revolver was also left untouched on the kitchen counter. There was no sign of a forced entry, indicating the victims may have known the suspect. Police found traces of bloody footprints outside the trailer.

Inside, the walls of the trailer were covered in blood spatters. Red stains hung down the curtains, on the windows and on the chairs. It was clear that whoever committed the crime was extremely agitated. These were not the acts of a typical robber who was motivated by money.

Detective Smith rationalized, "To stand there and beat someone to death with a hammer; bam, bam, bam, fifteen or twenty times, you have to be pissed off."

However, what was most puzzling was the vomit on the carpet and around the toilet, which had been left by the murderer. It almost appeared that the assailant had a difficult time carrying out the vicious acts. Such evidence points to the fact that the murderer might have fantasized about killing the women, but when it came time to actually commit the crime he became sick to the stomach. Police theorized the killer probably knew the two women.

Detective Smith promptly phoned Mark Barton to inform him that his wife and mother-in-law had been murdered. There was very little emotion from Barton. Smith then asked if Barton could visit the crime scene in the morning. Without any hesitation, Barton agreed.

The next day, Barton and Debra's father reached the campground parking lot at the same time in separate cars. Detective Smith stood in front of the rented trailer where the two women had been slain. He saw the two men talking a short distance away. The older man was visibly shaken, holding onto Barton's shoulder as the two of them walked cautiously toward the detective. When they reached the steps Detective Smith could see Spivey's face was an ashen color. His eyelids drooped and he took large heaving gulps of air, as if trying to prepare himself. His knees buckled slightly as Smith extended a hand to steady the man.

Barton in contrast appeared quite calm; he even had a hint of energy in his steps. As he made a gesture to shake the hand of the detective he said, "I've never been here before."

Smith thought that was an odd opening statement.

Soon Barton was not only a suspect, but the only suspect. Investigators believed that Barton's motive was the life insurance policy that he had taken out on Debra, surmising he had planned the killing earlier. The life insurance policy would be a handsome payoff and then he would be able to pursue his relationship with the other woman he was seeing. They had found out about Leigh Ann Lang. Another theory they had was that Barton came to Alabama to ask Debra for a divorce and she refused, prompting the killings. Unknown to Barton, investigators had already talked with another visitor to the campgrounds, who saw a man leaving Debra's trailer the night before. He was described as about six feet, four inches tall, about 240 pounds, dark wavy hair with a receding hairline, most likely in his forties. It was not a very detailed description, but it certainly fit the brawny Barton.

How many times a month do you see someone that size around here? Smith asked himself.

Barton was coolly uncooperative with police. When investigators asked if he would submit to a polygraph test, Barton flatly refused.

Barton later explained in a deposition why he refused to take it by saying, "First of all, I've had a lie detector test before, whenever I sought employment at the 7-11 convenience store. And afterwards, I felt raped; I felt violated…I knew that it was not admissible in court. I knew that these people were not on my side. They had already lied to me several times."

He referred to another case, comparing his situation to that one, saying the defendant in the case had not passed a polygraph test, and protesting vaguely, said, "I thought that lying people might do that to me.

"They told me that they wanted to give me a six-hour lie detector test and ask me about my relationship with my wife and with my girlfriend and just get inside my head and ask me about all kinds of things. I asked them if I was – if I passed such a lie detector test, would it clear me as a suspect. And they said no. For all those reasons, I said no, forget it."

Barton was just as uncooperative when asked to submit to a blood test and give a DNA sample. Again, he refused quite defiantly. Detectives tried to question him, but he always seemed to give rehearsed answers. He always stuck closely to his story and never offered up any new information or speculation that he might have had. Detectives thought Barton was trying to figure out where they were coming from and what they had on him. If he couldn't control the conversation, he either stopped talking or switched to another subject. Frustrated detectives saw a pattern form as they continued to question Barton. As one investigator described it, "For every question he was asked, he would come back with ten questions of his own."

On the night of the murders, Barton claimed he was at home in Atlanta, three hours away, with his two children. Although Barton said he was home with his children that night, police found he could not prove that he had not left the house while the children slept. They theorized there was enough time during the night for him to have driven from Atlanta to the Alabama lake, committed the murders and returned before the children awoke. Plus investigators believed Barton could easily have entered and left the campground unnoticed. The murders had occurred on Labor Day weekend when the park was crowded with hundreds of campers and a live band.

Investigators had immediately seized the floor mats in Barton's late-model Ford Taurus, because there appeared to be bloodstains on them. However, they were not able to examine the rest of the car for several days. During that time they allowed Barton to keep it, asking him not to clean it. When investigators returned two days later, they sprayed the car with Luminol, a chemical that is used to test for the presence of blood. Unfortunately, it was discovered the car had been cleaned, ruining any potential evidence. Barton explained the cleaning by claiming he had spilled a soda in the front seat. The gas and brake pedals also appeared to have recently been conditioned with Armor-All. They tested other parts of the car and several spots tested positive for traces of blood, including the steering wheel, the console, the gear shift lever knob and the top corner of the driver's door which all had minute traces. Further tests found blood on the floor of Barton's garage, where the car was parked, on the kitchen wall and in a sink near the kitchen in Barton's house. The areas where blood traces were found indicated Barton had had blood on his hands.

One investigator asked Barton, "Mark, how do you account for the traces of blood that we found?"

Barton answered, "Well, my wife had cut herself with a kitchen knife, that must be where the blood in the house came from. As for the blood in the car, sometimes while driving, I would pick acne on my leg until it bled."

Investigators confronted Barton about his newly cleaned car. They believed it was done intentionally and Barton's chemistry knowledge assisted him in doing a thorough job.

"Are you familiar with the compound, Luminol?" an officer asked.

Although he was a chemist, Barton looked puzzled. "I've never heard of it. What is it?" Barton answered.

Police were skeptical about his reply, which seemed unlikely.

Later, contradicting himself, he explained, "I had seen it on an episode of *Colombo*."

He did offer them a challenge, "If there is a ton of blood in my car, why aren't you arresting me? Well, why am I not in handcuffs?"

The police had to admit there was too little blood present for them to press charges and arrest him. It was then discovered that Barton had called up the company that made Luminol and asked lots of questions about the product's composition.

At that point, Detective Wynn finally decided the only way to nail Barton was to get him to confess. Wynn drove out to Barton's house along with two police photographers. As Wynn entered Barton's house, Barton asked, "What the hell is going on here?"

"We're going to take some pictures Mr. Barton."

"Uh, how many pictures?" Barton asked.

Detective Wynn stepped in closer, their noses nearly touching and said, "Mark, it's all over. You did it. I know it and you know it." Wynn jabbed his index finger into Barton's chest, despite Barton's taller size.

There was silence.

"Did you hear me Mark? It's all over. You've been caught and there isn't a thing you can do about it."

Again there was silence, as Barton coldly stared at Wynn.

Unfortunately, the traces of blood found in Barton's car weren't enough for the police forensic department to run conclusive DNA tests. As Barton continued to sit in stony silence on the couch, Wynn had no choice but to leave.

"I'll be back," Wynn vowed. "I'll be back."

The police began to examine Barton's alibi. They returned to try to talk to Barton's children. According to Detective Wynn, that was mistake number two. Getting to the two children in their home proved to be too difficult.

"It just isn't done that way. You take them out of the home and away from the father," Wynn later recounted to newspapers.

Finally, investigators got a break. They obtained a time-stamped receipt from the local all night mini store near Barton's home, indicating that Barton had not stayed with the children the entire evening. The receipt showed he had left the house around 10:00 p.m. Once again, Barton gave an excuse. When presented with this damning evidence Barton said that he had gone out for just a few minutes to buy some beer for himself and candy bars for his children.

Wynn's reaction to Barton's explanation was, "Who feeds their children candy bars at ten o'clock at night?"

Barton didn't budge.

In retrospect there were other mistakes made by investigators, including not seizing the love letters Barton had written to Leigh Ann Lang while still married to Debra. The letters spanned more than six months' time. One witness, who described seeing a man fitting Barton's description at the campground, was never brought to look at Barton in a police lineup.

Barton continued to refuse to admit to the killings, at least to the police. It was later reported that he told his brother-in-law, "They won't take me. I'm not going alive." Shortly thereafter, Mark Barton purchased a gun.

Debra Spivey and her mother, Eloise, were laid to rest in a family plot in October 1993. Those in attendance at the funeral included only family and a smattering of friends. As the eulogy was read in the large Baptist church, Mark Barton sat in the last pew with a blank stare on his face. People in attendance described his demeanor as "cold as a cucumber." Detective Wynn also attended the funeral and tried to stare him down, but Barton averted his eyes.

When the service was over Barton rushed out of the large wooden doors of the church before most of the other mourners had even risen. Waiting outside was Leigh Ann in a Mustang convertible, with the top down. Barton didn't bother to open the door, he just vaulted himself into the seat next to Leigh Ann as she gunned the motor and the two of them sped off down the two lane road. The stereo was turned up loudly enough for onlookers to hear the lyrics of the music.

The detective warned Leigh Ann's mother, "Get your daughter away from him. He'll hurt her."

No one was ever prosecuted for the brutal beatings and deaths of Debra Spivey Barton or her mother, Eloise Spivey. According to Captain Wynn, a twenty-three-year law enforcement veteran who has put four people on death row and has prosecuted approximately fifty other homicides, "Investigators made some very costly errors right from the onset of the investigation."

Barton never wavered in his declaration of innocence. "He was a pretty cool character. That was part of the problem; there was never a crack in his façade," another investigator observed.

Not long after Debra's funeral, Leigh Ann moved in with Mark. As the insurance company dragged its feet on the pay off on Debra's insurance policy, Barton and Leigh Ann often bickered. The company suspected Mark was the murderer and were hesitant to pay. They offered to pay the full amount of the policy, provided all the money went into a trust fund for the couple's children. Barton refused. Eventually, they compromised. The company had no alternative but to pay off the policy. The check issued to Barton was for $250,000. The other $350,000 of the original $600,000 policy had been set aside for Debra's children.

Despite the warnings from Detective Wynn, Leigh Ann married Barton. They moved to Morrow, Georgia, where their neighbors knew nothing about his first wife's murder. His second marriage, however, gave little promise of a happily ever after life. Whenever they fought Leigh Ann picked up and left. Neighbors gossiped about the marital unrest between the two, and about Barton's strange behavior; he was constantly on his computer.

After Barton remarried, he periodically called the investigators and taunted them, asking why he was a suspect in the slayings.

"It was a game to him. He got mad at me one time because he couldn't convince me he didn't do it," Smith said. Once, Smith said, "He told me 'that he would never go to jail'."

Several months after the murder Barton drove 100 miles from his Georgia home back to Alabama to tell Cherokee County investigators he had remembered why there had been blood in his car. It was his own, he said, explaining he had cut his finger the summer before, but when asked to give a DNA sample, Barton refused again.

In February 1994, Barton's daughter, then two and half years old, told a day-care worker that her father had sexually molested her. During the mental evaluations that followed, a psychologist said Barton was "certainly capable" of committing homicide. However, given the child's age, it was difficult for state attorneys to build a solid case around her against Barton, so he was never brought up on charges. Somehow he kept custody of both children.

Leigh Ann continued to stay with Barton despite the allegations that he sexually abused his own daughter. Nor did his ordering her around seem to dissuade her. But when she finally did begin to pull away from him emotionally and physically, she had sealed her fate.

The façade began to crumble when in the fall of 1998, Leigh Ann told him she was leaving. Among many of his erratic and odd behaviors toward her and his own children, one day Barton killed the family cat, and then pretended to take his children to look for the "missing" pet. By this time, he'd blown through the life insurance money and the family was having a tough time making ends meet.

Leigh Ann left Mark with the children in April of 1999, but later on Barton somehow convinced her to return.

They moved into a small apartment in the city of Stockbridge, Georgia, located in the northern part of Henry County, in the mid north region of the state. For the second time Mark Barton would paint a picture of middle class normality for an unsuspecting community. With his new wife and two young children in tow, Barton settled in Stockbridge, the last destination in Barton's volatile personal history. Located eighteen miles from Atlanta and twenty minutes from downtown Atlanta, Stockbridge was the locale in which Mark Barton's murderous mind would plot the destruction of many lives.

chapter two

A Venture into Day Trading

Brent Doonan, born on August 8, 1973, was a quiet child, always thinking and finding ways to learn from those around him. He was the second son born to parents Kenny and Sue Doonan of Great Bend, Kansas. After the birth of his younger sister, Jennifer, Brent became the middle child, sandwiched between his older brother, Brian, and his baby sister.

Located in the South Central region of the state, Great Bend, Kansas, sits on the bank of the Arkansas River along the Great Bend, where it got its name during the days of the Sante Fe Trail. From a trading post along the Arkansas River to a small military post, Fort Zarah, Great Bend began to grow with the move westward after the Civil War. The town of Great Bend formed in 1870, and was known as a cow town, with everything from Texan cowboys to shootouts outside saloons, with tumbleweeds passing through dusty streets in the breeze. Great Bend's cowboy days were followed by the boom

of the oil industry then followed by the location of a World War II
Army Air Corps training base. Great Bend, Kansas was reminiscent
of any American small town, with its town square, its special fire-
works every Fourth of July and Ellinwood's After Harvest Festival,
held every third week in July. Great Bend was a hometown that
turned out fine American boys like Brent Doonan, and furthermore, was as American as apple pie.

Wichita, one of the largest cities in Kansas, located at the west-
ernmost edge of the state, was named the "All American City," three
times; an identity it probably shared with other homey towns
throughout the state, like Great Bend. Regardless, both Great Bend
and Wichita's inhabitants, the products of their safe and comfortable
communities, would learn that their all-American upbringings
could not prepare them for the shock of a psychopath, a murderer,
in their midst. No one could have predicted that the Doonans
would encounter Mark Barton, who attempted to murder Brent
during his shooting spree. But this was not the first time that natives
of the peaceful state of Kansas would be exposed to a violent criminal. They would also be faced with the horrors of one of America's
most sadistic serial killers and psychopaths, the BTK serial killer,
short for Bind, Torture, Kill.

The idea of a quiet, serene all-American city housing a sadistic
psychopath for over thirty years, as was the case with the BTK killer
in Wichita, is quite frightening. On December 1, 2004, the BTK
killer, whose real name is Dennis Rader, was arrested for the murder of ten people, in a strangulation spree that had started in the
1970s. Consequently, for the past thirty years, the residents of
Wichita lived in fear of the possibility that the BTK would strike
again. When he was finally caught, people wondered how a psychopath, for some a neighbor and co-worker, could go undetected
for over thirty years. The devastation that Dennis Rader had caused

throughout Wichita and Kansas, like a tidal wave in a small pond, would be followed by another breaking wave from Atlanta in late July of 1999 that would horrify people who had watched Brent grow up.

Brent's mother remembers him best as a child that she could give a spoon to play with and watch as he found a dozen uses for it. Like most boys his age, Brent loved spending time outdoors, playing with friends and chasing after his older brother, Brian. During the day, he would most often be found in the backyard tinkering in the garden or playing on the swing set. On most nights, he was down the street playing "hide and go seek" with his pals.

It did not take too long for those around him to notice that Brent was the athletic type. At the age of two, he began snow skiing. A year later, he learned the art of water-skiing and by the age of five he had joined the kids' wrestling club.

As a grade-schooler, Brent quickly began to develop his caring yet very competitive personality. There was not a game or sporting event in which he would settle for anything less than first place. Kickball, dodge ball, baseball – you name it and Brent was playing it and playing it well. He enjoyed life and most of all, he enjoyed the challenges it offered. As one could imagine, his parents often found it difficult to keep up with his activities.

One year during his early childhood, Brent's parents even asked him to give up wrestling for a season. This would free up the family's weekends since all of the tournaments were held on Saturdays. For the sake of his family, Brent hesitantly agreed. Each day at school, he listened to the other wrestlers talking about the wrestling practices, but he resisted the urge to start up again.

Everything was fine until the night before the first tournament. When he could stand it no longer, he walked into his parents' bedroom and said, "Mom, Dad, I can't do this. Do you think you can get me in that tournament tomorrow?" That tells you almost every-thing you need to know about Brent Doonan. His father said, "Would you believe with no practice, he took first place at that tournament? Well, he did."

By middle school, he was developing into a well-rounded young man. He continued to be very competitive in sports, while at the same time he was also learning the importance of working hard and mak-ing good grades. On days when he was not tied up in athletic events, he often went out to the family business to sweep floors or find other odd jobs that he could do in an effort to make a few dollars.

In 1986, at the age of thirteen, Brent became the youngest per-son to take a class at the local community college. Six months later, he passed the class and earned his PADI, open water scuba diving certification. Later that year, he learned how to barefoot water-ski, as well.

Over the course of the next few years, he went on to enjoy a very productive and successful high school experience. He first became president of his freshman class in Great Bend, Kansas while maintaining good grades and working part time at a local restaurant.

A year later, his family moved to Wichita, Kansas, where he was welcomed into the sophomore class of Kapaun Mount Carmel Catholic High School. To the delight of his parents during the next three years, Brent became a star athlete and honor student. He immediately made the varsity football, wrestling and golf teams. Along the way, he also began dating his high school sweetheart, Janette, whom he dated for three years.

In football he was recognized by receiving city league honor-able mention status for his abilities as a wide receiver. He was a member of the varsity golf team that won two state championships his junior and senior years. His greatest athletic achievements, how-ever, were found in his wrestling abilities.

Throughout his high school wrestling career, he was beaten less than ten times. He won the city league, took third place at state and won back-to-back state championships his junior and senior years. Following his senior year season, he participated in the National High School Wrestling Championship in Pittsburgh, Pennsylvania

In order to participate in that tournament, each wrestler must have won first or second place in their respective state tournaments. Brent began that tournament as a state champion; he walked away as a High School All-American by winning third place. Ultimately, he was voted athlete of the year by his high school faculty.

Beyond his success in athletics, Brent worked hard to maintain a 3.80 grade point average. He was a member of the National Honor Society and was well liked by his teachers.

Outside the classroom, Brent kept busy helping out at his father's truck dealership and working to achieve a pretty lofty goal: While most fifteen year olds are busy learning how to drive a car, Brent was busy working on his Federal Aviation Administration pilot's license. A few days after his sixteenth birthday, Brent achieved that goal. The following year he earned his multi-engine and instrument ratings as well.

Following his high school graduation, Brent attended Indiana University in Bloomington, Indiana, where he majored in Finance and Real Estate. While at IU his college days proved no less hectic than his high school years.

By his sophomore year Brent was on the dean's list, received the Alpha Beta award for excellence in academics and athletics, joined the Phi Gamma Delta fraternity and became an officer for the Phi Eta Sigma National Honor Society. He also maintained a very active social life and was quite popular with the girls.

When school was not in session, Brent spent his time back at home in Wichita, Kansas. During the summer months he was employed as a driver for a local concrete company and also for a regional trucking company. Although it sounds odd for a person studying finance and real estate to be employed as a truck driver, it offered Brent the opportunity to stay close to his tight-knit family, while at the same time learning the importance of a hard day's work.

During his junior and senior years, he continued working hard to maintain good grades, but also worked at giving back to his community. He was elected President of the Honor Society and Treasurer of his fraternity. He was placed on the Campus Judicial Board of Directors supported by the IU Dean of Students. While on the board, Brent helped determine the appropriate disciplinary action of those students who broke University policies.

Along with coaching wrestling at the local boys' and girls' club, Brent participated in a wide variety of charitable events with other members of his fraternity. By his senior year, he had turned twenty-one and like most his age, spent a good deal of time at the local taverns partying with his buddies and chasing girls. In spite of being occasionally mischievous and fun-loving, he continued to remain focused on his grades and other achievements. After four exciting years at Indiana University, Brent graduated with a 3.50 grade point average with a Bachelor of Science degree in Finance and Real Estate.

Following a couple of rounds of interviews with a Big Six accounting firm in Chicago, Brent began working for them in the summer of 1997. At the time he lived with a couple of college friends from Indiana University.

Brent loved the bustle of the big city. It was a complete change from the small town in Kansas where he grew up. The magnificent night skyline, the great restaurants and nightclubs gave the city an exciting atmosphere. There was never enough time to do and see everything. The young man was enjoying everything about his Chicago lifestyle.

Working as a business valuation analyst, Brent started his career at an accounting firm in downtown Chicago. His office was on the seventy-sixth floor of a building on Michigan Avenue, with a window overlooking Lake Michigan. The view was stunning to see each morning. The work he was doing was challenging and he was learning a great deal every day. He always took his job seriously. He would often take business trips to other cities. When these opportunities came Brent would dine at some of the finest restaurants and see the sites.

Although he put a lot of energy into his work, Brent also played equally hard in his social life. At the time he was living with a couple of college friends in a three story flat in an area known as Wrigleyville. From their apartment they had a perfect view of the upper deck of Wrigley Field. Joining his twenty-something friends, Brent often hung out in the clubs and local bars. Together, they spent time after work hours drinking dollar beers, eating ten-cent wings, talking about women and the stock market.

These were good times for Brent. When many men his age were still trying to figure out what to do with their lives, he was living his dream. One day his firm sent him to New York on business. It was his first visit there and he ended up staying for two months working on the project. Brent enjoyed his stay at the very luxurious Waldorf-Astoria for eight consecutive weeks. Each night was spent dining in one upscale restaurant after another. By the time he checked out, he had amassed 200,000 hotel rewards points and it was all charged to his expense account. He seemed to be an up and coming young man on the fast track to success.

One evening he was dining with an associate from the firm at the lavish and extremely expensive Manhattan Ocean Club. His dinner companion, Matt, asked what the budget was for dinner. He was young like Brent and didn't know how the expense reports were handled.

"We don't have a budget. Just keep it reasonable and we'll be okay," Brent said.

After scanning the menu, Matt and Brent made their decisions and gave the waiter their orders. When the waiter left Brent said, "Matt, if you were so concerned about the budget why did you order the lobster of all things?"

"Well, I've never had lobster and it's real cheap here, so I thought I'd order it."

"What do you mean cheap?"

With a dead serious look on his face, Matt responded, "The lobster is four to five pounds tonight and it only costs twenty-nine dollars".

Smiling, Brent covered his mouth with his napkin, trying not to make his companion uncomfortable. "Matt, the lobster is twenty-nine dollars a pound!"

A bottle of Chardonnay, along with Matt's lobster and a tip, totaled nearly $250.

While Brent was enjoying his life in Chicago, his sister Jennifer's boyfriend called him from Kansas. He was calling with an offer of a new business opportunity. Brent didn't know Scott Manspeaker very well. Scott was an outgoing, high-energy redhead in his early twenties, whose friends considered him generous and a bit of an ambitious dreamer. Scott did, however, seem to give the impression he was making a great deal of money. He was a day trader.

Day trading, at that point, was a radical departure from how stocks were traditionally traded. In the past, investors usually took a buy and hold approach; at least that's what most of the brokerages and advisors preached. The ruling theory for more than a hundred years was that you bought a stock and held it forever. There would be down cycles where stocks would lose their value, but the good solid stocks would just continue to grow in value. A day trader would bet on minute by minute moves of stocks and buy and sell on their short term fluctuations, rather than waiting years or decades to sell. This new idea intrigued Brent.

Until the advent of high speed digital phone lines, the Internet and the ability to link directly from your computer to the various stock markets, day trading wasn't possible, at least not on a minute by minute basis. Since Scott was linked directly to the markets, he didn't need to wait for a broker to call him back to tell him what price he'd paid for a stock, or what he'd sold it for. With a simple click of the mouse, Scott could buy or sell a thousand shares in an instant. Trades were immediate, as were gains and losses.

Until he met Scott, Brent considered himself an investor. He rarely held equities for more than a few weeks. He had invested in the traditional manner by using a licensed stockbroker to place his orders. His background dealing with the stock market was limited.

The business opportunity that Scott offered Brent was tempting. At the time Scott had just quit his job as the office manager of a firm where he was day trading. During the next year or two, he planned to open his own office with a partner, stock it with computer terminals and teach eager students how to day trade. Revenues would come from three sources: fees for teaching students how to run the programs and how to trade minute by minute, charging small commissions on those trades and charging fees for the convenience of using the equipment and space. Of course he and his partner would also conduct their own day trading transactions. In Scott's mind it was a win-win-win proposition, and he was asking Brent to be his partner

Brent didn't understand why someone would day trade and the idea of him investing several hundred thousand dollars to open an office seemed like an extremely expensive gamble. To be able to make a profit from that kind of investment seemed a formidable task. Yet Scott was persuasive in his pitch to Brent. According to Scott, each of them would be able to make several thousand dollars a day. From the numbers Scott began describing, the offer began to sound more appealing.

Each time the two young men discussed the idea, the profit potential seemed to grow in Scott's mind. He had soon convinced himself that they could make two million dollars a year. Brent was more skeptical, feeling a healthy six-figure income would nicely suffice. His role would be to run the office and Scott, with more day trading experience, would execute the trades and train the students.

However, in a business where fortunes are made and lost in a matter of minutes, Brent was still apprehensive. Being the more prudent of the two, he wanted to experience the inner workings of a thriving day trading office before agreeing to the proposal. He wanted to see an office that had been in business for some time, was making a profit and was focusing on day trading. So later that year, setting aside their ambitious excitement, Brent and Scott flew to Montvale, New Jersey. They were going to visit the offices of All-Tech Investment Group, a firm that fit Brent's description perfectly and the one that Scott claimed to be the best.

The president of All-Tech, Harvey Houtkin, was known as the "father of electronic trading," though the industry was still in its infancy. He was credited with utilizing the NASDAQs Small Order Execution System (SOES), as a means of wrestling some of the wealth away from the predominant brokerage houses and placing it into the hands of the average investor. Brent and Scott were given a complete tour of Houtkin's facility and a short but compelling course on day trading.

SOES is a high-tech system of broadband phone lines that link the individual investor directly to the stock markets, something the large brokerages obviously did not find appealing. Over a period of years, Houtkin had single-handedly fought the brokerages to allow individual investors to place their own orders. In exchange, according to the final agreements, individual traders would be allowed to link directly to the markets, but each was limited to no more than 1,000 shares per trade. Firms like All-Tech in essence became mini-brokerages, charging fees for training and for executing transactions for individuals using their equipment and office space.

The history of trading stocks had begun a hundred years before, when large brokerages placed all the trades for their clients and deducted their own commissions on those trades. Because of the advances in technology, many individual investors cut out much of the commission and began trading almost directly using online systems with Internet discount brokerage houses, such as E-Trade and Ameritrade, who charge a fraction of the traditional brokerage fees.

This was fine, but the individual investor still wasn't linked directly to the markets. Very often, trades took too long even at the online brokerages. Split second opportunities were lost as a result. There was only one way an investor could trade in real time instantaneously, by using SOES and special programs designed for that very purpose. The day trading business was born.

Day trading is an incremental exercise. Using thousand-share blocks of stocks, a quarter of a point would yield $250 to the trader, less the $50 in commission to the house. A very good profit for only a couple of minutes worth of work. If a person could repeat this success consistently, the profits in a single day could be in the thousands.

Houtkin was compactly built, like a boxer, dark haired, sharp in his dress and had a somewhat intimidating manner. He exuded confidence and had the swagger and gait to match. He strode in quick heavy steps through the offices, past the traders who were busy pounding on computer keys, he spoke with a booming eastern accent and said, "To illustrate why someone would day trade with All-Tech instead of with a traditional brokerage, let's use this example. An investor, as opposed to a day trader, purchases one thousand shares of stock at seventy dollars a share. Assume this investor has done his homework and decided the stock looked promising."

As he led the two young men through the maze of computer terminals and endless octopus-like power cords and phone lines strewn through the office, he continued, "Now suppose that this company had also recently reported stellar earnings and Wall Street analysts had rated the company a 'strong buy.' However, a month after the investor bought the stock for $70,000, the Securities and Exchange Commission (SEC) launches an investigation into the company based on 'irregular accounting practices.' By the time the poor schmuck reads about it, the stock has fallen like a sixteen-pound bowling ball tossed out of a ten story window to forty dollars. And within another week, the price is down to fifteen dollars. In the course of a few days, the 'long term' investor, frozen into inaction by fear, hoping against all hope that the bloodletting will end and the stock will eventually return to its previous price and higher, has lost $60,000; not to mention the brokerage commissions."

Though Brent considered himself an "investor," he only held his picks for a week or two at a time. He fully understood what Houtkin was saying. It was the very reason he didn't buy and hold long term.

Houtkin continued. "On the other hand, a day trader purchases the stock at the same price, seventy dollars per share and notices that the stock is beginning to fall pending a news announcement. He or she might end up bailing out quickly at sixty-nine dollars and take a loss of only $500. In short, there are differing risks and rewards associated with each scenario. For the long term investor the profits are often much larger, but so are the potential losses. The day trader doesn't make as much on each trade, but his potential losses can also be much lower. Or, they can lose thousands in the blink of an eye as opposed to months or years."

Houtkin wasn't trying to downplay the potential pitfalls and Brent liked his candor. By the end of their day-long visit Brent had gained a great deal of insight into day trading. He now understood the allure of capitalizing on intra-day movements in stock prices. He knew the basics about the software programs, training courses and branch operations. The only thing that remained was for him to make the commitment. If he did go in with Scott, they would essentially be operating as a branch of All-Tech Investment Group, but they would still be in charge of their own business, similar to a franchise. Success would bring untold wealth in time and failure would mean a rapid bankruptcy. Brent was about to make the most difficult decision of his young life, only one year out of college.

Weeks had passed since their visit to All-Tech and Brent found himself falling right back into the routine that was his accounting job. Scott had made his decision long ago and was beginning to pressure Brent. If Brent wouldn't become his partner he would have to find someone else. Either way, Scott was going to do it and the sooner the better.

One night, while the two talked on the phone, Scott said, "Brent, have you made your decision yet?"

"No."

"I hate to keep pressuring you, but I've gotta know if you're coming in with me or not. Man, we are missing out on one hell of an opportunity. Did you see what the market was doing yesterday? I'm telling you, it's really beginning to heat up and we're going to miss it all. Is it the money? What is it that you don't see?"

"It's a lot of things. Yes, it's the money too. My father is going to have to co-sign on the loan for me, which makes me very nervous. It would kill me if I failed him in addition to blowing my own future."

"You have to stop dwelling on failure. You gotta face your fears head-on and walk right up to them. Picture yourself with wheel-barrows of money - it's a much better way to think."

"I know. You're right. But I worked very hard in college to land this job. I've been able to save a lot of money. The pay is good and I have great benefits. And I like the people there. I love Chicago too. We don't even know what city we would start the business in yet. You, on the other hand, have nothing to lose."

"Screw this then! Why didn't you tell me all this before you let me drag you to New Jersey?"

"I didn't say I wasn't going. I'm just thinking out loud, I guess. I know it isn't fair to you, but can you give me another week? I promise I'll decide by then."

"Okay. One week."

Brent questioned what he should do. He had a nice job, steady income, business trips and other perks. He loved living in Chicago.

A week passed and still no decision. Scott was threatening to find another partner and was becoming angry about Brent's indecision. The demand for day trading was skyrocketing. Investors were pour-ing into All-Tech training classes, both at a national level and at the branches, which were opening at a rate of nearly one every month, according to Scott. Company training classes were overflowing and according to Houtkin, every All-Tech branch was obscenely prof-itable.

Eventually, Brent put his fears and reservations aside and made the decision to make the commitment to the day trading idea. When Brent finally told Scott his decision, Scott was ecstatic. He and Brent both felt they could communicate, be successful in the rising business climate and make a lot of money together. Neither could guess that all too soon they would meet a man who would change their hopes of finding good fortune in one fateful day.

chapter three

Fortune's
Tricky Smile

Brent and Scott, with youthful exuberance, looked excitedly toward the future. The first order of business was to determine the best city in which to start an All-Tech branch office. Brent began by using the library to research possible sites by cross-checking the cities with existing All-Tech offices. He knew they would do better if there was no competition. They would need a large population base with a relatively high per capita income from which to draw prospective traders. All-Tech required their traders (Brent and Scott's clients) to open their accounts with a minimum of $50,000, so traders could make good incomes and still be able to devote time to trading.

Brent thoroughly read *Demographics Daily, Fortune* and *Forbes* magazines and a variety of other sources. His first inclination was to base the business in Chicago, but All-Tech already had a large established office there, as well as ones in Seattle, Boston and Dallas. However, they didn't have offices in Atlanta, Denver or Kansas City. The two men agreed on Atlanta, despite their unfamiliarity with the area.

Anxious and a bit naïve, Brent didn't realize the move and the business start-up were going to be far more difficult than his initial decision was. First, he had to inform his current employer that he was leaving and give them notice. In the meantime, he continued to work on valuation projects, while variations of the original All-Tech contract continued to come in over the fax everyday. There were many negotiations and changes. So many things required a great deal of give and take from both sides.

For Brent and Scott, every week spent negotiating meant further risks of competition in the new market they'd chosen. They could not begin to trade through All-Tech until the contract was signed. It took until the first days of the fall to end the negotiations and seal the deal and by end of it all, everyone was exhausted.

Once the deal was signed there was plenty to do, though neither Brent nor Scott was familiar with Atlanta. Office space needed to be rented, they had to attend All-Tech's training courses and there was the challenge of passing the brokerage exams. In December, Brent left his accounting firm and spent most of the month with Scott at All-Tech headquarters in New Jersey in preparation for their opening.

In the evenings, they spent any free time studying for the brokerage exams and finding out how to run the office. Their "to do" list went on and on. They needed to learn how to open new accounts. Marketing and advertising had to be studied. They would need back office support to master the new software programs. There was a lot to be done in a short amount of time, but their youth, high energy and enthusiasm for a new challenge pushed them onward.

In the classroom, they learned the reasons to *trade* as opposed to *invest*. Earnings announcements and financial documents were the

investor's bible, not the day trader's. Stock fundamentals were dis-
counted and were replaced with supply versus demand.

The key to making money as a day trader was to focus on what
a stock was doing that very second and where you thought it might
head in the next three minutes. Brent referred to it as, "planning for
the un-forseeable." Given the advanced computer technology at
their disposal, there was absolutely no time lapse between stock
trades. They were viewing every movement in stock price and actual
trades on a second-by-second, trade-by-trade basis. Day trading,
they were rapidly learning, was a distinct industry requiring explicit
skills. Brent was also learning that traditional stockbrokers despised
day traders. Day traders jokingly thought stockbrokers were concerned about their jobs.

A good day trader's rules for success included going home flat:
to liquidate all of one's holdings at the end of each day. Each trader
should be in cash by the time the closing bell rings. If not, if a trader
holds stocks overnight, he is turning a trade into an investment.
Other rules included: cutting losses, riding profits and treating trading like a business. Another no-no was to trade in the middle of the
day when volume is usually slow.

The trick to day trading is "riding momentum," but a day trader
must be nearly psychic to catch that momentum before it's visible.
If the trader waits to see the momentum, by the time he's in, the
trend has changed. All of which makes for a very difficult learning
curve, not to mention a very expensive one as well.

Brent and Scott were faced with a myriad of decisions, and even
the small ones proved arduous. What kind of phone system to buy?
Should they purchase or lease equipment? Should they purchase or
lease a copy machine? How to choose a contractor to install the
CATV cable linking the computers to the hub? How do routers and
hubs work in computer networking? The list seemed endless. The

two men were literally writing the abridged version of "How to
Start a Business."

*Those were very tense days. All partnerships can be difficult, but when
you're both only in your twenties and you've borrowed a lot of money from
banks, as well as your father to start up, the stress can be overwhelming. I was
worried about passing the brokerage exams. There was so much to learn both
from a technical and business standpoint. At times, I despaired that I had
made the wrong decision, though I didn't share those feelings with anyone.*

*Scott wasn't only my partner, he was my roommate, as well, so we were
practically joined at the hip. That meant there was no time for arguments or
disagreements, though I remained silent when I disagreed. Through it all
though, we were becoming very good friends. I learned that we both needed
to trust each other's judgment; we both learned when to defer.*

*Less than three weeks before we were scheduled to open, I passed the
second of the two required exams. Scott still had one to go and then in March
he passed it as well.*

*I still cannot believe we actually pulled it all off. But then again I have
always just plowed ahead when I wanted to achieve something, not giving in
to anxiety about how it would all work, just doing what had to be done and
trusting. If I gave a project 110% and I failed, so be it; if I did not and did
not accomplish my goal it would be my own fault. When you hide from risk,
you also hide from rewards. There is no middle ground.*

Brent and Scott chose to open their office in the upscale
Northeast Buckhead region of Atlanta along busy Piedmont Road
NE in the Piedmont Center building. The Buckhead region of
Atlanta is made up of numerous small neighborhoods spread amongst
intertwining roadways that run past shops, restaurants and businesses.
The northeast portion of Piedmont Road intersects with Peachtree
Road NE, two of the major streets along which Buckhead's businesses

and commercial industries were growing. Peachtree Road NE, the Broadway of Atlanta, intersects with Piedmont Road NE before it winds north from downtown Atlanta continuing on its course through the rest of Buckhead.

The premiere and fast growing section of Atlanta, Buckhead, and its streets had humble roots. It was named after a settler's tavern. Henry Irby's general store and tavern, Buckhead, accordingly gained its name after Irby killed a large male deer, a buck, and mounted its head on the wall for all the travelers passing through to see. The name stuck and so did the prosperity of Buckhead as a community, as Irby's tavern had been a popular rest stop for travelers during America's early wilderness days. Both Peachtree Road, once lined with the grandest homes in Atlanta, and Piedmont Road, originally an early settler route that connected farms, had also developed beyond their quotidian southern roots.

This section of downtown Atlanta was experiencing the same boom as the stock market during the bullish months throughout the later half of the nineties. From Buckhead's hip east village, lined with Atlanta's hottest nightspots, the Miami Circle design district off of Piedmont, to the Lenox Square Mall, the high end shopping mecca for the southeast, just off of Peachtree Road NE, and on to South Buckhead with galleries popping up right and left, soon to earn its hip name, Sobu; Buckhead's development was a force to be reckoned with. It was also the type of scene that would attract any twentysomething entrepreneur; it was the perfect place to start a business, be young and enjoy life, but it wasn't cheap.

Advertising, Brent and Scott soon found out, cost a lot of money. By the time the office opened, the two men had spent twenty thousand dollars on ads designed to bring in new clients. They splurged on a beautiful grand opening seminar/dinner at the upscale Hyatt Regency in the heart of Buckhead. Crisply starched white linen table cloths were draped over the tables with stunning floral arrangements in the center of each one. Fine china place settings framed with sterling silverware and large wine goblets were meticulously arranged, each topped off with a lace and linen napkin. No expense was spared. It attracted 350 curious guests, who sat ten to a table.

The main attraction was All-Tech CEO Harvey Houtkin, who spoke for over an hour as the excited group of potential investors hung on his every word. During his speech he used material from his then recently published book *"Secrets of the SOES Bandit."* Audience members asked many questions, particularly with regard to the success rates of day traders. Houtkin's answer: "I would guess over thirty percent, but I don't have an exact number."

When others asked questions about the technology used in day trading, Houtkin simply said that All-Tech's proprietary trading system, ATTAIN, leveled the playing field between the pros and the average investor. Houtkin was smart enough to know that the system was too complex for the average investor to understand, so he simply dealt with the technology aspects in broad strokes. The dinner was a huge success.

Brent and Scott opened their new business's doors the next day and the offices looked very impressive as intended. There were only ten computers, but to fill all the potential spaces would have cost another $40,000. They would have to start conservatively and work their way up to the desired full capacity of thirty-three traders.

Rows of black high back leather chairs filled the room; each had been placed neatly against the shiny surfaced Formica trading tables. Expensive carpeting lay beneath. Every workstation had a terminal with a giant 21" monitor. Very clean, efficient and impressive. On one wall were four large simple round black and white clocks, one for each time zone. The office was a statement in reserved elegance.

The phones rang steadily from the very beginning. Eager would-be day traders called and one by one Brent signed them up for training classes. Their first class or "boot camp" as they referred to it was filled. Ten anxious traders lined the trading floor that Saturday morning in the spring of 1998. Though they represented a diverse background of education and ethnicity, all were men and each had the same goal: to learn to compete in the intense new world of day trading.

They taught the trainees everything that Scott and Brent had learned and new calls continued to flood in. Quickly it got to the point where the two men couldn't answer the phones and train. So Scott oversaw the training while Brent manned the phones.

Within a month, they were generating decent revenues, though they weren't yet profitable. Brent believed it would only be a matter of time. Brent's decision to "go for it" turned out to be the right move and Scott's intuition about the markets heating up could not have been more prescient.

The year 1999 marked one of the hottest stock market periods in history. It was becoming absolutely crazy. Dot-coms were coming online in droves. IPOs, initial public offerings, were moving twenty, fifty, even a hundred dollars a day. NASDAQ was nearing 5,000 for the first time in history and the DOW blew by 10,000.

In September of 1997, it had hit 7,945. By 1999, when All-Tech was peaking it had hit 10,336 and month later it jumped yet another 400 points.

Moms and pops, housewives, tradesman and even laborers were making fortunes. Brent felt a rush going to the office everyday. In fact, he couldn't remember a time when he was so eager to wake up early and get "at it," yet, once in a while he did feel a twinge of nervousness about the mounting pace of success.

I had heard my grandfather many times speak about the crash of 1929 and the frenzied year or two of trading prior to that debacle and though I gave no thought to any kind of crash, I remember thinking that investors then, as now, must have been absolutely giddy with the prospects. Not unlike then, many people were buying far too much on margin (borrowing). In those days you could buy $1,000 worth of stock for as little as five dollars, so everyone was leveraged up to their collars.

One thing that has remained constant since October of 1929 until today and will be the same in another fifty years, is that the stock market consists of a herd mentality. There are stampedes to get in and certainly to get out. My own irrational exuberance wasn't so much in making stock trades, it was wrapped up in the totality of it all; I was becoming a successful entrepreneur, the market was frenzied, everyone seemed to be winning, I was making some solid day trades and I was helping to run a fantastically exciting business. I was firing on all cylinders.

Brent's and Scott's All-Tech branch was growing rapidly. Many of the first students were now trading and demand for new clients was growing steadily. Eventually the two held boot camps on a monthly basis, usually with filled classes. Their goals for that first year were simple: try to help new traders become as profitable as possible, while at the same time, paying down their debt. They were succeeding at both and Brent was beginning to breathe easier about his father's name on the bank loans. Brent and his father, Kenny, had a fabulous relationship. Kenny was a successful business owner and he called Brent several times a week to check in. He was very proud of his son's success and when the business started to really take off Kenny was just as excited about it as Brent. He congratulated and encouraged both men and he was a sincere listener when things weren't going well. He always told Brent, "Just try to give it your best. That's all anyone can ask." And Brent was determined to follow his father's advice.

I strive for success, never happy with second place. If I don't accomplish something every single day, or at least learn something of value, I don't feel like I'm contributing to my own future or anyone else's.

The thought of how, in high school, I won two state wrestling championships, took third in another year and was an All-American, kept passing through my mind. I won honorable mention status as a football player and was on the state championship golf team.

In college, I joined a fraternity and was the treasurer. I was president of the national honors society and won a seat on the campus judiciary board, graduating with a 3.5 grade point average and a degree in finance and real estate. I also coached a boys wrestling club.

Later in Chicago, even though I was busy trying to succeed in my profession, I taught a fourth-grade business class once a month as an outside business mentor who came in and lectured.

I am driven about whatever I go after. I'm also a little high strung, which I guess is good for the energy level I needed. And being raised in a religious family, I knew the importance of what my father always called, "the greater you," the part in all of us that must contribute, give something back in order to be whole. These attitudes and perspectives served me well when Scott and I were both putting in seventy-plus hours a week at the brokerage. I always had my father's encouragement, my faith and my persistent nature to guide me in my journey.

It would eventually take Brent three years to repay the business loan, which had been the agreement with Kenny. Oddly, this subject was fodder for one of the very worst arguments Scott and Brent ever had. Scott wanted to hang onto the money for five years, giving them a greater cushion. However, Brent agreed with his father that the sooner they were debt-free, the better.

It could not have been a headier time for the two. They had, perhaps luckily, started their business just before one of the wildest rides in stock market history, truly catching the wave before it was visible and then riding it as it crested. When the market was rewarding audacity for the average investor, day traders were the most daring of all. Sophisticated trading software had become an essential tool. Brent did little of the trading, concentrating on operations and Scott who was trading often said, "I'm not a gold digger, I just provide the shovels. I just want a little piece here and there."

The initial public offering (IPO) market continued to boost the markets to astounding heights. Average men and women became overnight multi-millionaires.

Brent and Scott watched as the boom spread and dot-coms began springing up like weeds in fertilizer. Stocks like Amazon, Yahoo, eBay and Red Hat, among hundreds of others, made their way to Wall Street via the IPO market. Hundreds of thousands of investors and executives alike were relishing the newfound demand for these high-flying Internet companies. Companies that were only a year or two old were more capitalized than some of the Blue Chip giants that had been in business for fifty years or more.

The Wall Street investment banks that brought these stocks to market were enjoying overnight returns at an average rate of 71 percent during these years. The investment houses, mutual funds and wealthy investors lucky enough to receive pre-opening shares were astounded to watch their investments double or triple in a matter of days, sometimes overnight. Stocks that closed one day at $80 a share could easily open the following morning at $100 or more. The markets were flying high.

Those getting rich were getting very, very rich and that included some of the day traders. Holding stocks overnight had always been taboo in the day trading world, but now it could be downright tragic. Tens of thousands could be made or lost from the close of the market one day to the opening the following day.

At the same time the dot-coms were making their debut, many of the stocks that had been trading for some time began to display volatility as never before. On one occasion, Brent traded Yahoo for a $19 per share profit. In less than fifteen minutes the stock that was trading at $150 per share rose to $200 per share range. A twenty or thirty point move in a matter of minutes was not out of the ordinary.

Month after month new money poured into the markets. Amateurs and professionals dumped hoards of cash into stocks, all hoping to get on the gravy train. Many people took out second mortgages, dipped into savings accounts or ran up enormous credit card debt, all in the hopes of striking it rich like their neighbors.

Brent's and Scott's business was surging. The business of day trading continued to attract investors not only in Atlanta, but also in almost every major city in the country. By December, in Atlanta alone, several other day trading firms had opened in order to cash in on the rising demand. It looked like Brent and Scott would soon be close to filling out their goal of thirty-three traders. It was a thriving time. Their computer systems were handling remote accounts from clients in North Carolina, Tennessee, Colorado, Kansas, Florida, Alabama and Hawaii. Brent had hoped to become the largest and most successful of the twenty All-Tech offices across the country. It looked as if they were going to meet that goal. However, Brent knew that success usually comes with a price. By this time though, he badly wanted to believe in their success.

He told himself not to be so much of a doubting Thomas. After all they were working hard and as a result the business they had built was doing remarkably well.

Then one day, several weeks later, Brent answered a persistently ringing phone.

"Hello, All-Tech Investment Group. This is Brent Doonan. How may I help you?"

Using the standard questions Brent had asked a thousand times before, he asked "Are you currently trading?"

"Yep, I sure am," the gravelly voice came back.

"What system are you using and are you trading with a broker or online?"

"Been doing a little of both. I used to be a chemist, but I'm semi-retired now. I've been using another company, but I'm looking for a better way to trade."

"What is the problem with your current brokerage?"

"Whenever I place an order, it takes too long to fill it."

"Well then, you've called the right place indeed," Brent responded. "Our system is linked to the stock exchanges in real time via high speed phone lines. You'll have instantaneous access to the markets."

Based on his first responses, Brent began to think his caller was inexperienced so he kept the questions coming.

"What share size do you typically trade?" Brent asked, hoping the man would respond with anything over 100 shares.

"It depends, but usually it's in the 3,000 to 4,000 range," the caller replied.

The man's response trumpeted in Brent's ears. People who trade in ranges that size are either seasoned professionals or wealthy individuals looking for some excitement.

"Would you be willing to come down to our offices for a system demonstration? Are you aware your minimum account needs to be in the fifty thousand dollar range?" Brent asked eagerly.

"Actually, what I would like to do is to start trading with you as soon as possible. Shall I make the check out to your company?"

"Well, if you're going to use our software on our premises, you'll need to attend a training class. Unfortunately, we just started one Saturday, so you missed that one."

Sounding disappointed, the caller said, "Oh, that's no problem, I don't care if I miss a couple of days. If I pay for the entire class can I go ahead and attend on Monday? I really want to use your computer software."

"It's a bit unusual," Brent said, trying to keep the excitement from his voice. He paused, took a deep breath and went on hoping vehemently his caller would share his enthusiasm and commitment and would want to be a part of All-Tech. "I don't see why not. If that is what you want to do, go ahead and come on in and we'll get you started. Do you have our address?"

"Yes."

Brent tried to keep his voice even and serious. If the caller actually showed up for a class he would have been the quickest client Brent had attracted to that date. Whether the caller showed up that day or not, he seemed very interested, Brent mused.

"Good, okay then all I'll need is your name and your phone number," Brent said.

"Sure. This is great news. My name is Mark Barton and my number is..."

After hanging up the phone, I pondered the likely outcome of the call. I was afraid Barton would not show up for the three thousand dollar training class without even meeting me. On the other hand, I could not believe how excited he seemed at the possibility of using our software. Mr. Barton, it appeared, was not about to wait another month.

chapter four

Incongruous Impressions

While visions of success swirled in his head, an energized Brent anxiously awaited All-Tech's new client and trader. He wished he had thirty Mark Bartons who were willing and able to trade in blocks of 3,000 to 4,000 shares all day long.

Mark Barton strolled into the Buckhead offices dressed in casual clothes: khaki shorts and a knit golf shirt. His wardrobe seemed to fit his "happy-go-lucky" attitude. At about six feet four inches, with dark hair and weighing roughly two hundred and thirty pounds, Barton had a very impressive physical presence, but radiated a friendly aura. The first thing he did was stride up to Brent, give a big toothy grin and extend his hand.

"You must be Mark Barton," Brent said and smiled back.

"How did you know?"

"Intuition, I guess. We use a lot of it around here. Come and have a seat," Brent said. "You'll need to fill out our enrollment forms and then I can get you started."

While Barton sat in a large leather chair in Brent's office using a clipboard to fill out the papers, Brent's and Scott's visible excitement grew. Both were eager to have their new student get started.

"We seemed to really click, Scott," Brent said as they stood off to one side. "I only talked to Barton briefly on the phone before he showed up today, but he said he is a semi-retired chemist. He's just recently gotten into trading and apparently he's done very well. When I told him his minimum account balance needed to be $50,000, he just said, 'Shall I make the check out to All-Tech?' This guy's loaded and experienced. And he seems like a really good guy."

After Barton had filled out all the necessary paperwork, Scott and Brent sat down with him in the manager's office to talk with him about his goals and plans as a day trader. When asked how he planned to trade and fund his account, Barton replied, "I would like to trade in 'big blocks,' as I like to call them," he chuckled. "I hope to fund my account with a large initial transaction," he finished.

Before he sat down in the training class, Scott and Brent thanked Barton for coming in so promptly and showing such an eager interest in All-Tech Investment Group. Still in a state of disbelief regarding Barton's fervor and urgency to begin trading as soon as possible, Brent and Scott asked him if he really wanted to start in the current training session, since he had missed a few classes. They offered to allow him to wait to train with the next class in a couple of weeks.

"Here's my check," Barton's quick response caught Brent and Scott off guard. It was as if Barton wanted them to stop delaying him. Furthermore, he seemed not to want to be questioned concerning his decision. "Now then, can I start?" he finished, smiling confidently.

Brent and Scott looked at each other briefly and smiled. They both seemed to be thinking that in contrast to the way new traders had conventionally responded to the prospect of day trading, regarding it as a very serious decision that required time in order to be certain, Barton's confidence and eagerness was uplifting. They introduced him to the instructors of the training session that was in progress and left him to get acquainted with his classmates. From behind the glass window, Brent and Scott watched the training class, as Barton effortlessly joined the boot camp in progress. He joked with his classmates, adding a lighthearted mood that counterbalanced the jitters of the new venture. That day marked Barton's start down the road of his day trading career.

Barton's radiant smile and laid-back outlook on life meant a lot to Brent and Scott, because they had attracted the type of client that would be a pleasure to work with and instruct. More importantly, Barton was elated to have the opportunity to join the new breed of investors known as day traders and his ebullience seemed contagious. Barton was an instant hit with his fellow traders, and over the next few days he acted as the comic relief that let some of the pressure out of the high stress atmosphere of day trading. He became known as a man who had a talent for making light of fortune's ups and downs. Funny and gregarious, he often had Brent and Scott laughing at his stories and jokes. Moreover, he seemed unfazed and able to handle the frantic pace of the organization. He made himself comfortable among a diverse group. Some were lawyers, others doctors, some retired; only one was a chemist. Their one common bond was they were all disillusioned with the traditional forms of investing and intrigued by day-trading. Mark Barton and all the others believed they had found the perfect place to try their hands at taming Wall Street.

In the weeks that followed, trader Mark Barton quickly joined the ranks of the rest of the "live traders" who were now engaging in this new rapid-fire method of investing. Besides being the only chemist, Barton had one other quality that distinguished him from everyone else in Brent and Scott's All-Tech offices. While most "newbies" took their time becoming accustomed to trading by making only a couple of trades per day, Barton wasted no time.

Though the market was hot, most of the newcomers started out executing conservative trades tallying three or four a day in the hundred to three hundred shares per trade range. But Barton immediately placed ten to fifteen orders daily and it wasn't long before that number jumped to fifty a day, each in the one thousand-share range. After all, as he told everyone, he was a seasoned trader. He repeatedly said, "Ah, that's nothing." He gave the impression he could handle the potential huge losses that could happen when he traded this way. Day after day, Barton sat in the middle of the trading floor clicking his mouse at a furious pace, jumping into and out of the markets hoping to cash in on the market frenzy. Meanwhile Brent and Scott were tasting success beyond their wildest dreams.

Throughout the remainder of that first year, our business grew rapidly. We held boot camps on a monthly basis and usually filled each of the classes. Slowly, however, we moved the classes to every six to eight weeks as the office reached its capacity. Our goals were simple: try to help new traders become as profitable as possible while at the same time paying down our debt as we went along. I believe Scott and I did our best at both.

The years 1998 and 1999 were the most explosive years the stock market had ever seen. It was a feeding frenzy. Every day each of the thirty-plus terminals at All-Tech were humming with activity. Mark Barton, like the rest of All-Tech and other investors across the nation, found himself in the midst of the largest stock market advance in the history of the United States. All of the computer stations at All-Tech were filled, in addition to Brent and Scott handling remote accounts from clients in states as far flung as Colorado and Hawaii. In two short years, Brent and Scott managed to cultivate the Atlanta company into the most profitable of All-Tech's branches. Brent and Scott were continuing assiduously to pay down their massive debt and Brent had finally begun to breathe easier about the bank loans. They could not have asked for a better course of events; no one could.

Brent and Scott hired an assistant to help with the overwhelming load of paperwork. Kathy Van Camp was a bright, attractive, middle-aged woman who knew nothing about the stock market, but was searching for a new challenge. She proved to be a quick study. Kathy flashed through most of the financial and investment encyclopedias and occasionally sat in on a boot camp class. She gave Brent a great deal of comfort with her strong work ethic and the pride with which she conducted herself. She was committed to the firm and became a great asset to the company. Kathy fit in nicely with Brent and Scott and lightened their large work loads considerably.

However, even with Kathy's help, Brent and Scott found it difficult to trade their own accounts. It was becoming increasingly more difficult to field phone calls, help the traders and to trade themselves when huge amounts of money were at stake and could be lost in a matter of seconds. They realized they would have to make a decision. Either they could run the office and not trade, or sell the business. The market was peaking and there wouldn't be a better time to sell. Realizing they could get the most out of their investment if they cashed in now, they both agreed that this would be the best decision.

Choosing an Atlanta business broker, Tom Santoras, to help them arrange the sale, all three men were confident the sale would bring top dollar. Under Tom's guidance, Brent and Scott pulled together all their financial statements dating back from the first day they had opened their doors until the present, in the early part of 1999. The revenue chart of the Atlanta branch of All-Tech showed a positive incline from the first day, as month after month the company's profitability had been steadily increasing; a great selling point to have in the midst of a valuation. The demand was still growing. While Brent and Scott continued to focus on the markets and their traders, Tom went about creating business valuations in preparation for the sale.

Barton had been trading at All-Tech for a year by the time Brent and Scott had grown confident that the business they were building was succeeding. Like most of the other traders, Barton's experience was that no one wins 100 percent of the time. It's a numbers game, make money on six of ten trades; just don't lose all of your money on the four losers. The best advice in a nutshell is to hold on to some of your winnings.

A typical day for Barton was usually an intense experience. On some days he made three, five or ten thousand dollars; on others, he lost equal amounts or more. He maintained his sense of humor and buoyancy throughout, with his dramatic wins and losses putting him at the center of attention on the floor almost daily.

When the market was going his way, everyone knew it by his boisterous, outgoing and likable disposition. By then the joyous but somewhat childish man had been nicknamed "The Rocket." Over the course of his tenure, Mark Barton and Brent Doonan had developed a strong relationship, almost a friendship. Brent and Scott laughed with him when the market was good and felt his pain when it wasn't.

As with other clients, Brent occasionally invited Mark out for dinner or drinks. Barton was different from the rest, though. He always declined, saying that he was a committed family man and preferred to spend time with his wife and children.

"No thanks," he would often say. "I'm going to go home and play with my kids." Brent found that commendable and was never offended.

According to Barton, he was a Cub Scout leader, a steady churchgoer and a friend and father to his two children. He was often seen taking his kids to soccer practice or coaching his son in Little League. The family lived on a typical middle-class street, which housed a blend of newcomers and longtime residents. At home, he was always on the computer. He had even set it up by the window, so he could watch his daughter ride her bike while he played the market. To those who knew Mark Barton, he appeared to be the perfect father, one who chose his family over his friends.

I was different than Mark. Though I did want to get married and have a family someday, I was still only twenty-four years old and like any single twentysomething male, I enjoyed, whenever possible, lots of other activities outside work. I had purchased a Harley Davidson softail motorcycle, which I loved to ride out in the country. Scott and I often enjoyed waterskiing on the weekends and, of course, I loved the nightlife, especially in Buckhead. At heart, I was still a small-time Kansas boy who was, perhaps, growing up too fast.

Though Barton seemed to be the perfect father and husband, he did seem to have one prominent character flaw, as Brent noted. He appeared somewhat controlling over his wife of six years, Leigh Ann, although he expressed being very much in love with her. During his daily calls to his "sweetheart," he usually began the conversation by saying, "Honey, it's me. Go ahead and pick up the phone," which led Brent to believe he would not allow her to answer the phone. There were other subtle clues, but Brent didn't want to pry. It was certainly none of his business.

Neighbors later said Barton was conspicuously less than neighborly. On occasion, if someone would wave to him, sometimes he'd acknowledge them and sometimes he'd act like he didn't see them. The children often spent more time playing at the neighbors' house than at their home. His daughter was cute and adorable, often carrying her pet cat draped on her shoulder. His son seemed more withdrawn, very often immersed in video games. Leigh Ann was thought to be very nice.

Although Barton was an aggressive trader, whose style, like few others, kept pace with the frantic stock market, his non-profitable days were beginning to far outweigh his profitable ones. All too often the market failed to cooperate with his method of trading. He, like many of the others, was beginning to break the cardinal rules: holding positions overnight, trading into the slow portion of mid-day and failing to cut his losses. By March of 1999, Barton had drained his entire trading account and because he'd been using margin, he owed Brent and Scott nearly $11,000. However, Brent and Scott still had faith in Barton, as he was a determined individual who seemed capable of getting through a difficult time. "Don't worry," Barton assured them with a quirky look on his face, "I'm good for the debt." However, with his account wiped out, he had no choice but to stop trading. He would be back, he promised, and assured them he would make good on his debt.

In April 1999, Barton returned to All-Tech to reassure Brent about the money he still owed them. With a smiling face and a bouncy energy, he told Brent that he had managed to develop a new soap and had made a fortune from it. His trading losses were nothing more than inevitable bumps in the road. He wanted to return and vowed to be more cautious the second time around. That day he repaid the money, replenished his account minimum and started trading.

However positive Barton's intentions were, they never materialized. Despite his attempt to start anew, Mark soon fell into the same method of trading that had previously wiped him out. Once again he began trading in a very haphazard fashion. He didn't try to build up gains slowly. He was trading large amounts of money in the hopes it would be a fast and profitable payoff. Although he managed to make a few good trades, over time, his losses far exceeded his gains. Within a month or two he again met with the same fate as before, and by June, his account was once again empty. This time he owed Brent and Scott $30,000. At the end of the last trading day, an awkward conversation followed. After shutting off Mark's computer, Brent spoke to him about the situation.

"Mark, what happened?"

"Brent, I am so sorry. I was too aggressive again, trying to recoup massive losses in only a few weeks. Instead of swinging for singles and doubles, I was trying to crush home runs."

"For the time being," Barton continued, "I'll resume my business as a chemist. I'll go back to work with my partner and soon I'll develop another product that will help me get back on my feet. I'd prefer to continue trading, but I guess I'll just have to do what I can."

To Brent, it seemed to be no big deal; Barton acted in much the same manner as he did before. But that was that. The upbeat and jubilant man who sat in the middle of the trading floor had turned his computer off for the last time. Brent sighed as Mark walked out the tall glass doors of the office and into the courtyard; it marked a sad day in the history of All-Tech Investment Group. For Mark Barton the financial scars of the stock market had taken their toll, while Brent and Scott were left holding the bag on the $30,000 debt he owed. There were no hard feelings between the two as Barton left All-Tech. He was still on good terms with Brent; they had shared a mutual respect and business relationship.

That night before closing, Brent sat down and broke the news to Scott. Scott knew that Mark had drained his account, but didn't realize that he was in the red five figures. They had fallen prey to someone who was at best a loser or at worst a con artist.

"Why did we allow him to trade again? How could we have been so stupid?" the two pondered.

"I thought at first, when he paid us back, it was just a fluke. Besides, I tend to trust people, especially those that I like. I made a bad call." Brent thought a moment. "On second thought, he's a big boy. Mark was the one that was begging to trade again. Mark was the one who assured me that money was no object. He's the one who said that he didn't listen to a word of what we tried to teach him. I believe he's good for the money and I like him. If nothing else, he'll repay us and then we'll go our separate ways. Somehow, I have a feeling this isn't the last time we'll see him."

"I hope you're right."

Like many who had gone before him and many who may yet follow, the stock market had gotten the best of the forty-four-year-old Mark Barton. But through it all, Barton had managed to remain strong in the face of adversity. His smiling face and obvious addiction to the thrill of trading had been evident from the moment he first walked into our office a year before. In the year or so that I had come to know Mark, I do not recall ever seeing him upset. I hoped his positive outlook would get him through this tough time and hoped to see him again under better circumstances.

In May of 1999, Brent and Scott received their business valuation from their broker. Though the true worth of a company is never known until a willing and able buyer comes to terms with a willing and able seller, their office had been valued at $7.9 million.

The two men decided to put the business up for sale, needing only to find a qualified buyer. The timing was great. The market was still hot, but Brent knew it wouldn't last forever. Both men had shown a propensity for "moving with the heat." Scott's early gut feelings about the market in 1997 had proven right on. His timing in his day trading was always one step ahead of the curve, jumping into the momentum before most people saw it coming. The same could be said of putting the company up for sale. They were going to move ahead of the current heat and get out before the market inevitably declined.

As spring turned to summer, the search for a buyer continued and life went on as usual at All-Tech. The demand for trading was beginning to soften slightly, but was still busy, so they hired a new college graduate, Meredith Winitt, as a second assistant to help Kathy. She was a bright twenty-two-year-old, who had an exceptional academic record and was excited to start her first big job. Brent planned to have her assist in marketing and system demonstrations, but she had to obtain her brokerage licenses first.

In the meantime, despite Barton's withdrawal from the market, Mark Barton and Brent managed to keep in contact over the weeks that followed his departure from day trading. If only for a few minutes, they routinely touched base and kept the lines of communication open. Even Kathy occasionally called Mark to check up on him. Except for the brief period following his change of address, Barton responded quickly anytime someone from All-Tech called. According to Barton, he was working aggressively on a new chemical product. He kept assuring Brent that he would swing by the office "one of these days" to repay his debt. He seemed profoundly embarrassed and sincere.

Unbeknownst to his friends and debtors at All-Tech, Barton's home life, like his business life, had become more unstable. Barton was

living with Leigh Ann and his two children in Morrow, Georgia, a
suburb of Atlanta. It was February of 1998 when Barton first walked
into All-Tech Investment Group. From the time Barton began trading at All-Tech, in February, his family life began to decline, culminat-
ing in Leigh Ann's expressed desire to leave Mark in the fall of 1998,
as Leigh Ann began to realize who she had married.

Leigh Ann left Mark with the children in April 1999, about the
same time he'd walked out of All-Tech. Soon after, somehow Mark
convinced his second wife to return. When she returned they
moved into a small apartment in Stockbridge, Georgia, but there
wasn't much left to move. At a yard sale in April, Barton tried to sell
the sofas in his home for ten dollars apiece. Barton then went to a
Jehovah's Witness minister for help. Barton explained to the minister that his wife was ready to leave him, but he couldn't stop gambling on stocks. He said he would wake up in the middle of the
night and be worried he had inherited some kind of undefined
mental imbalance from his father.

In late July, Brent received a visit from Barton. By that time it
had been several months since they had spoken. Brent was inwardly
hoping the visit would resolve the money problem they had with
him.

"Hey buddy, where have you been?" Brent asked, extending his
hand.

"Here and there. We moved into an apartment in Stockbridge,
so I've been busy with that."

"Why? I thought you loved that big house."

"Naw. To tell you the truth it was too big, too much upkeep. We
decided to downsize," Barton said. "Hey, I'm working on a new soap
with a partner. When I get it produced, I'll make a fortune. It's something very unique."

Barton seemed to be happy and Brent was glad to see him

again. But in reality, everything Barton was telling him was a lie. No partner existed. No soap was going to be manufactured. The motive of moving was not to simply downsize. He was not working as a chemist. Barton also neglected to tell Brent that he had been trading again, only at a different brokerage.

Over the past three months, when Barton claimed to be working as a chemist, he was trading, just across the street from All-Tech Investment Group, at Momentum Securities, located at 3500 Piedmont Road, where Barton found relief from his previous debts. Somehow Barton had managed to raise enough cash to start a new account at Momentum, but not enough to repay his debt to Brent and Scott.

It seems odd that he and Brent did not see each other again, despite Barton working nearby. What was even stranger was that the manager of Momentum Securities never called Brent to check on their new trader. For most professionals it would have been important to have known how well or poorly Barton had performed, and also whether he owed them any money. The Momentum office seemed to take Barton's good past performance on faith, although they knew that he had previously traded with All-Tech. Of course, as Brent knew, Barton could be a charmer. During the first part of June, Barton filled out the necessary account paperwork, opened his new account at his new firm, and began trading again. When he opened his new account, Barton listed his net worth being at $750,000, including $250,000 in available cash. Perhaps the managers at Momentum Securities were just happy to have a new and experienced trader on board and wanted to leave well enough alone. Yet Barton hadn't learned from his overeager trading methods at All-Tech; he was losing money again.

Between June and July, Mark Barton fell into the same trading routines that had cost him so dearly over the previous year. He borrowed "on margin" $100,000, which he quickly lost and another $87,500 was lost trading stocks. By June tenth, Barton owed Momentum $187,500 on top of the $30,000 he owed Brent and Scott. Later that afternoon, Barton left Momentum as if it was just another day. He shrugged off the huge loss, saying he would soon get back on his feet. When Barton got home, he put on his Boy Scout Leader's uniform and went to a troop meeting with his son. Later that evening he and Leigh Ann quarreled over money again.

chapter five

Hell
Fire

Thursday, July 29, 1999, began in much the same manner as any other summer day in Georgia. By 10:00 a.m., the heat rising off the pavement on Peachtree was meeting with the humidity weighing down from the clouds. The day was steamy, even at that early hour; there would be no climatic reprieve until the sun set that evening.

Brent daydreamed that it would have been a perfect day for him to take out his Harley for a ride, or for him and Scott to play hooky and go out to Lake Lanier for some waterskiing. But he knew he had to concentrate on the difficult business scene. There hadn't been many new buyers interested in All-Tech and it was beginning to look like there might not be any in the next coming weeks. The market had been sliding slowly for the last two months and, on this particular day, it continued its downward trend. Traders were suffering monetary defeats and the mood of the office personnel was glum.

Still, Brent was determined to make the best of the heat, in
more ways than one. Brent wore his favorite outfit to work; he
wanted to feel good about himself, and one way to act the part was
to dress it. The double-breasted black coat and loose fitting slacks
looked sharp and felt great on him. The crisp royal blue shirt and
bright red tie glowing from underneath the jacket had become his
favorite "look" for quite some time and more often than not, the
color combination had brought him good luck. Brent wasn't super-
stitious, but he was an optimist, and despite the declining market, he
felt he had a lot to look forward to.

That night he planned to meet with his friend, client and real
estate agent, Sofia. Mortgage rates were going down for the first
time in years and Brent had saved enough to comfortably afford his
own home. Sofia had found a unit in a new condominium complex
just down the street from Brent's office, with a great view of
Buckhead from the top floor unit he wanted.

Brent had also been looking forward to an upcoming skydiving
expedition he had planned with Scott and Kathy, their assistant.
After much consideration, they decided they were going to take the
leap together. That coming Saturday, they were to go on their first
dive. Brent was excited and the thought of hurtling through the air
at 120 miles per hour alleviated the feeling of stifling heat that was
hovering over Atlanta.

Despite Brent's good luck efforts and his hopeful outlook, the
NASDAQ had dropped to triple digits and looked to be heading
lower. Though traders at All-Tech had been taught how to "short"
stocks during a decline, most were uncharacteristically holding positions from the previous day. Those who were not were glued to their
monitors, eager to see if the negative momentum would turn their
way this morning. They were losing money by the minute. Shirt col-
lars were being unbuttoned, ties were loosened and handkerchiefs

were being applied to sweaty foreheads, even with the air conditioning blasting inside to offset the muggy southern climate.

On that same day at 11:30 a.m. Rick, one of the few traders at
Momentum who smoked, sat outside in the courtyard of the office
building. He had a cigarette between his lips and began fumbling in
his pockets for his lighter. Suddenly a burly hand thrust out from
behind him. A thumb flipped the lid of a Zippo lighter and held it
to Rick's cigarette. Rick turned to see Mark Barton.

"Thanks Mark. Hey, where the hell have you been?" Rick
Penly asked.

"Oh, I've been around," Barton said, then, in an apparent reference to the bad market he continued, "Rick, are you going to stick
around for the blood bath this afternoon?"

Before Rick could respond Barton was already walking out of
the courtyard with two knapsacks draped over his shoulder. Mark
seemed to be in a hurry. He was going to visit some old friends, say
hello to former colleagues and repay a few outstanding debts.

Later that afternoon, at about 2:15, Barton strolled into the
Momentum Securities brokerage office in the seven-story building
where Momentum was located. The office was filled with clients
working at computer terminals. Momentum management had
expected Barton to wire some additional funds into his account. As
one of the traders, Jesse, left the trading floor and headed towards the
elevator, he noticed Mark standing in the hallway with a big smile
on his face. The two men exchanged pleasantries and then went
about their business.

On the surface, it was business as usual when Mark made his
way into the Momentum Securities office that Thursday afternoon.
Upon entering the trading floor, he first met with Marci Brookings,

one of the office workers. Barton approached the reception desk, where Marci was sitting, and informed her that he was there to make a wire transfer into his account, but said he first wanted to speak with the manager, Justin Hoehn, to ask if he could trade again. He explained that he could have $200,000 wired into his account. Marci told Barton that Justin was out, but she offered to call him on his cell phone.

When Barton got Justin on the phone, Hoehn said, "Hi Mark. Good to hear from you. I'm at the store, but I'll be back in fifteen minutes. As long as you're wiring money, go ahead and do some trading until I get back."

Barton managed to keep himself busy for the next fifteen minutes by sharing idle chatter with some of the traders. They spoke briefly of the market that day, the weather and other non-threatening chit chat. He briefly spoke with Joe Skipper, another trader. He had a smile on his face, looked Skipper in the eyes and asked how he was doing. Skipper responded, "Great."

Thirty minutes later, Justin still had not returned and Barton was getting visibly anxious as he walked into the room where they took coffee breaks. Kevin Dial, the branch co-manager, noticed that Mark didn't seem to be wearing his traditional smile. His face was unusually tense; his eyebrows were furrowed together above his nose, and sweat beads were forming on his forehead. Barton was becoming impatient. He decided he did not want to wait any longer for Justin.

He and Kevin were making awkward small talk about how bad the market was that day. Then, while the two men were standing side by side, Mark Barton suddenly turned to Kevin and said, "It's a bad trading day and it's about to get worse."

At first, Kevin probably thought Mark was talking about the market. But as Kevin turned to look at Barton, he realized something was terribly wrong. Barton faced him with a heavy semi-automatic hand-gun in each hand. The scene was so out of place and surreal, Kevin couldn't grasp what was happening. Before he could react, Mark had pressed a Colt .45 automatic to the middle of Kevin's back, then quickly shoved a Glock 9 millimeter into the center of Kevin's chest. Barton fired both guns at the same time tearing lemon-size holes through both sides of Kevin's body.

The sound of the two gunshots echoed throughout the office. Blood exploded outward over the nearby desks and onto the four time zone clocks on the wall. The bullet had pierced Kevin's heart and left lung. His body immediately went limp and dropped to the floor. He was dead. Barton stood motionless and expressionless, his arms hanging at his sides still holding the two guns. The gun bar-rels each had thin streams of smoke drifting out of them. Barton's hands and shirt sleeves were soaked with blood. Blood freckled his face.

Everyone in the office stared in disbelief. There was total silence in the room, for one terrifying moment, in which no one breathed or even tried to say anything. All eyes were on Barton as he stood over Kevin's body. In an instant the silence and stillness turned to pandemonium, as the traders and workers began running, yelling and pushing each other in every direction. Everyone was scrambling to find an exit as their minds began to process the horror of what they just witnessed and the danger they were now faced with.

Barton watched. He seemed to relish the power he had over the others at that moment. They were weak, helpless and completely at his mercy. His life had been determined by the stocks he was trad-ing. He had no control of how well or how poorly they did. He always just had to accept what effect they would have on his own life. Now he would be the one determining what everyone's future would hold.

He began seeking out more victims. Barton started to shoot down the line of work stations. Andrew Zaprzala was hit and then James Jordan. Zaprzala hit the floor and thought; *We're all going to be killed here.*

Jordan got to his feet and made a mad dash to the door. Barton squeezed off another round at him and he was hit in the arm. He stumbled out the door.

Justin returned from running his errands and had just entered the hallway when he saw Jordan come running from the office, bleeding and calling for help. His face was white and he sounded frantic. A large circle of blood stained his jacket under his left shoulder.

"Jesus man, what in the hell is going on?" Justin asked.

"Someone is shooting up the office! Run, Justin, run!"

Justin turned instinctively and followed the man, who ran down the hallway toward the outer doors. Muffled cracks of gunfire were still resonating from the office. He got to a phone and dialed 911.

Scott Webb was in an office training a newcomer, Brad Schoemehl, when they heard the shooting. Webb opened the door and said, "What the hell is going on around here?" Seeing Brad, Barton turned towards him and fired. A bullet from Barton's .45 tore through Webb's chair, ripped through his right lung and lodged in his chest. Barton again fired into the office. Two bullets struck Schoemehl. The first hit him in the back; the second went through his shoulder.

Barton turned his attention to the reception area. Marci quickly tried diving under a heavy steel desk, but Barton aimed at her and squeezed the trigger. The bullet grazed her shoulder as she hit the floor short of the desk. Towards the front of the suite Russell Brown tried to take cover, but was shot three times.

Barton was on the move. He was rushing around the trading floor firing indiscriminately at anyone he could find. He was shooting with a gun in each hand, as if he was a cowboy in a movie. One by one, loud shots rang from both barrels. The air began to smell of sulphur and smoke. Some people hid behind desks, others managed to make it to the exits. Barton took aim at those who were lying on the floor and those who darted away from him. As he walked back through the room looking to finish off his victims, he paused for a moment to shoot out what had been his computer terminal.

Edward Quinn had been struck in the neck. He might have survived the single gunshot wound had it not been the path it followed. Quinn had turned as the bullet hit so that it exited his body and re-entered the back of his neck, where it cut the jugular vein and an artery before leaving the left side.

Two traders, Joe Skipper and Glenn Miller, made their way to an inner office. They quickly pushed a heavy desk against the door. Miller picked up the phone and dialed 911. Gunshots could be heard behind the closed door.

Linda Batch fortunately had gotten through to a 911 operator. She was locked in her office with one of Barton's victims. "There is a man bleeding in my office," she yelled at the operator. She had already given a description of the shooter, saying he was a white man wearing a pink shirt.

From the third story office Skipper and Miller were trying to escape. Just then, the door began to shake under the pounding and the body weight of Mark Barton. The two men watched as the heavy steel desk began to inch further into the room and the door slowly opened more and more. They both pushed back hard on the edge of the desk, but the door continued to nudge further into the office. Barton was using his entire 240 pounds to force the door open. The two men used all their strength and weight to keep the door from opening as Barton continually pounded against the door. He tried to get a glance of the two men through the crack of the door. It was still not wide enough to fire off a round.

Just as Joe and Glenn were expecting the door to fly open, the banging stopped. For a couple of seconds it was silent and the two men stood their ground holding their breath. Then the silence was suddenly broken. Two bullets ripped through the door, one whistling inches by Glenn's ear. Both bullets missed them and embedded themselves into the dry wall next to the window. Again it was silent. Barton had given up on the door and returned to the trading floor. The window would be later used by police to get into the building.

Barton walked back through the trading room. Schoemehl and Zaprzala lay on the floor, pretending to be dead. Barton shot Webb at point blank range and fired a third bullet into Schoemehl's right forearm. Fortunately, for some unknown reason, Zaprzala was ignored.

As Barton walked away, Schoemehl feared he was bleeding to death. He tried to move his hands and feet to make sure he wasn't paralyzed. When he didn't see Barton he decided to take a chance and made a run for an exit. He ran down a hall toward an insurance agency.

"I've been shot!" He screamed. "There's a maniac on the loose."

Hot shell casings sat in pools of blood around the victims. Some of the wounded lay motionless on the floor. Moans of agony could be heard throughout the room. Barton calmly reloaded both of his guns with new clips, fresh bullets. Then he picked up his knapsack and tucked the two guns inside, slinging it over his shoulder. Although the shooting had lasted more than ten minutes, no police were visible on the street.

Joe and Glenn were still locked in the office when four people started banging on the door to be let in. They opened the door and let them in. One of the six used a cell phone he found on the floor to call 911. He explained he was in a back room and they were trying to break a window. The operator asked for basic information: the address, the phone number, how many people were shot, but the man couldn't answer.

Nathan Degyansky took the phone from the man and said to the operator, "Ask me the questions."

In the background, the five were desperately trying to break the office window. They picked up a computer monitor and threw it into the window, but it wasn't heavy enough to crack the safety glass. Then they tried a file cabinet, which also failed. Finally, on their last try they threw an entire computer against it and the window shattered into hundreds of pieces onto the street thirty feet below. They looked out and then down. It was long way to the concrete sidewalk below.

"Everybody's able to get out of there now?" the operator asked.

"It's a twenty-foot drop" Degyansky said. "I don't know what good this going to do us."

He told the operator that of the six of them in the room, only Marci was shot and her shoulder wound didn't appear to be life-threatening. The operator instructed him to keep pressure on it to stop the bleeding.

"We're not going out of this room until the police arrive. We're scared," said Degyansky.

The others in the office began throwing trash and paper out the window to get the attention of police. They kept shouting, "We have an injury here!"

Still on the floor, Zaprzala heard the front door open and close. He believed that Barton had finally left. He saw Webb bleeding profusely, still slumped in his chair. Zaprzala saw him still breathing slightly.

"Scott, Scott – how you doing?" Zaprzala called out.

Scott didn't answer.

Reaching for the top of his desk, Zaprzala grabbed his mobile phone. He nervously hit buttons. Two and half minutes after the first call to 911 from a woman in the building's management office, Zaprzala got an operator on the line.

"Momentum Securities in Buckhead. We've been shot," Zaprzala said.

"Someone's been shot?" the operator said.

"A whole bunch of people have been shot."

"What is the address?"

"It's Momentum Securities."

"Momentum Securities. You work there. Are you playing on the phone, sir?"

"No, I'm shot."

"Why do you not know the address of where you are? Do you work there?"

"No, I'm a day trader."

"You're a decorator. And it's called Momentum Securities. What is your phone number?"

"404 – I can't remember."

"How many people have been shot?"

"About a dozen…send help, please."

"I will."

The operator stayed to try to keep Zaprzala calm until police arrived. He then asked her to call his wife.

"You're not going to die, you're going to be all right," she answered. "You just stay on here with me and talk to me."

"I can hear talking now."

"You can hear what now, baby?"

Police officers burst into the office, shouting at Zaprzala to raise his hands.

"I can't," he said. "I'm shot."

In the midst of the chaos, Mark calmly organized his knapsack. Within minutes, Barton was making his way across the street towards the All-Tech offices, his next target.

chapter six

Blood Bath

The clock in the middle of the room read 2:55 p.m. when Mark Barton opened the tall glass doors that led to the All-Tech trading floor and slowly made his way into the room. The office was full of clients and workers. The trading floor was enclosed on three sides by glass walls. On the 1,800 square foot floor were thirty-five trading stations, along with three large conference tables. A large office and a small conference room faced the trading floor, where on a typical day between thirty to forty clients could trade. Each room was separated by glass panels.

Despite the turbulent market, it was business as usual for Barton's former colleagues. Several said hello to him as he passed them, then quickly focused back on their trading. Fred Herder had sat side by side with Barton day after day trading at the computer terminals. Herder noticed that despite the air conditioning, Barton was sweating profusely. Today Barton didn't seem to want to talk shop with his fellow traders. He specifically singled out the working staff saying he hoped they weren't out doing errands. The staff was all in the building that day, spread throughout the office. Meredith Winnit was seated in the entryway at the reception desk. Scott Manspeaker and Kathy Van Camp were in the main office and Brent was in the conference room giving a system demonstration to a potential client. After he entered, Barton immediately tried to get Brent's attention.

I made eye contact through the glass with my old friend at around 3:00 p.m. Hey, it's Mark, I thought. I smiled and waved, nodding my head toward my client, hoping my friend and colleague would understand that I was in the middle of training. At that point, we needed all the clients we could get.

Instead of sitting in the waiting area, Mark motioned to me to come out with the same quirky smile he'd always had. Again, I shook my head and gestured to the trainee. Then Barton began pacing outside the glass. Back and forth he walked, occasionally glancing into the trading floor with an impatient look. Finally, he stopped pacing and rapped on the glass loudly with his knuckles, pinching his face up, giving me almost an angry look. Good God, I thought, what does he want? I had no choice but to excuse myself to my client and at least acknowledge Barton's presence.

I nodded my head to him as if to say, okay and motioned for him to come in. As he swung the door open, he suddenly looked excited, as if he was eager to share some good news. Perhaps he'd perfected his soap, I thought. Maybe he was finally here to repay his thirty thousand dollar debt.

"Hey Brent, I need to talk to you. It's important. Can I have a minute?" he asked.

"Yes Mark, just a minute." I said, hoping he would leave me alone and maybe go speak to Scott. But as he closed the door, he turned back smiling broadly and said, "Hurry up Brent. You're really going to love this!"

I'm going to have to go see what he wants, I thought, waiting for the appropriate place to interrupt my trainee.

While Brent finished up with his new client, Barton walked into the break room, grabbed a couple of soda cans out of the refrigerator and went to say hello to a couple of his colleagues.

"Hey Mark," one of the traders blurted.

Another asked, "Where have you been? You make too much money or what?"

"Not really," Barton replied as he wiped the superficial smile from his face, advertising the fact that he was not too talkative today.

As the idle talk with the traders subsided, Barton quickly made his way into the main office. For a few brief moments, he exchanged pleasantries with Scott and Kathy while acting as if nothing was wrong. It was good to see them, he said. They returned with the same. Standing in the doorway, Barton was dressed in his typical khaki shorts and polo. Scott started to become fixated on Barton's arms. He noticed red dots that speckled Barton's forearms, the collar of his shirt and his hands. Scott was trying to think what Barton might have been doing earlier in the day. *He must have been painting and splattered himself.* Abruptly, Barton told them he would be right back. He turned and headed towards the doorway, stopping short of leaving the room. He nonchalantly grabbed the controls of the three neutral colored blinds that covered the long glass panels that separated the office from the trading floor. Scott and Kathy watched in wonder as he slowly twisted the rods and closed the blinds before leaving the room. As he walked out, Barton closed the door behind him. Kathy turned to Scott with a perplexed look on her face. They both felt something strange was happening. Before she could say anything Scott jokingly said," What's he going to do, kill us?" The two let out a half-hearted laugh and then shrugged it off and continued to work.

Barton walked across the trading floor back to the conference room. He had an unusual expression on his face. Opening the door he said, "Brent, come here quick. Really, you're gonna love this!"

My first thought was that he was going to give me a check for $30,000. That would have certainly made my day considering how trading was going. I could see that he was excited. Perhaps his big new product had brought him a windfall. I decided to put my meeting on hold for a couple of minutes and informed my client that I would be right back. In turn, Mark turned to the man and politely asked, "May I get you something to drink?" I declined but the client answered, "I'll take a Coke." In the rush to meet with Mark, my mind was stirring. Maybe he had developed another product. Maybe he had made a fortune doing something. "Who knows," I was thinking to myself when Mark returned and gave the man a Dr. Pepper. I was so caught up in the excitement of the moment that I failed to realize the man received a Dr. Pepper when he had requested a Coke. However, the potential client said nothing as I excused myself to see what Barton was so excited about.

As I headed towards the main office, he followed close behind me. While engaging in random small talk along the way, I noticed that Mark could have cared less about what we were discussing. He was anxious to get the meeting underway and remained composed about the business at hand. In retrospect, there appeared nothing peculiar about Mark's mannerisms other than the fact that he was in a hurry. He was dressed the same and acted the same as he always had. Although, as we approached the office, I thought it odd that the blinds and the door were closed; they were always kept open so that we could watch the trading floor.

Upon entering the office, I noticed Scott was sitting behind the desk and Kathy was working at a computer on another table with her back to us. Looking at us over her shoulder, she gave us an inquisitive look, but did not say anything and continued working on her computer, not wanting to be rude. I had taken two or three steps inside the office when I turned and faced Mark as he calmly closed the door. Suddenly, an uneasy feeling crossed my mind. With the blinds closed, I felt shut off not only from the office, but from the world.

Mark turned and stood in front of me, roughly four feet away. Though I was nervous, I tried to be positive. The fact that he entered the room with the remnants of a smile on his face gave me some reassurance that he was up to something good.

Making eye contact with me, as he turned from closing the door, Mark's smile faded, giving way to a cold, blank stare into a vacant nothingness. It was as if he was looking through me and not at me. "Well what is it?" I asked, hoping to hear something good come out of his mouth. Ignoring my question, he spoke in a cool calculated tone, "Today is going to be visual."

I had but a brief second to ponder his carefully chosen words as he was on the move. What's that supposed to mean? *I thought as I replayed his words in my head. His words and his expression did not match his initial jovial and excited demeanor. I had not even finished repeating his statement when it registered to me that something was terribly wrong as I watched Mark Barton.*

Brent's entire world would change in the next three seconds, as would Scott's and Kathy's. By the time Mark Barton pulled his shirt out of his shorts to reveal two large handguns stuck in the waistband, it was too late. Like an outlaw in a bad western, he crossed his left hand over to the right and his right hand over to his left and pulled out a nickel-plated .45 caliber and a black 9mm. At first, Brent thought it was another one of Mark's childish pranks. *They were cap guns, kids' toys*, he thought. By the time it registered that they were real, Barton was taking aim.

Barton fired both guns into Brent. The first, a .45 caliber hollow point slug (very deadly, developed expressly for the purpose of killing someone, the bullets are intended to mushroom out and become larger as they exit the body) slammed into his abdomen just below the sternum. As the bullet ricocheted through his body, it tore through his liver, spleen and diaphragm before exiting out of his back, two inches from his spine. It missed his heart by less than a millimeter.

The 9mm, also loaded with hollow point bullets, hit Brent in the elbow and bounced up his arm, and before it could mushroom out, the bullet came to rest in his tricep muscle just short of exiting.

I saw a bright flash and then another and another, which sounded like a loud but muffled pop or a car backfiring. Suddenly my feet were knocked out from underneath me, like I'd been taken down quickly, surprisingly, by a larger, faster opponent in one of my old high school wrestling matches. I don't remember hitting the floor, nor did I feel any pain. The next thing I remembered was lying face down on the carpet asking myself, what in the world was that? What is happening to me? Then I felt the warm thick blood pooling up around me. I began to panic, I was in shock. My God, this is real! That son-of-a-bitch just shot me! As the sounds of gunshots continued to ring out, I felt the pain intensifying. I felt like I'd been hit in the chest with a sledgehammer, as my stomach tightened and strained in agony. I couldn't move.

Lying on the floor in terrible pain, with my face turned to the side, I could see the two spent casings; they told me everything I needed to know. I was going to die. My God, I'm going to die here on the floor. I knew I was losing a great deal of blood because I was growing lightheaded and though the pain was excruciating, I could feel my arms and legs beginning to tingle, and the pool of blood around me was crawling out in a larger and larger circle, soaking through the carpeting as it advanced. I wondered if Scott and Kathy were still in the room. Had they been shot? Were they alive? There were no sounds.

Barton had not come just to see Brent. Lying helpless, Brent heard two more loud shots ring out. One struck Kathy in the temple, going through one side of her head and out the other temple. Blood flowed down her throat and shoulders and soaked into her blouse. Her facial artery, that essential lifeline which crept up her jaw to supply the color to her cheeks and feed the brain, had been severed.

Another shot and Scott fell motionless to the floor by the desk. Scott had one bullet lodge in his abdomen and another hit his wrist, fracturing his forearm. The spittle at the corner of his mouth was red and his eyes were closed.

The way I landed, I couldn't see Scott or Kathy. Both were behind me. I didn't want to move so I couldn't look for them. Barton would see that I was alive. So, I lay facing the computer printer, exactly the way I landed. I saw the shell casings, the blood flowing under me. I am now ashamed of my thoughts as they jumped around quickly: escape, survive and worry about the others later. But I suppose that's what goes through everyone's mind when they are dying or wounded - survival.

Brent was sprawled on the floor with his eyes closed. Playing dead might be his only chance, but what if Mark continued his rampage? If so, could Brent really stop him anyway, even if he wanted to? Could he even bring himself to his feet? Would he even be alive in the next few minutes?

Barton stepped back toward the door, plodding purposely across the carpet to the trading floor. The five shots that hit Brent, Scott and Kathy only took five or ten seconds, though in Brent's mind he had been lying on the floor for an eternity. Outside the office on the trading floor, people were reacting to the gunshots.

Some thought that someone was banging on filing cabinets or that some equipment had fallen over. No one was expecting to hear gunfire that afternoon. Brent was helpless to do anything, he couldn't move even to the phone. He could only hope the shooting would end there.

Fred Herder saw Barton walk out of the office holding two guns. Barton moved alongside the twenty-five-foot-long row of trading desks where the traders sat facing each other. As people began either to run or to duck down behind desks, Barton immediately began firing wildly throughout the room.

Barton first found Nell Jones sitting outside a door. She looked right into his eyes and described him as "someone who was very calm and determined. He looked like he didn't have any feelings." He pointed a gun towards her and pulled the trigger at point blank range. The bullet whizzed by her head and missed her entirely. She was able to escape when he turned to shoot at the others.

Jamshid Havash was sitting at a table just outside the manager's office. He didn't have time to run before he was hit in the back by a bullet that killed him instantly. Red blood slowly covered the white shirt he was wearing.

Across the table, Yuzef Liberzon and Fred Herder started to move, but Barton moved faster. Herder tried to duck under a desk, but he was shot in the back. Herder fell to the floor and lay in a fetal position. Liberzon was struck by a bullet in the side of the head, his blood spraying the wall next to him. He fell to the floor, critically injured.

Barton turned to his right and walked toward another table of computers in the middle of the room. Three traders on one side scrambled out a side door next to the table and ran down a breezeway that led to the parking deck. On the other side of the table, three other traders were trapped. Mike Ford dropped to the floor and hid beneath a table. Next to him, Allen Tenenbaum tried to crouch beneath his work station, but Barton fired a bullet into his back, killing him.

Dean Delawalla tried to run to the door to follow the others who had escaped. As he was running a bullet struck him in the middle of his back and came out his chest. The bullet's trajectory carried it into his throat and out a second time above his left eye. As he was falling, Barton shot him again in the right buttock. He was already dead.

Barton moved back to the front of the room, firing one gun then the other. Joseph Dessert was standing at his work station at a table near the front door. He was facing Barton, when Barton squeezed the trigger of the .45 twice. One round hit Dessert's right shoulder and another struck his upper chest, killing him.

At the same table were Harry Higginbotham and Sang Yoon. Barton shot Higginbotham in the head and Yoon in the arm. A bullet struck Meredith Winnit in the back, while she was hiding behind a partition in the reception area,

Bam, bam, bam followed by thump, thump, thump. The bullets slamming into flesh sounded like someone pounding on a watermelon. It was incessant. Barton simply shot people as they sat on the floor frozen in fear. Though the entire front wall of the office was made of glass, Barton's precise shots never hit it. Barton kept firing at anyone he could find. After he emptied the clips from each gun, he proceeded to reload them. He announced, "I certainly hope this doesn't ruin your trading day!" Then he started to shoot again.

At that point my only thought was survival; finding help. Should I play dead? Should I try to help the others? I could still move my right arm and slowly move my legs, but would I have the strength to pull myself up and if so, would that just exacerbate my wounds? A hundred thoughts raced

through my mind as I continued to hear the gunfire - a hundred thoughts, but no logical answers. The sound of the gunfire was making me nauseous. As if things weren't bad enough, I wanted to puke. I think the only thing that kept me from vomiting was the intensity of the pain.

I told myself to think like the All-American wrestler I had been in school. I'd been up against the wall plenty of times and always found a way to win. I never walked away from a bully or a fight either. It was in that moment that I remembered something my father had told me long ago, "Face your fears and they will disappear. Run and they will always chase you." I knew in that instant that I would survive. Somehow, I would survive. I realized that instead of seeing my entire life flash before my eyes or seeing a bright alluring white light, as people who have survived near death experiences often say, I was seeing possibilities. Perhaps I could fight Mark and wrestle the guns away, save some lives maybe. I also realized that the panic that had initially swept over me was gone. I was thinking clearly, rationally. I held no hate for the man; my thoughts focused solely on staying alive.

But the more I thought about it, the less chance there seemed of subduing the maniacal 240-pound Barton. I might have been a wrestler, but taking away two powerful handguns from a man who outweighed me by eighty pounds was a stretch. I decided I would make a run for it.

There were three possible exits. One was inside the conference room next to the main office door where I was lying, which led to an interior hallway. If I could crawl out it would lead to a back stairwell. If I went out through the conference room, I could exit the building through the main entrance and out into the street for help. The other choice would be to go out a side door into the courtyard below. We were on the second floor of the building. Doing this, however, would mean having to cross the trading floor. Mark was still somewhere on the trading floor. I continued to hear gunshots. Okay, the conference room is my only chance, I thought to myself while knowing that I risked further injury or death if my plan went sour. There was no time to be scared.

By now my adrenaline was kicking in. I knew it was time to move. My mind wanted to live; my body reacted to my mind. I willed myself to rise on my unstable feet. Using my hands to push myself up onto my wobbling legs, I instinctively clutched at my chest; blood was pumping through my fingers, I couldn't stop it. Again, I was feeling weak and lightheaded. I managed to bring myself to my feet and then lunged for the door.

Quickly, I turned the brass knob and opened it. This was a terrible mistake. Barton stood on the other side. Though he was facing the trading floor he took careful aim at anyone who dared to stand up and run. One by one he squeezed off rounds trying to pick off arms, legs and heads, anything visible. Looking past his shoulder, the horrible reality of the room asserted itself.

What should I do now? Lie back down and play dead? If Mark turned around and saw me, he would surely finish me off, perhaps a bullet to the head this time. Just then, I saw one of the traders jump up and make a dash for the door. He was too slow and Mark shot him in the back. Seeing that, I decided to make a run for it, I had no choice. I could save myself and maybe others if I could just get to another office to use a phone or outside to get help.

As I started toward the door, Mark raised his gun once again and took aim at a woman. She was directly in front of him with nowhere to go. Lunging through the doorway, I used my good shoulder to ram into Barton. It was just enough of a surprise to knock him off balance, his shot crashing through a computer monitor, narrowly missing the woman. The spent shell casing careened off a desk, bouncing, pinging until it came to rest on the floor.

My body block was only temporary as Barton spun around and righted himself. By then, though, I was rounding the corner of the conference table. I heard two more shots; one searing through my left arm, the other hitting just below my left shoulder blade, coming out on the left side of my chest: My fourth wound. Suddenly everything was happening in ultra-slow motion.

Despite being shot four times, Brent did not give up. He had but one thought on his mind, to live. He said he didn't feel the third and fourth bullets; most likely he was in shock at that point. He was acting out of pure animal instinct. Playing dead was no longer an option. Brent dashed into the conference room and toward the doorway. His life would depend upon what happened in the next few seconds. For reasons unknown, Barton turned back to the trading floor instead of continuing his hunt for Brent. Perhaps he would come back to finish him later or he thought he had already finished him off.

Not knowing the extent of my internal injuries, except for the pain, I continued along my escape route. As I stumbled towards the hallway, I managed to attract two followers. Upon witnessing my flight from the office, one of the traders fell in behind me as I headed out the door. A few seconds later another potential target decided she would take her chances and she headed towards the hallway also.

After opening the door and entering the long narrow hallway, I faced another decision. Should I turn left and head towards the main building exit or turn right and head for the stairwell. If I go out the main exit, surely he will see me, I thought, but I had to make a decision; I had no time for questions, the throbbing pain that shot through me reminded me of my deteriorating condition. I bolted down the hall toward the rear stairwell, with all the strength I could muster. Fumbling up against the walls, feeling my way along, I left a trail of dark red smears over any surface I touched.

Although I had been down this path a million times before, it felt as if I was in a surreal version of it. The hallway colors faded and the walls and the carpets seemed to vanish, as I found myself in a world of blacks, grays and whites. The bright fluorescent lights in the ceiling hovered over me; their emittence was clouded by a misty haze of gray and white. Looking down that very long strange hallway, I questioned whether I would have the strength to make it to the end. I would later find out that at this point, I'd already lost two pints of blood. At the time I did not have the presence of mind to register that my blue shirt had already turned a dark brownish red.

As I made my way down the end of the hallway, I could see the stairway door with nothing blocking my path. With my right arm held tightly against the bullet hole in my abdomen, I ran as hard as I could. At the end of the hall I made out a dark rectangle, the door. Clutching at the hole in my stomach I stumbled towards it, bracing myself against the wall as I made my way, aware that I could no longer feel my legs as my left arm hung limply at my side. I turned back to see if the killer was still behind me. He was not. I breathed a sigh of relief. I also noticed that the two people who had followed me out were no longer behind me.

Just before I reached the door, which was still ten or fifteen feet away, I came upon the elevator utility room, an option I'd completely ignored in my plans. Next to the elevator was a five-by-five-foot room that separated the hallway from the elevator. Using everything I had, I pushed the heavy brown door open and successfully got inside the room. If I could get into the elevator in front of me, Mark would not find me. I kept stabbing at the button, hoping that the elevator would arrive. I anxiously waited for the slow moving service elevator to reach my floor. As I listened to the methodical slow whirr of the moving elevator, I kept looking back over my shoulder for Mark as I continued frantically to push the button.

Although I could hear its movement, the unhurried elevator was not making its way to my floor anytime soon. "Come on! Come on!" I quietly whispered, pleading with the piece of machinery. I got on my knees as I desperately tried to pry the doors open with hopes that at least I could find some sort of protection in the event that Mark had followed me down the hallway. It was no use. The elevator must be on one of the top floors, I thought, starting to panic.

As I waited for the elevator to arrive, I felt my body becoming weak. It was nothing but pure adrenaline that had gotten me this far, I figured. The rush was wearing off and for the first time since the shots rang out, I felt the chill of death wash over me. "This is it," I thought to myself while doubting that I could go any further. I am going to die in this little box and no one will ever know until it's too late. I was scared, scared of dying and scared that Mark was hot on my trail.

Still on my knees from trying to pry the elevator doors apart, I crawled to the entrance door hoping to take a peek down the hallway. Opening the door of the small room slightly, I saw a woman running towards the end of the hallway. She was not injured, but was obviously panicked. I started to gesture to her to duck into the room with me. She was only three feet away when Mark came into view behind her.

Oh my God, I thought, as he raced up to her pointing the gun to the back of her head. There was nothing I could do. I felt weak and could no longer stand up. I had never been as desperately helpless as in that minute. I pulled back in fear of being seen and realizing I had no way to help. I slowly closed the door. As the shot rang out, my stomach churned both in sympathy and fear. I would later discover that he shot her in the head at point blank range, killing her instantly.

Please God, don't let me die. I don't want to die, I was pleading. I had not made eye contact with Barton and did not know if he had seen me. Then in the instant he pulled the trigger, God answered me - the elevator doors opened.

Brent managed to crawl into the elevator and began to furiously push all the buttons, trying to close the doors. When they finally did begin to close, the door to the small room opened. Barton dashed towards the open gap in the closing elevator doors. As the two elevator doors nearly touched, Barton stood on the other side aiming the .45 through the crack. Miraculously, the doors closed completely before a shot rang out. Later police would discover that Barton had pushed the elevator "up" button, perhaps with the intention of hunting Brent down or finding more potential victims on the floors above. They would never be sure.

The scene on the trading floor was horrifying. Bodies were spread randomly around the offices. The four time zone clocks, like those at Momentum, were splattered with blood, as were the walls and desks. Barton had shot with astounding accuracy, most of the victims either shot in the back or in the head. In most cases, Barton had been standing within five feet of his victims, so he himself was covered with their blood. Barton stood in the center of the room, guns held down at his side. He had a serene look on his face, as if he had just completed a difficult task with precision and success.

By now, police had responded to the Momentum 911 calls coming from across the street. As Barton slowly walked towards the front door, one man was lying wounded on the floor facing in the direction of the doors. He had his eyes closed, his hands clutched together and he was praying. He was preparing to die as Barton's footsteps got closer. He held his breath, anticipating a final shot, but the room stayed silent. Barton continued walking past him and disappeared out the door.

In the midst of the still ensuing chaos, no one knew if the shooter was still somewhere in the building or had gotten away. Chris Brennan had survived the gunfire. He was at All-Tech that day for a three week boot camp seminar. Since he was not a full time trader, he was stationed in the corner of the room farthest from any exit. He and a small group of people had huddled together in the corner during most of the shooting. Seven out of the eleven people that were unharmed were in that corner. Brennan later nicknamed it the "Amen Corner."

Following the shooting, Brennan grabbed his cell phone and called 911. He told them that there had been a lot of shots fired and seven or eight ambulances were needed. A bunch of people had been shot and were dead or wounded. The 911 operator asked for his location. He gave her the address. She asked for the phone number, again he complied. Then she stated police were already there. However, no help had arrived at All-Tech. She was wrong. Police were at the site of the first shooting.

Outside police were running towards the doors at the Momentum offices. Little did the police know that Momentum Securities wasn't the only crime scene, as pools of blood spread out in circles from fallen bodies and seeped into the carpets across the street at All-Tech. The scene was total mayhem, no one sure where the killer was or who would get shot next. As civilians stood outside watching the commotion, some started running. Meanwhile across the street Barton simply got in his green mini-van where he parked it. He put his duffel bag on the passenger seat and merged his van into traffic on Piedmont Road. Within minutes the killer disappeared undetected, leaving behind one of the most gruesome crime scenes that Atlanta had ever seen.

chapter seven

Mortal Wounds

Brent Doonan rode a slow elevator to freedom crouched on all fours like a wounded animal. By this point he felt so weak, he knew if he allowed himself to lie down he would not be able to get up. But he also realized he now had a fighting chance and had to draw upon any remaining strength in his body. After what seemed an eternity in the upward moving elevator, it suddenly stopped and the doors opened onto a hallway. Brent didn't know which floor he had reached, because he had pushed all the buttons and couldn't read the floor sign.

Peering down the hallway, swaying on unsteady feet, Brent reasoned that if he could make it into one of the offices, he would be able to get help. *Why hadn't the police arrived?* he agonized. As he took his first steps, it became painfully obvious that the adrenaline surge that had gotten him here was not going to last. His wounds were taking over. Using the hallway walls to maintain his balance, Brent turned to the right and began his torturous journey to get help. With no more than one hundred feet to go, he saw an office door looming at the end of the hallway. Brent was so close. He knew he had to push himself onward. As he made his way down the hall he left a trail of blood behind him. Looking around Brent gasped. If Mark was following, the blood he smeared along the hallway walls would give him away. Brent needed help. He reasoned that with all the horrific commotion, surely someone heard something!

In fact, people did hear the gunshots. In the midst of all the chaos, a motorcycle officer, John Caber, en route to Momentum Securities, had heard the sound of gunshots. As an ex-marine, he knew the distinct sound a gun makes and was trying to find its source. He quickly whipped his cycle into the parking lot of the office complex and turned off the engine, listening for the sound again. But the gunshots had fallen silent.

Caber thought maybe the sound had come from across the walkway in another building, but he was unsure. Pulling out his gun, he left his motorcycle and raced to the scene on foot. A man was running towards him. His face was streaked with purple and red bruises and he had a look of panic in his eyes. "Call the police!" the man kept shouting. As Caber got closer he saw security guards running inside the building. Caber crossed a walkway, got to the emergency exit of All-Tech and peered inside to the trading room. He could not believe his eyes.

One man was lying on the floor with a bullet wound in his cheek. He was silently trying to feel places on his body to determine where he had been shot. A few feet away another man lay on his back, his eyes wide open and fixed. Caber ran to him. He leaned forward and began to perform CPR. "I've never done this for real before," Caber whispered to himself. When Caber pressed on the man's chest, he could feel the man's ribs cracking. He tried to fill the victim's lungs with air, but it traveled right back out. The man was dead.

With a sense of defeat, Caber stood up and looked around the room. He saw another man lying on the floor not moving. The curious began rushing into the room. There was an eerie silence. The onlookers, frozen in disbelief and shock, were trying to process the horror they were seeing: a massacre.

As he looked around the room, Caber noticed something on the floor. It was a 9mm bullet, a hollow point. Caber recognized it since he owned a 9mm handgun. Nearby, he saw a shell casing from a .45 caliber bullet. He shook his head. Two different guns.

Near the front of the room a young woman was slipping into shock. She had been shot in the hip. People were trying to cover her with clothes to keep her warm. Towards the woman's left was a man with bullet wounds in his chest. Dead. Caber looked into the manager's office and saw blood all over the wall.

Caber grabbed for his radio. He stated his location as being in Building Eight, and told of the wounded, requesting immediate assistance. However, his pleas were seemingly falling on deaf ears. The superior officer informed Caber that he was in the wrong location and that he should report to the Securities Center office complex immediately.

Stunned at the response, Caber again repeated that there were dead and wounded in Building Eight and he needed immediate assistance. The other officer mistakenly told him he was in the wrong place.

Both brokerage firms were now scenes of mass chaos as police scrambled to understand exactly what had just occurred.

A lone phone began ringing in the All-Tech office, the noise startling several people. Someone picked it up, thinking it might be

the police or the paramedics. The caller was Derek, the office manager of All-Tech in Kansas City, casually asking if he could speak to
Brent.

"Don't you know what just happened here?" the voice yelled.

Derek was startled, "What's the matter?"

"There's been a shooting and the shooter is still in the building!" the voice on the other end frantically replied.

"Okay," Derek said, "Do not hang up this phone. I'll help you.
Where's Brent, where's Scott?" Derek was urgently trying to piece
the event together.

"I don't know," the man replied in a voice that was already starting to crack, "But someone saw Brent get shot."

In the background, Derek could hear people screaming. He
could hear others crying. It was chaos, utter chaos. It was chilling.

"Just keep this line open," Derek explained to the frantic voice
on the other end, "I'll be right back."

Meanwhile, Brent, moving slowly toward the end of the hallway, realized he wasn't going to make it. Filled with fear and disappointment, he believed he was coming to the end of the strength he
summoned, but he still desperately wanted to live. Weak and barely
able to stand he turned back and inched towards the elevator.
Nearing the elevator entrance, he glanced to his right as his heart
pounded in his chest. There it was, an office, right next to the elevator. Somehow in his bleary struggle to find help, he hadn't noticed
it before. As his suffering increased, he stumbled into the office and
yelled, "Help! Help me! I've been shot!"

A man in another office behind the reception area said, "Is this
a joke?"

Shaking with pain, bleeding profusely, Brent slumped to the
floor in the doorway, his small burst of energy fading fast with his

hope, and said, "No. This is not a joke." His torment and anxiety mounted. Lying in the middle of the entrance way, he cried out, "Please help!" A moment later, a woman named Carolyn found him and began yelling to the others, "Help! Help me in here! A man has been shot!"

Randy, another employee, ran over, recognizing Brent as one of the traders on the third floor. Carolyn frantically dialed 911, as other workers dashed into the room

Brent cried out, "Quick, get me out of the doorway!" Scared that Barton was searching for Brent, he pleaded, "Hide me! Hide me! He's after me and if he sees me we're all dead!"

At first they were hesitant to move Brent for fear of further injuring him, but Brent continued to beg them to get him away from the door. By then several people were on their cell phones calling 911, telling the same story different ways. A man had been mugged. A man had been beaten. Someone was shot, maybe others as well. In answer to the operators' questions all replied, we don't know who or why.

"A man has been shot and he is lying on my floor bleeding to death," Carolyn told the 911 operator.

"Okay ma'am, I understand. Tell me your address."

"I don't know the address. We're in Piedmont somewhere," Carolyn said.

"Ma'am, we have units en route. Please calm down."

"What do you mean you have someone en route?" Carolyn said. "I am just now calling you."

In fact, dozens of officers were on their way, but not to All-Tech. They were responding to other emergency calls from Momentum Securities. Meanwhile, Officer Caber, the officer who had heard the gunshots from the All-Tech office, had been calling for backup since he arrived. He told the other police whom he contacted that he didn't know how many were dead, wounded, alive or if the killer was still in the building. He stated his position as building eight and requested immediate assistance. The superior officer to whom he was speaking continued to inform him that he was in the wrong location and that he should report to Momentum Securities.

Stunned, the officer at the site repeated his plea. He stated he could see at least seven wounded or dead. Again the call came back to report to Momentum. This miscommunication went on for what seemed like a long period. Crucial minutes passed before officers understood both Momentum and All-Tech were under siege. Meanwhile, the confusion and chaos continued.

After unsuccessfully trying to contact 911, Chris Brennan went to Scott's office. He saw that Scott had been shot in the stomach and tried to reassure Scott that he would be okay. Kathy was also lying on the floor; she had been shot in the temple. Since Chris heard people say that Barton was responsible, he asked Scott where the files were located where they kept the traders' names. Scott tapped his fingers against a filing cabinet. Chris opened the drawer, looked inside and pulled out Barton's file.

Meanwhile, Brent, who was lying on the floor in another office, had begun gasping for breath. The scene was bedlam. What had started out as a typical middle of the week workday had become a nightmare. No one knew what to do. No one had medicine or compresses, or knew what kind of medical procedures to apply. They were totally unprepared for a catastrophe of this magnitude. Some stood in shock covering their mouths with their hands, others were frozen in fear.

Finally, a woman named Serena stepped up and took control, trying to calm everyone down. She thought perhaps Brent was in the middle of a business deal gone sour, some angry client getting revenge. Or perhaps the young man at her feet was the result of a drug deal gone bad.

"Do you have AIDS?" Serena asked him, as she knelt down beside him. Brent answered with a resounding no and another plea for help.

"I'm going to find something to stop your bleeding."

Serena quickly ran into the office kitchen and began searching for a cloth to help stop the bleeding while Lynda turned her attention to Brent.

"What is your name?" Lynda asked.

"Brent Doonan."

"Brent Dona?" She asked, unable fully to comprehend Brent's slurred speech.

"No, Doo-none," Brent tried to articulate.

"Do you know who did this to you?"

"Yeah, Mark Barton," Brent mumbled while fighting his intense pain. He was, in fact, starting to slip into unconsciousness. As Lynda continued to throw a barrage of questions at him, all he could think was, *I am about to die and all this woman is doing is interrogating me.*

Hoping to get to the bottom of the ordeal, she continued asking questions, "Why did he do this?" Brent had no idea. "Where is he now?" Lynda asked in a concerned tone. Again, Brent had no idea. "Okay," she said, "Just hang in there; help is on the way."

While waiting for Serena to return, Lynda started to pray aloud. With her hands on Brent's body she asked God to save him, and then came the answer. Lynda felt that God spoke through her touch. She felt the spirit through her hands as she continued kneeling over Brent, praying at his side. At that point Lynda told him, "You are going to be just fine. I can feel it. Just try to relax."

My left arm was paralyzed. It lay by my side like a piece of meat; no feeling. It was no longer a part of me. Though a bullet was still wedged inside my tricep muscle, I could move my right arm. I had experienced broken bones and torn tendons before, but nothing ever compared to this level of pain. The hole in my chest was the size of a walnut. I felt like a stake had been driven through my heart. Every inch of me throbbed and pounded. On the outside of that hole, it felt as if someone were lighting my skin on fire with a blowtorch. I had trouble swallowing and breathing. I didn't know it at the time, but given my circumstances, it could actually have been much worse. Normally, hollow point bullets make a small entry wound, but then the soft bullet expands as it exits; leaving gaping wounds the size of softballs. Barton had been standing so close to me that three of the four shots went through me and into the office walls. They never had time to expand. I guess my lucky outfit had paid off.

Despite the pain and the fear, there was another part of me that kept saying, "Stay strong." A voice deep inside me was convinced I could make it. It's almost as if I was three people; one was the physical body, one was the emotional aspect and the other was the spiritual. So far, the spiritual had overcome the other two weaker parts of me.

At that moment, Serena returned from the kitchen with a roll of paper towels. "This may not be the ideal dressing, but it's all we've got," she said as she applied pressure to Brent's wounds with the towels. At least the paper towels were clean and would be absorbent. Continuing to press the towels to his chest, Serena and her co-worker, Russell, held them tightly against the gaping hole. In seconds, the paper towels were soaked with blood. She tossed those away, tore off several more sheets and applied those. By now, another woman at the scene, Carolyn, had been in touch with the 911 operator for the second time and had correctly given the address and the name of the office complex. Finally, the police were on the way.

While Lynda, Serena and Russell sat by Brent's side, trying to stop the bleeding, Serena spoke softly to Brent saying, "I don't want you to be uncomfortable." She then untied his tie, loosened his collar and gently stroked his forehead. Brent thought of how his mother would gently stroke his hair and forehead to soothe him when he was a sick child. Serena's gentle touch calmed him.

A few minutes later, Lynda decided it was time to assess the damage. She asked Brent if she could open his shirt to look at his wounds. He weakly nodded yes, though he was frightened about what their reactions might be. Lynda gently unbuttoned his shirt, which was sticky with blood, and pulled the fabric back.

She placed two fingers on Brent's throat feeling for a pulse. She waited. Nothing. She turned to Serena with a hopeless expression, her head shaking back and forth. As Brent's shirt was laid open, the facial expressions of all three changed dramatically from concern to sheer horror. "Oh my God," Brent murmured, peering from behind his lowered eyelids, "it's worse than I imagined."

At that moment, I thought all was lost. Seeing the horror on their faces and feeling I was going to die, I tried to forgive Mark Barton. Maybe he was nuts and did not know what he was doing. Maybe he was possessed by demons or had forgotten to take some medication. It might have been a chemical imbalance or a brain tumor. Who knows? In that moment I thought about forgiveness, but I couldn't, I knew those are the things people think of right before they die. I didn't want to die, so again, I managed to pull myself up from my negative thoughts. Above all, no matter what, I had to think positively. I focused on living.

By now, ten or fifteen minutes had passed and there was still no sign of help. Each passing second seemed like a minute to Brent; each minute felt like an hour. He was giving it everything he had to hang on, but the struggle was taking its toll.

"Where the heck are they?" Brent asked weakly, knowing the EMTs should have responded by now.

"We don't know," Lynda replied, "But they are on their way. Carolyn is on the phone with the 911 operators right now."

"They've got to hurry or I'm not going to make it," Brent pleaded.

"We know. Calm down, you're going to be just fine," she confidently replied while stroking Brent's forehead.

"Ah the hell with it, I'll go myself," Brent said, frustrated that it was taking so long yet scared that he couldn't make it any longer. "Here, help me up," hoping that something could be done.

"Just stay put, they are on their way," Serena chimed in.

All those present knew Brent was in no shape to go anywhere. Thoughts of doubt began creeping in Brent's mind as he wondered how much longer he could continue. At first, he thought he could hold on for as long as it took for the EMTs to arrive, but now he was not so sure. He needed to alert his family, he thought, in the event that he couldn't make it. *This is bad, really bad.*

"Could you please call my father?" Brent asked Lynda.

"Of course. What's his number?"

Lynda left and Serena continued to tend to the holes in Brent's body. Brent had four entry wounds and three exit wounds. However, Russell and Serena could only apply compresses to four of the wounds. All the while warm blood continued to pool around Brent as he lay there.

The 911 operator had stressed to Serena to keep Brent as alert as possible. She began questioning him.

"Do you have any medical conditions that I need to know about?"

"No."

"Are you allergic to anything?"

"Yeah," Brent replied, "Bullets."

For a split second, there were actually chuckles. The expressions on their faces were worth a million dollars.

"Do you have diabetes or anything like that?"

"No, but I am allergic to morphine. Don't let them give me any of that," he said in a feeble voice.

Then Brent grew silent. Serena grabbed his arm and tried to get a pulse. Nothing. She asked Brent to squeeze her hand, but he could hardly move his fingers. Serena frantically tried again for a pulse. This time she got one in his neck.

Lynda returned with the bad news. "I'm sorry Brent, your father's out of town," she said in a somewhat discouraged tone, "but his receptionist is trying to reach him," she reassured him.

From the floor, Brent lifted his right arm and motioned Lynda closer.

"Can you try my mom?"

Brent whispered the number to Lynda, but again the results were disappointing. Several attempts to reach her on her cell phone failed as well. Lynda left a message at both numbers. The thought of dying without his family was inconceivable, but it was becoming very possible. *I might die surrounded by total strangers*, Brent thought.

"Could you try my brother?" he pleaded one more time. "Try my father's office and ask for Brian."

Lynda dialed the number again, but she was told Brian was out of the office in another part of the country attending a business meeting, and his father was out of town working on the family vacation house. Lynda pleaded with the receptionist to call the hotel where Brian was staying. She kept repeating it was a dire emergency.

She hung up the phone and kneeled beside Brent. "I don't know if they will reach Brian, but I asked her to call his hotel and told her it was an emergency. We can only wait now," Lynda told him.

Brent was drained physically, emotionally and spiritually. More than half an hour had passed since he'd been shot, and he knew the odds of surviving were quickly diminishing. He'd seen it on the news a hundred times. Most trauma victims die if the paramedics don't get to them in the first fifteen minutes. He knew the faster he got medical attention, the better the chances that he would live. Brent was nervous about his survival. Surrounded by a group of people who had no medical knowledge and whose only first aid supply was a roll of paper towels, he was aware of how tenuous his grasp on life was.

"I'm not going to make it, am I?" Brent asked, as he looked at the three of them.

"Yes you are!" Serena said sternly. "You're going to be just fine. Just hang in there with us."

At that point, Serena and Russell had surveyed the injuries, quietly comparing notes on various wounds. They had a relatively good idea of which injuries were entry wounds and which were exits, which were life threatening and which were not. Although they weren't trained for this type of situation, they had done the right thing. If the paramedics arrived in time, Serena and Russell could provide valuable information that might help save Brent's life.

A ringing phone broke the silence and startled the group. Lynda jumped up and raced to the desk. It was the hotel calling back from Wyoming. The woman seemed oddly uncooperative though, asking what the problem was. *What did it matter,* Lynda thought, *it was a serious situation. Wasn't that enough?*

"It is a family emergency. His brother has been injured and I need to speak with Brian right now!" Lynda said emphatically as if she'd known him for years.

"Okay," the operator responded. "I'll have him call you back."

"That's not good enough. I'll hold."

Minutes passed. Silence filled the line. Finally a male voice came on the phone.

"Hello?" the voice said.

"Is this Brian?" Lynda asked.

"Yes. Who is this? What's wrong with Brent?"

As Lynda recapped the events, she could hear the person on the line grow more anguished. Brian began to cry, his words slow and unrecognizable.

"Brian, this is not the time to fall apart. Your brother needs you to be strong. He's been shot several times, but he's alert and he's going to make it! The paramedics will be here soon," Lynda said.

"Can I talk to him?"

Lynda pulled the cord across the desk. Brent stretched his good arm. The cord was too short, so Lynda became the operator relaying the conversation between the two brothers. Brent could almost hear his brother's voice as Lynda relayed the words. "Brent, you hang on buddy. Don't give up on me, damn it. Don't you die! Do you hear me?" Lynda looked over at Brent and repeated what he was saying.

"Brian, I love you," Brent said in a whisper. "Tell Mom and Dad how much I love them too." Lynda did not report to his brother that Brent's voice had trailed off. Once again there was silence.

chapter eight

A Nightmare Unfolding

Brent's father, Kenny, was at the family's lake house working outside in the yard. His phone was ringing incessantly, but he was too far away to hear it. Brian hadn't been able to reach either of his parents, so he began trying to get in touch with some friends. He was hoping they would know where his parents were. Suddenly, cell phones began lighting up all around the lake house. Finally, at the marina, a friend of Kenny's answered his cell phone and Brian told him the bad news about Brent being shot. Allen jumped into his jeep and sped over to the Doonan home. He saw Kenny in the front yard gardening, rushed over to him and told Kenny, "You have to call your office." Kenny at first thought it was an unimportant business matter. Focusing back on his garden, he said, "I'll call them later."

"No, Kenny! I mean right now," Allen yelled. "Something terrible has happened to Brent. There's been a shooting in his office."

Kenny's faced turned ashen. He dropped the rake on the ground, ran into the house and raced for the phone. He called the All-Tech office, but the phone just continued to ring, no one there answering. Next he tried to call his wife, Sue, at home. There was no answer there either. The answering machine clicked on, but Kenny didn't want to tell his wife the news about their son on the answering machine, so he just said, "Sue, something's happened to Brent. Call me at the lake as soon as you get in."

In a desperate attempt to get in contact with someone, Kenny dialed his secretary; she told him the little about the shooting she knew. "No one knows if Brent is alive or not."

Kenny wanted to stay at the lake until he had spoken to his wife, and they had coordinated their next moves. He turned on the television. Information slowly began to pour out about the massacre, but the details were very general. It was chaotic coverage of a chaotic event. There were no reports about specific individuals; so far they only knew several people were dead. He put his head in his hands and began to sob. This was a nightmare unfolding and the worst part was that he didn't know if Brent was alive or one of the dead.

Sue, who had been shopping for the last hour, had just arrived home. When she walked over to the answering machine, it indicated there were fifteen messages. Her heart began pounding. Something was terribly wrong. There were never more than one or two messages on the machine. She tried to brace herself as she pushed the message button. Skipping through the first two messages which seemed insignificant, she came to one from Derek in the Kansas City branch of All-Tech. Before his message was finished, Sue rushed into the bedroom and began packing a suitcase. After she threw in some clothes and toiletries, she returned to the answering machine, hearing Kenny's voice.

Derek's phone rang. It was Kenny. Almost simultaneously, Sue called on another line. Both parents were talking at once, both wanting information. Derek was trying to explain what he knew about the shooting, but it got lost in the frantic desire of each parent. "Derek," Sue yelled into the phone, "Hang up on Kenny and talk to me! Just hang up on him!"

On the other line, Kenny was also yelling, "Hang up the damn phone and talk to me! Tell her I will call back!"

Derek tried to communicate to them both at once. "Okay, listen folks," he said in a level-headed tone, "I'll tell you both at the same time. There has been a shooting in Brent's office. I know for a fact that Brent has been shot, but I don't know where he is or what condition he's in. I don't know much more than that. Some nut went on a rampage, I think. A lot of people got shot."

A minute later when their conversation was over, Brent's parents frantically began to make their ways to Atlanta from two different cities.

Meanwhile, back at the Piedmont Center, Brent's blood pressure had dropped to nearly nothing. His skin was blanched, but he was still conscious. No paramedics, no doctors, not even a first aid kit had arrived. The only thing they had to stop the bleeding, the roll of paper towels, was almost gone.

"What religion are you Brent?" Serena asked.

"I'm Catholic."

Serena began to recite, "Our Father, who art in Heaven, hallowed be thy name. Thy kingdom come. Thy will be done…." Everyone who was there repeated the prayer, including Brent. They followed it by reciting the Hail Mary.

As I lay there, I remember thinking how fortunate I was to have such good people around me. While praying aloud, my words slowly started to slur. I had lost a lot of blood, my condition was worsening and my motor skills were failing. Shock was beginning to set in and I knew it. As I spoke, my words slowly spilled out, but the words I wanted to say would not cooperate.

The word "hurt" came out as "cold," "help" came out as "day" I was slip-
ping and those around me knew it.

Brent had started to lose consciousness but he pulled himself
back by trying to concentrate on anything that would keep him
awake. His mind wandered back to his childhood years. He remembered an afternoon religion class. On that day, Father Dan spoke to
the class about dying. Brent could hear his words, "I just want you
to remember one thing. I am going to dedicate our hour today to
one simple thought. When you pray at night, pray for the grace of
a happy death."

Father Dan had gone on to tell the class about people on their
deathbeds who had positive experiences. He told the story of one
man who was dying at home and was surrounded by his family.
They had come from all over the country to be with him. As he lay
in his bed dying, he turned to them and simply said, "I am so glad
you are all here with me. This is the first time we've been together
in nine years. I feel no pain." Minutes later, the man passed away
with a smile on his face.

Brent never forgot that story and had always asked for his own
happy ending in his prayers. Now his mind flashed back to his
remembered feelings of serenity as he prayed.

At that moment, I began to make peace with dying. No longer did I
fear death. I only feared missing my family and friends. I'd only been on this
earth for twenty-five years. It didn't seem fair. I realized so clearly for the first
time that ultimately all we have in life is a limited time. It's just that sim-
ple. And my time was up. But I still had so much I wanted to do. Mostly
though, I would miss my family. I realized in that moment that people need
the presence of another human to die, preferably a family member, just as they
need the presence of another human to be born.

Over the course of my life, I had prayed about nearly everything. Sometimes I begged and pleaded for certain things to happen. At other times I begged for nothing to happen. I prayed, almost nagging for certain solutions and I made my share of deals with God. For the most part, my prayers were answered. Now I realized I should have prayed for time. Prayed to grow to a ripe old age and then, like Father Dan's old man dying in his own bed, I could say, "I am so glad you are all here with me. I feel no pain."

When death is close you begin to understand many things that were never apparent, things you never bothered to examine or pay attention to. When you're twenty-four you believe the world goes on forever. There is no rush, because time seems infinite and we end up wasting the present in so many ways. Now lying there, my strength fading, questions came to me. Had I used my time fully? Whatever success I had hoped for, I realized that there would never be a more meaningful, but subtle range of sounds, than I had been able to hear every day, if only I'd listened more closely; paid more attention to the beauty around me. I would never see a wider field of vision or more intricate and lovely structures or more subtle colors, if only I'd been still and aware.

In the end, I concluded, you have to let go of yourself and just become a witness.

It was now 3:40. Forty minutes had elapsed since the shooting started at All-Tech and still no police or paramedics had arrived. As Brent slipped in and out of unconsciousness, Serena, Russell and Lynda remained at his side kneeling next to him. They were surrounding Brent in a semi-circle, praying. While praying, Serena periodically stopped to ask questions, hoping to keep Brent alert. Brent struggled to answer, but it was no use. His words made no sense and he was choking on his own blood; gasping for each breath. Russell, who wasn't Catholic, simply said, "Lord please take my angel and give him to Brent. He needs all the angels he can get."

Suddenly Russell's eyes widened. He stared for a moment, and then shouted to Serena and Lynda, "Hey, did you see that?"

"Yes, yes, I did! I did!" Serena answered.

They both had seen a spirit. Later they described it as a willowy face with his eyes closed. His head was tilted, as if in prayer. To Russell it was Brent's angel. To Serena, it was the spirit of Christ. Serena saw the spirit descend down into the room. His face, which hovered behind Brent's head, was partly shrouded in a white cloak; his hands were placed on Brent's head.

Suddenly a man name Franz, who had been in the back room praying for Brent, entered the office and said, "I know he's going to be okay. The Lord told me." Serena's painful tears slowed. Russell's hand felt light, he had prayed to the angels and they had responded. Now he sensed them trying to pull his hands away from Brent wounds. It was as if they were saying, *it's okay, you can let go now.* Although they did not know it, Brent had been praying, also.

Slowly Russell and Serena removed their hands from the gun-shot wounds. The steady stream of blood that had been pouring from Brent had slowed to a trickling. Everyone in the room was stunned. Brent's face was deathly pale. Was it a miracle or was Brent simply running out of blood?

I knew that I was speaking directly to God and he was listening. He was telling me to calm down, that I would be fine. My thoughts, which had been flooded with fear, were now tranquil. I couldn't be sure that God meant I would live or if he meant I would be with him. Either way, I felt safe.

Earlier, while the police were searching the offices of Momentum for the shooter, Barton was killing people inside All-Tech across the street. Although the victims had called 911 only fifteen minutes after Momentum's phone call, it took over thirty minutes before a superior officer finally acknowledged that two separate shootings had occurred. Shortly thereafter, officers began swarming the All-Tech building.

Eventually, the first SWAT teams arrived at the scene. In the heat of the chaos, they all crowded into the same elevator. They were heavily armed, wearing flak jackets, hobnail boots, plastic face shields and their helmets. Almost immediately after it started up, the elevator suddenly stopped; it had gotten stuck between floors. Having exceeded the weight restrictions, they were stranded and remained so for a short period of time. Maintenance men had to be called to rescue them. However, at that point officers outside the building were cordoning off the area, so that when the maintenance men arrived, they were refused entry. By 3:45 the team still hadn't gotten on their way. Meanwhile, Brent was mortally wounded upstairs.

Finally, the SWAT team managed to get to the upper floors. Guns drawn, they burst through doors and ran into the offices. Pointing their guns first one way then the other, they began positioning workers against the walls, yelling at them to tell them who and where the shooter was. "Everyone put your hands in the air," they shouted. As they went through the room moving the employees against the wall, they held their guns poised for the possibility that the killer could be anyone. Amid all the chaos, officers were cautious and apprehensive. Although the police command had a complete description of Barton, they had failed to communicate it properly. Thus, most of the officers who were searching for the shooter didn't know exactly what or who to look for; instead they treated each person they came into contact with as if he might be the gunman.

The door slammed open in the office where Brent Doonan lay

holding on to his waning strength. In rushed several police officers, pointing their guns at Serena, Lynda and Russell, yelling and moving them up against the walls as they scoured the room searching for the perpetrator. While looking down the barrel of one of the officer's guns Lynda yelled, "Hey look, we are victims here too! You guys are wasting time!" She was obviously upset as the officers moved about the room. "And get me some help up here for this guy. He's wounded badly!" she screamed. The officers turned and quickly fled the room continuing their hunt. They left Brent lying there hoping that the paramedics would soon follow.

Serena was sure the paramedics would arrive in a minute or two. *They would certainly be following the police,* she thought. Five minutes passed, then ten. Silence filled the room. After fifteen minutes, Lynda dashed to the phone and dialed 911 again.

"Where the hell are the paramedics? The police have been here for fifteen minutes. I called you a half hour ago for God's sake! A man is dying here!"

"Ma'am, please calm down. They are in your building," the operator answered.

"Yeah, you told me that before, but they still haven't gotten here!" She hung up the phone.

In fact, the paramedics were in the building, but were attending to the victims on the lower floor. For some they arrived in time, for others it was too late. Aware that they were fighting the clock, they had set up a triage area. They would try to save the savable first and deal with the dead or about to die later. Victims were classified as emergent, urgent or non-urgent. The emergent and non-urgent were told to wait while the EMTs tended to the urgent. First, they applied thick gauze pads to stop the bleeding. Some were then administered morphine for the pain and started on IV drips with fluids. Some people struggled to stay alive; others were being placed on gurneys and rushed outside to waiting ambulances. Although each was critically injured, Scott, Kathy and Meredith, along with a handful of others, were all still alive.

The trading floor looked like a slaughterhouse. Jamshid Havash had taken a bullet in the back. His body lay near his computer. A few feet away a second victim's body was spread out like a child making an angel in the snow. Allen Tenenbaum had a gunshot wound to his upper back, torso and right shoulder. Next to him was Dean Delawalla, who had been shot five times, in the head, neck, shoulder, back and buttocks. The woman Brent had seen running down the hall near the elevator had been shot in the head. Her body lay where she was hit.

Though the flow of his bleeding had stopped, for the next fifteen minutes, Brent Doonan was literally drowning in his own blood. The bullet on the left side of his chest had torn a hole in his lung. The wound was causing his lung to fill with blood and that began to close off his air supply. With each breath he took, his nose and mouth filled with warm blood.

I felt like I was submerged underwater in a cold lake with the only source of oxygen being a narrow straw peeking just above the surface of the frigid water. My body was very cold. I struggled to breathe through the small opening in my throat. Each exertion for a breath returned a mixture of air and liquid. I would try to breathe out through a gurgle of blood. Unable to take a full breath, I had now resorted to a series of shallow breaths, each time choking and coughing on my own blood. It occurred to me that I might drown before I bled to death. Oddly, I feared that outcome more. I had always thought growing up that the worst possible way to die would be to suffocate or drown, but not in my own blood. Each time I choked out more blood, I could feel myself going into a panic mode once again.

In an attempt to comfort Brent, Serena kept wiping his forehead with a damp paper towel and continued to wipe the blood from his nose and mouth. Finally, the office phone rang and Lynda quickly answered it.

A voice said, "We have a doctor in the building. What is your location?" Lynda quickly gave directions.

"Stay put. The doctor is on the way," the voice said and then the phone went silent.

Moments later EMTs stormed into the room. They began to strip off Brent's clothes to assess the damage. Then while setting up IVs, one of the paramedics yelled for someone to bring in a pack of cigarettes. While they quickly infused Brent with life sustaining fluids, someone returned with a pack of Marlboros. The EMT quickly tore off the cellophane wrapper and used it to form a vacuum over Brent's wounds, in an attempt to seal off the bleeding. Though not the most ideal method of wound care, it was the only method the EMTs had left. The paramedics had used all their sterile patches downstairs and they had nothing else with which to seal the wounds.

Now my chance of survival hinged on the ability of the medical personnel, who finally had arrived. Though the EMTs were rapidly tending to my injuries, they appeared to me to be in slow motion. The room was nothing more than a black and white cloud with people moving about. I had fallen into severe shock; my body was shutting down, the bright lights, shining from the ceiling, told me that I was still alive. The people were moving about the room, but I had no idea what they were doing. My body was numb, but the pain in my chest was too much to handle; I could barely breathe. I'm just going to pass out, I said to myself unable to hang on any longer. They can take care of me from here on out.

A tall, gray haired man entered the room. He asked the paramedics, "How's he doing?"

"He's lost a lot of blood."

The man knelt down, placed his hand on Brent's shoulder and looked over Brent's wounds to try to assess his condition. He said in a heavy southern drawl, "Son, I'm Doctor Harvey. I'm a trauma surgeon. Keep your eyes wide open and on me and I'll get ya fixed up." Brent could barely see the man through his glazed vision. He was clearly losing consciousness.

But the doctor ordered him, "Listen to me, if you keep your eyes open you will live. If you close them, you die!"

Standing up abruptly the doctor turned to the medics, "Get him ready!"

The doctor's advice penetrated Brent's fog.

My father always told me that failure was okay; without it we probably wouldn't have light bulbs because it took Thomas Edison thirty-three tries, or thereabouts, to stumble onto the invention. Thirty-two tries had been failures. Without failure, we don't learn anything. I was failing in the biggest way now. In the game of life, you don't get thirty-three chances. I could only hope that the learning curve would be in proportion to that which I had to give up.

Then, as quickly as the EMTs arrived, they were packing up to go. Sliding a wooden board under Brent, the medics lifted him onto the gurney. Knowing that the building was still not secure and that Barton could be lurking in one of the offices, Dr. Harvey stood up and said, "Okay, get him out of here!" As the stretcher raised, the wheels locking in place, Lynda, with a concerned look on her face, reached over and tucked a piece of paper into Brent's waistband.

"When you get to the hospital, someone please call his family. Their phone numbers are on this slip of paper," she told the EMTs as they prepared for the journey to the hospital. Before they rushed Brent out of the room, she quickly added, "He's allergic to morphine."

For those who had tried to summon help, the worst was finally over as the EMTs wheeled Brent from the room. Some stood silently wondering if Brent could make it. Others fought back visions of Brent being in a coma or of being severely disabled if he did make it.

I was on the stretcher and we were rolling down the hallway, the same hallway I envisioned myself dying in. Though my eyes remained open, I was in shock. I told myself to keep fighting. I had lain on the conference room floor for an hour while desperately clinging to life. I had struggled to survive despite knowing that my condition was growing worse and worse. Now, I told myself, is not the time to give up. I pleaded with myself. I had come too far. Dr. Harvey's words echoed in my weary mind, "Keep your eyes open and you will live; close them and you will die."

In the distance came the sound of the officer's yelling.

"Make a hole! Make a hole!" voices were shouting as they rushed Brent down the hallway and into the awaiting elevator. For the second time that day Brent rode an elevator to possible life or death.

chapter nine

Desperate Hours

On the side of Building Number Eight was an old fashioned instrument; a large, round, white-faced, plastic thermometer with a Coca-Cola logo in the center. The dial registered ninety-seven degrees, with a humidity of nearly ninety percent.

Officers in police cars were parked in the street, by the side of the buildings, in alleys and in intersections and were trying to make sense of the chaos. Civilians were screaming, running in all directions and crouching behind cars. Onlookers pointed to the commotion, trying to figure out what was happening. SWAT team members dressed in battle gear shouted, "Go, go, go" and quickly disappeared into the building. The police had yet to cordon off the area, so curious spectators continued to pour in, making logistics even more difficult. Helicopters were flying overhead, using their loudspeakers in fruitless attempts to get the bystanders out of the area. Police helicopters flying over the business district just made the scene more surreal.

Several large ambulances were now outside the building awaiting the injured. EMTs kept rushing out wheeling one person after
another on gurneys. Workers still left in offices counted how many
people were taken out of All-Tech and shook their heads in disbelief. The medics were hurrying all around the area searching for any
wounded, patching up those they found as best they could. The real
issue was trying to get the victims to the hospital as fast as possible.
Time lost could be crucial to survival. Brent Doonan, among others, had been mortally wounded for more than an hour.

The warm sun blistered down on Brent's face as the paramedics
raced him out to the ambulance. He had lost vast amounts of blood
and was in deep shock. Though the temperature was in the nineties,
he was covered in heavy wool blankets, in an attempt to calm the
contractions his body was going through. The doctor quietly told
the medic he felt Brent had a fifty-fifty chance of survival. They
questioned that Brent would even live long enough to reach the
awaiting ambulance, let alone that Brent would hold on long
enough to make it to the hospital.

*I was shivering terribly and knew I was in shock. I was fully aware of
where I was. The sun felt good. Above me a helicopter hovered with its giant
blades whirring in slow motion; whop, whop, whop. I kept saying in my
mind, "You can do this. You can do this."*

*Perhaps this was the grace of a happy death. I loved to fly and today I
would be going for a helicopter ride to the hospital. If I died in the helicopter, it would be better than on the floor of a conference room, I thought to
myself while trying to find something positive about my rapidly deteriorating
condition. Perhaps my parents and my family would arrive in time so that I
could say goodbye.*

*My hopes were dashed however, when the EMTs hoisted me into the
back of the ambulance. I found out later the helicopter was a police unit taking aim at a man on the top of a building whom they believed was Barton.*

I kept hoping I would pass out so the pain would go away. But each time that thought occurred to me, I remembered the doctor telling me to keep my eyes open. Okay, I told myself, keep your eyes open and you'll get through this. I didn't want to look to the side where the walls of the ambulance were lined with emergency equipment; oxygen masks, needles, bandages, IVs with blood and fluids. I had always hated doctors' offices and hospitals since I was a kid – particularly hating needles. Now I knew this was my only chance at living.

"Okay. Let's go and make it quick!" Dr. Harvey, the doctor, shouted as he jumped into the back of the ambulance and slammed the door behind him. The ambulance pulled out of the parking lot and onto Piedmont Road. The street was now filled with police, FBI and SWAT teams, which made it difficult for the ambulance to move. The ambulance driver saw he was boxed in but there was no time to spare. The driver pulled out, pressed his foot firmly against the accelerator, and swerved into the oncoming traffic lane. He was making his own route in the traffic. One way or another, he was going to "make it quick."

Meanwhile, police continued searching for Barton throughout the building complex. Chris Brennan had given them the information about Barton that he'd found in Barton's file. The SWAT team scoured every office, looked on every floor of every building in the area. They found countless workers hiding in their offices and under their desks. Room by room these people were escorted to the street below. But there was no sign of Barton. The police manhunt flowed out into the streets. It was rush hour, but cars were meticulously searched. Three helicopters were able to survey the surrounding area from the sky. Unfortunately, the description of Barton's vehicle was inaccurate. Police were searching for a white van, while Barton's van was actually green. The description of Barton himself was also misleading, so none of the officers had a clear idea of what he or his van really looked like.

There was an added complication. Before police had focused their attention on him, Barton had already gotten into his van and disappeared into traffic. At that point there were no roadblocks, no police presence or any kind of obstacle for him. It was as if he was driving home from a normal day of day trading.

While Barton's van sped down Piedmont Road in the oncoming lane, at almost the same time, one of the EMTs in the ambulance tended to Brent's injuries. Dr. Harvey got on the cell phone and alerted the emergency room that they would be receiving two critically wounded patients, one male and one female, both requiring immediate surgery.

The EMT who was tending to me appeared to be moving in slow motion, though I'm sure he was frantic. Then I realized I could no longer understand what the doctor was saying. I could see his lips move, but only gibberish came out, all in ultra slow motion. I could no longer feel my arms, but my chest continued to burn. I struggled to keep my eyes open. In the background, the slight sound of a siren and the occasional horn-honk kept me hanging on. They were doing everything they could for me; I had to do the same for them.

Under normal conditions, this trip would have taken fifteen minutes, today it only took seven. By the time we arrived the ER was filled with doctors, nurses and hospital technicians.

Two or three police officers and hospital security guards stood in the emergency room entranceway, securing the area for our arrival. "Okay, here we go. Here we go!" I said to myself as a slight burst of energy hit me. "I've made it!"

The sounds of rumbling gurney wheels and EMTs shouting instructions to each other filled my ears. Above, blurry but bright green tinted lights raced past me in the ceiling. Then, two large steel doors swung open and the gur-

ney came to an abrupt halt. Four men reached under me and on the count of three raised me up and onto a steel table. Two nurses stood beside me still holding plastic bags above their heads, one filled with blood, the other with a clear fluid. Needles no longer bothered me.

To Brent the room was blurry, probably because he was at the center of a swarm of fifteen or so medical professionals, while numerous others stood on the periphery, intensely watching the frenzied movement of their colleagues, ready to jump in if needed.

"We'll need chest X-rays stat," one medic called out. "Probably fluid build-up within the left chest cavity."

"I'm not getting much of a pulse," a nurse checking Brent's vital signs added.

All I could repeat to myself was to keep my eyes open, keep them open and in doing so I watched with my own horror, the look of terror on the faces of those attending to me. For some strange reason, though I felt nearly unconscious, I remembered a famous old Bill Cosby routine, where he tells of being on an operating room table and hears the doctor say, "Whoops." Even in my deathbed state I realized I was hanging onto anything that made me want to live: the hope of seeing my family and even a little humor.

Though it was unintentional, fear seemed to be the overwhelming emotion that was evident on the doctors' faces as I looked about the room. Normally, doctors aren't supposed to show alarm, particularly panic, but their grave expressions brought another wave of fear over me. I could feel what little adrenaline was left surge into my system.

Dr. Harvey appeared, accompanied by another doctor, Dr. Ferrier, and both started to assess the damage. Pain shot through my body as first they rolled me onto my right side and then back onto my left.

"This one went in here and came out over here," Harvey said.

"No, I don't think so, I think it came out over here," Dr. Ferrier said.

For several minutes they debated entry and exit sites of the bullets, try-
ing to determine the best surgical procedures. Eventually, I began to grunt and
groan as they moved me back and forth. It hurt so badly; I was ready to be
knocked out, regardless of the outcome.

Suddenly a nurse appeared at Brent's side and implored, as she
forced a tube into Brent's nose, "Tilt your head back. Tilt your head
back!"

She pleaded, "Now swallow. It's okay, swallow for me."

The tube that she pressed into his throat ran from a suction
machine a few feet away, into Brent's nose and down into his stomach. Brent gagged and choked as the nurse said again, "Come on,
swallow for me!" As Brent forced himself to comply, the nurse continued to jam the tube down his throat. As the tube reached his
stomach, Brent tried not to throw up, but it was no use. The nurse
quickly turned his head away from her as he heaved bloody fluid
across the table. "That's okay. It's okay!" she assured him as she surveyed the tube. "You are doing just fine."

By now Brent had been in the emergency room for over
twenty minutes. As he bent over Brent, Dr. Harvey briefly explained
the next procedure before he made a small incision in Brent's left
chest cavity and inserted a chest tube that returned approximately
200cc of bright red blood. The tube was hooked to a Pleur-Evac
and was being monitored for further fluid loss as the doctor anxiously waited for additional blood.

They had given me some pain medication other than morphine, but it
wasn't working. Agony was wracking my body in great surges. I felt as if my
entire body had been placed in an enormous vise.

Never had I been in so much pain. I thought I couldn't stand it. Then, an angel appeared at the end of my bed, though she was wearing a nurse's uniform. She had a million watt smile. Her long blonde hair spilled over her shoulders and framed one of the most beautiful faces I had ever seen. Wow, she was stunning, I thought, another reminder that life, even in its worst moment, can hold beauty.

Though she was standing at the foot of the bed, she was in the second row of doctors and nurses. Seeing my eyes open wider and look at her admiringly, she pushed her way to my side and gently began stroking my forehead while reassuring me I would soon be feeling better. In the midst of the chaos, suddenly I felt a little better, if only for a moment. An angel had arrived.

I had something other than the pain on which to focus my attention.

"Don't be afraid. You're going to get through this." Just then, we made eye contact. It was as if she knew exactly my fears about surviving.

This is better, I thought to myself. Perhaps this was the happy death for which I had prayed. She wasn't family nor was she even a friend, but somehow she managed to calm my nerves. She reminded me of the good things in the outside world, a beautiful stranger one meets along the journey of life, a person out to do something good for others.

Silently, I smiled about the whole scenario; a good looking blonde nurse had arrived at the eleventh hour to be my comfort and support; for the time being, could she be my lifeline?

Soothing thoughts managed to comfort me for a few minutes; they were gone in an instant. It hit me like a ton of bricks. 'Oh my God!' I said to myself, now completely embarrassed. 'She's standing here and I'm completely naked!' I wanted to cover up, but knew I could do nothing.

Then a doctor turned my head towards him, placed a small mask across my nose and mouth. "Take a deep breath for me," the man said in a tone that alerted me to what was happening. I obeyed his orders the best I could as I inhaled from inside the mask. I took another deep breath as I listened to the distant commotion around the room. Then the voices fell silent, the room turned black and my angel disappeared.

As Brent fought for his life, Barton became the focus of a statewide manhunt. Atlanta police were patrolling nearby areas and setting up roadblocks. Mayor Bill Campbell held a news conference, announcing that at the moment there had been nine fatalities because of the shooting in the vicinity. He identified the alleged gunman as Mark Barton, age forty-four. The mayor said the whereabouts of the suspect were unknown, but he should be considered "armed and dangerous."

Local stations interrupted regular programming to report the workplace massacre. News shows devoted coverage to it as soon as they knew. The entire state of Georgia and probably a large part of the United States now knew what had happened in downtown Atlanta and were now aware of the search for the suspect, Mark Barton.

However, police hadn't come up with any clues as to where Barton drove to after the massacre. As more time passed, the search widened. Police theorized that Barton could be holed up somewhere within a few miles of the crime scene or could be headed towards the state line. Each passing hour meant a better chance that Barton could escape.

As the sun began setting on Atlanta, Barton approached a woman getting into her car in the parking lot of a shopping mall in northwest Atlanta. As he walked up to her, he said, "Don't scream or I'll shoot you."

Before he got too close the woman ran. She found a phone and contacted mall security. At about the same time another woman saw Barton get into his minivan. Recognizing him from the news coverage, she immediately called 911.

A short while later, a police cruiser spotted Barton's green minivan and followed him from a distance. Barton didn't speed and seemed to be driving as casually as possible to blend in with the other motorists. Police suspected he had approached the woman in order to steal her car. He must have known that police were looking for him and now had a good idea of what kind of vehicle he was in. If he wanted to escape, the first thing he would have to do would be to get a different car.

Barton pulled his car into a gas station. A perfect place to find a different vehicle, he must have thought. He circled around slowly, through the parking lot, around the back, but when he came around he saw a police cruiser blocking the exit. Moving towards the front he saw another cruiser in the entrance way. Barton was boxed in.

Police units scrambled to the location. News crews, who had been listening to police scanners, raced to the scene. Police and news helicopters began to circle the area. No one was aware of Barton's duffel bag in the front seat of his vehicle. In addition to a Colt .45 and the 9mm Glock, the bag had a .22 revolver, a Raven .25 semi-automatic and 200 rounds of ammunition, enough to kill a lot more people.

"Are we certain it's him?" Sergeant Brady called to one of his patrolman.

"That's his van. It's the right plate and judging from here, he fits the description," came the reply. Brady and the other officers were kneeling behind their units with guns drawn, all eyes on the green van. Two gas station attendants were hiding on the floor behind a desk in the office.

"We have to be sure it's him," the Sergeant said.

"Only one way to find out."

The muscular Sergeant lifted the large bullhorn to his mouth. "Open the door very slowly, throw out your gun, then climb out and lie face down on the pavement!" his voice barked from the megaphone.

Silence. Barton sat behind the steering wheel, not looking at the police. He continued to stare out the front window into the sky, as if in a trance-like state

Again, the Sergeant yelled, "Barton! Throw out your weapon and get out of the van!"

"What are we going to do, Sergeant?" the other officer called.

"We're going to wait him out. He isn't going anywhere."

Just then, the air split with a single gunshot. The surrounding police all instinctively fell to the ground, pointing their guns at the van.

Getting up cautiously, they slowly approached the van. Looking inside they found Barton's body soaked in blood. Barton had placed the Glock to his right temple and the .45 to his left. He had planned to fire them both simultaneously, but was only able to shoot one. The hollow point slug went through his temple, into his sinus cavity and burst out the back of his head, taking half of his brains with it.

Pieces of brain tissue stuck to the ceiling. His body was held up by the seat belt. He was wearing tennis shoes and a belt with a Boy Scout buckle. A cell phone lay on the seat next to him. In the van were several tablets of an anti-depressant drug, a magazine, four handguns, several boxes of ammunition and a large amount of cash.

In the map compartment of the door, the officers also found a copy of Barton's updated will. He had removed his wife's name as beneficiary and changed that designation into his mother's name.

After Sergeant Brady and officer Dan Rinkley called in the finding and asked for an ambulance, they left the scene and headed directly to Barton's Stockbridge apartment. They knew from the information in the file that Brennan had given police that Barton was married, had two children and lived nearby. They wasted no time following up on this information and went directly to his house.

After knocking several times and shouting for Leigh Ann, Barton's wife, officers broke down the front door. There were no children in the room and Leigh Ann did not appear to be home, either.

Making his way slowly, gun drawn, Sergeant Brady went into the first of two bedrooms; the other officer went into the kitchen where a slip of paper lay on the counter. Reading it Brinkley called out, "Oh my God. Dan, come here."

"What is it?" Brady ran into the kitchen.

"Read this." he handed Brady the note he'd found.

To whom it may concern,

Leigh Ann is in the master bedroom closet under a blanket. I killed her on Tuesday night. I killed the children Wednesday night. There may be similarities between these deaths and the death of my first wife Debra Spivey. However, I deny killing her and her mother. There is no reason for me to lie now.

It just seemed like a quiet way to kill and a relatively painless way to die. There was little pain. All of them were dead in less than five minutes. I hit them with a hammer in their sleep and then put them face down in the bathtub to make sure they did not wake up in pain, to make sure they were dead.

I am so sorry, I wish I didn't. Words cannot tell the agony. Why did I? I have been dying since October. I wake up at night so afraid, so terrified that I couldn't be that afraid while awake.

It has taken its toll. I have come to hate this life in this system of things. I have come to have no hope. I killed the children to exchange them for five minutes of pain for a lifetime of pain. I forced myself to do it to keep them from suffering so much later. No mother, no father, no relatives.

The fears of the fathers are transferred to the son. It was from my father to me and from me to my son. He already had it. And now to be left alone, I had to take him with me.

I killed Leigh Ann because she was one of the main reasons for my demise, as I plan to kill the others. I really wish I had not killed her now. She really couldn't help it and I love her so much anyway.

I know that Jehovah will take care of all of them in the next life. I'm sure the details don't matter. There is no excuse, no good reason. I am sure no one will understand. If they could, I wouldn't want them to. I just write these things to say why. Please know that I love Leigh Ann and the children with all my heart. If Jehovah's willing I would like to see them all again in the resurrection, to have a second chance. I don't plan to live very much longer. Just long enough to kill as many of the people that greedily sought my destruction.

You should kill me if you can.

Barton had typed the chilling confession about eight hours before he had gone to Momentum and All-Tech.

Though Sergeant Brady was a twenty-year veteran, patrolman Dan Rinkley had just joined the force eighteen months earlier. He had never seen a murder scene. Viewing the children ages eleven and eight in their beds, lying side by side with their skulls and faces beaten beyond recognition, was tough. They were dressed in their pajamas with their toys neatly arranged around them. Everything was covered with the exception of the children's faces, which were neatly framed by the comforter.

Next to Barton's son were some Pokemon cards, a video game, a Swiss Army knife and some Boy Scout patches. There was a note lying on top the boy that read, "I give you my son, my buddy, my life. Please take care of him."

A doll with blonde curls, a teddy bear and a frilly dress were tucked neatly beside Barton's daughter. The pillow was soaked in blood, which was beginning to dry. There was another handwritten note lying on her which read, "I give you my daughter, my sweetheart, my life, please take care of her."

Rinkley, his hand over his mouth, rushed into the bathroom, where he leaned over the toilet bowl and heaved until he had nothing left but tart stomach bile.

Next the two searched for Leigh Ann's body. They found her body on the floor in the master bedroom closet. She was behind several boxes and under some clothes, presumably so the children wouldn't discover her. Like the children, she too was wrapped in a blanket. Her head was wrapped in a garbage bag. She also had a handwritten note lying on top of her. The note said, "I give you my wife Leigh Ann Barton, my honey, my precious love. Please take care of her. I will love her forever."

Back up ambulances were called and the two men retired from the scene. They took deep breaths and began writing their initial statements about the savagery they'd just encountered.

They wouldn't discover until later in the full investigation that Barton had taken his son for a haircut the day before, nor would the police know until after the autopsy that after he bludgeoned them to death, pulverizing their small brains into pulpy mush, he put both his children into a bathtub full of water to drown them, just in case the hammer didn't do the job. Then, after they had soaked for half an hour, he dried them off, dressed the children in their pajamas and neatly tucked them back into bed, face down, with all of their favorite toys around their lifeless bodies.

When CSI got to the crime scene they took more than fifty photos, attendants draped the bodies, put the mother and children on gurneys and wheeled them out of the apartment.

The suicide note was placed in a plastic bag for evidence.

chapter ten

Heroic Surgery

From 4:30 p.m. until nearly 9:00 p.m. a surgical team methodically tried to piece Brent Doonan back together. When a hollow point bullet goes through tissue and muscle, it doesn't travel a straight path – it twists and tumbles; a jagged lump of lead ripping, tearing and ricocheting off bone and tissue until it either comes to rest in an organ, or it passes through the body entirely. A slug may enter the abdomen, bounce around or break bone and become lodged in a joint–like a pinball.

In Brent's case, one bullet had tracked across his face, three had passed through his body and one lodged in his arm. However, since Barton had shot him from such close range, the hollow points of the bullets didn't have time to mushroom open before exiting his back. If they had, the holes in his body wouldn't be the size of walnuts as they were now, they would have been the size of oranges.

However, even with this stroke of luck, the operation was dangerous. First, Dr. Harvey inserted a catheter in through Brent's rib cage, which immediately returned a significant amount of blood. Then Brent was rolled onto his right side where he was prepped and draped. A ten-inch incision was made from the midline of his abdomen and stretched all the way around his body to the middle of his back. Upon opening the area, Dr. Harvey tried to make light of the situation. He turned to Ferrier and said with a hint of sarcasm, "Oh, lots of blood."

Approximately seven pints of blood had collected within Brent's abdominal cavity. After suctioning the blood from his abdominal area, the doctors saw that nearly half of Brent's liver had been destroyed and was bleeding profusely.

A lateral thoracotomy incision was made in the left chest wall, through the skin, tissue and muscle. On entering the left pleural cavity, Dr. Harvey noted that it was filled with blood. Dr. Harvey again turned to Ferrier commenting, "It got his diaphragm too." The doctors refocused on the chest area.

There were holes in the diaphragm and Dr. Ferrier had identified that the hole through the diaphragm had also torn through the lobe of Brent's left lung. This was repaired with a running continuous 2-0 black silk on a GI-needle. The lower lobe of the left lung was traumatized and doctors could not save it, so a wedge excision of a portion of the lower lobe was carried out using the GI-stapler. Since the lung had ceased bleeding, they now focused their attention back to the diaphragm, which continued to return a fair amount of blood. A second incision, roughly eight inches long, was made running from mid chest to Brent's beltline. From here, doctors could determine whether any significant damage had occurred to the major blood vessels. Though there was no significant damage to the "great vessels," the doctors noted a "thready pulse at this point" and Dr. Harvey began to massage Brent's heart, hoping it would continue to beat.

After noticing that one of the bullets had also torn through the mid-portion of Brent's spleen, rupturing it into three or four major parts, Dr. Harvey lightened the severity with some sarcasm, "And wait, oh, he's bleeding from his spleen." The doctor's grim humor stemmed from the fact that Brent appeared to be bleeding from everywhere, but it helped to ease some of the medical staff's tension. Minutes later, the spleen vessels were clamped and Brent's entire spleen was removed. A further search for bleeding revealed a fractured rib as well.

While the two doctors were busy assessing the damage caused by the bullets, the others carefully monitored Brent's vitals and continued with blood and plasma infusions. For a few fleeting moments, the bleeding seemed to be controlled and finally the pace had slowed. But then, with a touch of dry humor, Dr. Harvey again spoke up, "Oh, he's bleeding from his liver again," to which Dr. Ferrier replied, "Will you quit it!"

Over the course of the surgery, the two doctors diligently worked together moving from one organ to the next. As soon as one hole was stitched, Dr. Harvey always seemed to find another that continued to bleed. It was a constant battle to repair quickly the damage from one organ while slowing the bleeding from another. As the surgery neared its completion, Dr. Ferrier inserted two chest tubes to help with the drainage and carefully began closing Brent's chest in multiple layers.

Then Dr. Lourie, the orthopedic surgeon, returned to the operating room to repair Brent's arms. Dr. Lourie removed the bullet that was lodged just below the skin in Brent's right tricep then bandaged both arms and "packed open" the wound to allow for drainage. The bullet he recovered would later be given to police as evidence.

Though the human body holds an average of twelve units (pints) of blood, Brent, while in surgery, had already been given twelve units and continued to receive another four. Surgeons could not explain how he could have lost nearly his entire blood supply and yet still be alive. His spleen was gone, part of a lung, a portion of his diaphragm and a third of his liver.

By the time I arrived in ICU, Ruth, the nurse, already knew me well. Having been called in early for her shift, Dr. Harvey had taken her into the operating room to "make sure she knew what she was dealing with." She had been assigned to keep a close eye on me throughout the night. I was to be "monitored, supported and warmed" while I continued to recover. Fully aware that I had suffered tremendously at the hands of a crazed killer and lived through several hours of intense surgery, Ruth's goal was simple: to keep me alive for the next twenty-four to forty-eight hours.

Though swollen and pale, I now lay in intensive care asleep and unaware of my surroundings. A respirator kept my breathing stable while a dozen intravenous lines ran into my body, slowly pumping fluids and additional blood products.

To a random visitor, the scene would have looked like Dr. Frankenstein's laboratory. Brent's arms were tightly bandaged; a tube ran through his nose, another into his side under his ribs and on either side of the bed two IV bags were silently dripping blood and clear fluids through three needles into Brent's arms. The huffing of a respirator, not unlike an accordion without a keyboard, wheezed up and down thirty times a minute. Above, behind and to the right of Brent's head was a panel that rivaled NASA for technological effect. One screen showed a heart rate tracer bouncing up and down, leaving a wispy green tail as it traveled to the right. On another was a digital read out giving the nurses Brent's blood pressure. Others were monitoring, in red or green numbers, pulse rate, blood oxygen levels and respiration.

Under his gown, the grim evidence of the surgeon's scalpel and the lattice work of number 4-0 black silk sutures and G2 staples ran over a raw incision from the mid chest up to the "open packed" dressings on Brent's side and then again across to the middle of his back. The piece de resistance was the small trough-like path that ran across his cheek under his right eye, the footprint of a .45 caliber slug.

Brent's parents, Kenny and Sue, had watched live news coverage of the massacre while waiting for their flight to Atlanta. They knew from the phone call with Derek that their son had been shot several times, and for all they knew he might be already dead or dying. They also knew many others were injured and that there had been multiple fatalities – Brent might be one.

The Doonans felt impotent. Still hours from Atlanta, they could do nothing and they knew nothing. Then a glimmer of hope came as a Dr. Haley came onto the telecast to give a press conference from Grady Memorial Hospital in downtown Atlanta. It was the first public announcement other than the mayor's original abbreviated statement.

Kenny leaned forward closer to the monitor and listened intently as Dr. Haley briefed reporters on the condition of the shooting victims, but Brent Doonan's name wasn't mentioned. Kenny picked up the phone and got Dr. Haley on the line. However, the doctor knew nothing of a man named Brent Doonan. Kenny realized either his son had not arrived yet, had been taken to another hospital or was dead.

Before getting on the plane, Kenny only knew, at that point, that two men were reported killed at All-Tech. He didn't want to admit it to his wife, but his fears were that the two that were dead were probably Brent and Scott. Kenny frantically began dialing the numbers of every hospital in the Atlanta area.

If Brent were alive, would he be able to hang on until they got there? Was he suffering? If he had been killed, how would they go on with their lives? For two hours, they watched the saturation coverage of the event and agonized, knowing it would still be several hours before they would get any meaningful news.

The Cessna Citation II was ready to take Kenny, Sue, Brent's uncle Bob, sister Jennifer, Scott's father, mother and others from Scott's family to Atlanta. Finally one of Kenny's calls reached the Atlanta hospital where Brent had undergone extensive surgery. They knew now that he had been shot five times and the prognosis was not good.

After takeoff, the horror of now knowing exactly what happened to Brent filled the cabin. Scott's parents had heard that he had sustained one injury and would probably be okay, but they all had serious doubts about Brent. Most would spend the next hour and a half praying with their rosary beads.

Sue tried hard not to imagine life without her son. She couldn't believe she would live longer than him. The thought of him dying brought waves of nausea over her. She choked the feeling back and wiped her tears repeatedly, a virtual water tap that wouldn't close. Clutching her rosary beads, she also prayed. "Take me instead," Sue said to herself. "I will not be able to live without him anyway."

"Please Lord. Let my boy live. That's my boy," Kenny said quietly, clinching his eyes closed tightly, trying to visualize the face of God, trying to find a clueto whether He was listening or not.

"God, please don't let this be happening. Brent is such a good person. He doesn't deserve this. He never harmed another human being in his life. He doesn't deserve this, nobody does." Kenny kept saying the same thing over and over.

"Don't take him from us. He has so much in front of him."

Sue dropped the rosary beads in her lap and began wringing her hands. She stared at the ceiling of the cabin, then dropped her head in silence and thought about Brent.

It is said that there is nothing on the earth that is more inconceivably unbearable than to losing a child – nothing lonelier than to outliving someone you're used to loving.

As you mature, you come to accept your mortality. You know how fast it all went, the things you'd like to take back, the things you wish you had done, the regrets along with the small triumphs, but in the end you accept it though you certainly wished it all lasted longer than the predictable seventy or so years, perhaps not even that. But when you're twenty-four you don't think about death. You think life goes on forever and it's a ball. Everything is new, an exciting challenge; there's an adventure around every corner and perhaps love, maybe if you're lucky, a lifelong love and children and maybe even a little peace of mind and a sense of fulfillment. At twenty-four, your life should be beginning, not ending.

Sue could not stop crying as thoughts of her son raced through her mind. She thought her son would never know these joys and she would have to live the rest of her life without him.

The plane was approaching the airport as she said her last prayer: "God, I know he was your son before he was mine. If you must take him, thy will be done. But please don't."

As the plane landed and taxied to its stopping point, all nine passengers anxiously pressed their faces to the small windows of the Cessna. The parking area had been cleared except for police vehicles and three rental cars. The police offered Kenny an escort, but he declined, saying he could get to the hospital faster himself. He

grabbed his wife, daughter, his wife's brother, Bob, and Stan, the
pilot, a longtime friend, and piled into one of the vehicles. Kenny
put the gearshift into drive and spun the back tires in a half circle,
shooting the car away from the parking lot toward Northside.

In six minutes they were at the front door of Northside
Hospital. The hospital was crowded with police, a ghoulish reminder
of the reality they might have to face—that their son was likely dead.

Kenny, Sue and the others jumped out of the car and began to
run to the front door where they were stopped by a burly three-
hundred-pound security guard telling them they couldn't park in
front of the hospital. Kenny turned, pulled the keys out of his pocket
and tossed them to the guard.

"Here, you move it," he said sternly as he continued walking
toward the door.

Once inside another security guard confronted them.

"Are you from Kansas?" the guard asked.

"Yes."

"Good. I'll take care of you. Come with me," he said.

The family was ushered down a long gray hall into a small
office.

Kenny and Sue's world had gone to black and white as they
filed down one long stark hall after another. At one point, the gray
linoleum fused with a nearly identical hue on the walls. The overhead fluorescent lights, far too bright, exposed them in minute
detail, clearly showing the track marks of tears and puffy eyes.

The only variation from the drab visual of the hallways was the
occasional open door exposing the awful scene of someone who
was either very ill or nearly dead, hooked up to a litany of hoses and
monitors. The smell of alcohol and Lysol was pervasive; the only
sounds were the muted voices of characters on glowing television
sets screwed into the walls, high above each bed.

Kenny and Sue braced each other as they followed the guard, hoping for the best, but also steeling themselves to face the worst.

Finally, the guard stopped walking and hailed a passing doctor.

"Hello, I'm Dr. Harvey," the man said, extending his hand to each of the Doonans in turn. "I'm taking care of your son." That was the extent of the small talk. Harvey didn't know what he could say to comfort them, but he was anxious to meet Brent's parents and to be as honest as possible.

"How is he?" each asked simultaneously. "Is he going to make it?"

"Let's duck into one of the office waiting rooms." Dr. Harvey said, indicating a door nearby. Once inside he addressed the anxious parents.

"Please, please sit down," Harvey said, gesturing toward a couch. He sat in a nearby chair. "Brent was shot four times. He was hit in both arms, the abdomen and the chest. He also has a burn on his cheek from a fifth bullet."

Sue covered her mouth, tears forming in her eyes, as she gasped into her hand. "Oh my God," she whispered in despair. Kenny put his arm around her. Stan placed his hand on her other shoulder. It was even worse than they had anticipated. The gruesome reality of the shooting hit home. "So, how is he?" they asked, fearing the worst.

"The surgery took several hours. A team of specialists did everything they could – everything. He's in the ICU now and will remain there. The next twenty-four to forty-eight hours will tell."

To Brent's parents, Dr. Harvey sounded like an actor in a daytime soap opera, but this was very real and the victim was their son. "The next twenty-four hours will tell." That line was so uninformative.

"I wish I could tell you more," the doctor said. "It's really in God's hands—and Brent's, now. To be honest, he has about a fifty-fifty chance of surviving. The trauma his body has endured is nearly inconceivable.

We had to remove his spleen, part of his liver and part of a lung. He lost almost his entire blood supply as well. We did all we could do."

Kenny's head slumped forward. He sat numbly with his hand supporting his forehead. "We did all we could do?" he questioned, repeating Harvey's ominous words.

This was not a soft and gentle journey into an idyllic afterlife after a long lifetime, a warm glow, a simple transition into spirit. This was a brutal catastrophe, a maiming of body and soul, a ripping and tearing of flesh and bone, a wonderful essence yanked and jerked violently from the earth.

Again Kenny replayed the doctor's words, reaching the point of, "He is in the ICU."

Suddenly Kenny's attitude changed. Brent's father looked up and stared into Dr. Harvey's eyes. "You mean he's alive?" he asked in disbelief.

"Well of course he is," Dr. Harvey responded with a slight chuckle. "Nobody dies on my operating table."

"Oh my God! He's alive! Come on everyone! He's alive! That's the only thing that counts right now." He turned to his wife, "You know how tough Brent is. He would never allow himself the luxury of failing. He's going to make it, no matter what. I just know it."

Sue immediately perked up. "You're right. He wouldn't want to fail. When can we see him, Dr. Harvey?"

"Right away, but first, I should tell you that about a hundred of his friends are holding a vigil and are awaiting news. They are downstairs. Would you like to see them first?"

"Is Brent stable?" Sue asked.

"Yes."

"Then let's go see his friends."

The family got up and followed Dr. Harvey to a crowded room.

He excused himself to see his patient. Immediately Brent's family was inundated with questions from the anxious visitors. Scared, shocked and saddened they stared back at Brent's family, in nervous anticipation of the answers to their questions, "Is he all right?" "How badly is he hurt?" "When can we see him?"

Kenny repeated what the doctor had told them. Brent was in the ICU and they had to excuse themselves, but they would shortly return with more information. He added, "And thank you all for coming to support Brent."

As Brent's family was led to the ICU, it did not take them long to figure out which room was Brent's. Five nurses stood around bed number nine in the ICU, all tending to Brent. Then came the doctors, the four specialists that had worked so hard to try to save his life, each introducing themselves and offering condolences and best wishes for the family. One by one, they scribbled their cell phone numbers on business cards and handed them to Kenny. The last to introduce himself was Dr. Lourie, the orthopedic surgeon.

"Mr. and Mrs. Doonan," he said in a tone that spoke of his disappointment, "I was the last to work on Brent and I need to tell you...Dr. Harvey and Dr. Ferrier were in a hurry to get his wounds closed up so I didn't get much time with him." And then the news got a little worse as he explained the reality of the situation. "I don't know if Brent will ever be able to use his arms again...I just can't tell at this point," he said in a dismal tone as he spoke sincerely from his heart. "But we can always go back in and work on any problems," he added as he turned and left the room.

Once alone, Brent's family focused their attentions on Brent. With great trepidation, Kenny and Sue crept closer to the bed, wanting, but not wanting, to look.

When they did look, they saw Brent through whirring motors,

dials and switches, bags and IV lines hanging like spaghetti and a
pump whooshing up and down. There were tubes going into Brent
from three directions, stitches, staples, blood and a crease on his
cheek as if he'd burned himself with the edge of an iron.

Brent's eyes were closed; he was deep in a narcotic slumber,
unaware of his surroundings. A piece of tape ran from one cheek,
over his upper lip and onto the other cheek to hold the drainage
line in his nose. His mouth hung open, gaping like that of a fish out
of water – helpless. Two machines were strapped to his legs to massage them in order to keep the blood moving so there would be no
clotting.

As she stared at her son, tears dropped onto the collar of Sue's
gray knit blouse. She opened her purse, withdrew a tissue and blot-
ted her eyes. "At least he's breathing. There's hope."

Kenny stood there speechless, with his eyes wide open, holding
his breath.

Approaching his son, Kenny saw that all the color was gone
from Brent's skin. He appeared beyond pale, almost albino. There
were bruises on his forearms and neck and along the side of his face
where the bullet had grazed him. He could feel that his son's skin
was cold and clammy as he touched him on the cheek. It was as if
he were touching a cadaver. He stared down at Brent's arm bandages, already soaked in blood and in need of a change. Nearly every
inch of Brent's body was attached to some type of machine, the
largest of which was connected to a tube that ran straight down his
throat.

As Kenny pulled back slightly the sleeve of his coat caught the
seam in Brent's gown, pulling it back just enough for the family to
see the bright silver staples pinching a deep red incision in Brent's
chest.

Sue gasped as she fought the urge to start sobbing. Seeing her weaken, Kenny steadied her while helping her into a chair.

No amount of strength can overcome the emotion of seeing one's child on the verge of death. Kenny's cheeks were stained with tears. He could barely stand to look, yet he didn't want to move. Suddenly, vivid memories of the times he and Brent had shared began to flood Kenny's mind: fishing at the lake, rooting for Brent in his high school wrestling matches, watching him graduate from college, even Brent's funny habits. It was like he was walking through a family album. Kenny stared at his son, but he was in another place until he felt Sue's hand on his. Now he was thinking he didn't want to live himself, if Brent didn't make it. It was all so unfair. Brent had never harmed so much as a fly. He cared about people. He loved life and his was just starting to take off. Then Kenny began to agonize over his other son, Brian. Where was he? Was he okay? Was he on the way?

Standing there, the only thing that prevented the family from falling into the depths of despair was the fact that Brent was alive. Hope was the only remedy that could save them from a complete breakdown; no incentive was quite as strong as the possibility of hope – the possibility of a life snatched back by the hand of the Almighty. Brent lay there cushioned by his family's prayers, held in place only by His firm finger.

Downstairs in the lobby nearly a hundred people prayed for Brent. It was 10:00 p.m. when Brent's family returned to the waiting room where many of Brent's friends remained. Television monitors were blaring the on-going news coverage; most watched in amazement as the story continued to unfold. When the announcement that Barton had killed himself came on, the room erupted in loud clapping and cheering. Justice had been served. Later, at midnight, Brian, Brent's brother arrived.

By 2:00 a.m. most of Brent's friends finally went home, but his parents, Kenny and Sue, his sister, Jennifer, his Uncle Bob and his brother, Brian, remained on vigil, praying.

chapter eleven

Hazy
Perceptions

A t 6:00 a.m. on Friday, July 30, Brent woke up, opening his eyes
for the first time since the surgery. Though the tube in his throat
kept him from talking, and the straps securing his arms to the table
kept him from moving much, as he looked around the room and
heard his family break into cheers, a tenuous smile crossed his face.

Everything seemed very surreal. With my arms pinned down, I could-
n't pinch myself. Through a haze I could see the blurry figures of my family.
I was, after all, with those that I loved and if I was dead, so be it, this was
the way I wanted to go, my last vision that of my father, mother, brother, sis-
ter and uncle. Who can ask for any more grace than that? Death, like that
long corridor at the office, was poorly lit with all its secret and greater rooms
beyond. It was mysterious but peaceful.

Suddenly, a violent pain shot through my side and I knew I was alive
– unbelievable, I thought. I felt like I'd been eviscerated and my throat burned

with an intensity far beyond any strep throat I'd ever had. I kept gagging on a tube that seemed as if it was made of sand paper. I looked at my arms, seeing the bandages that were soaked in blood.

Then I began to feel the pulling and stabbing pain of the staples in my chest and side. I was alive, but I felt like hell — half-conscious, tumbling and falling —my body imprisoned. I lay strapped to a table, unable to move. My heart and lungs were frenzy feeding on a very short supply of blood and oxygen generated by the machine nearby. My chest muscles had amnesia, forgetting to rise and fall on their own.

Apparently, the drugs administered for pain were wearing off. My mind was rambling. For a few moments I felt I was back at the crime scene. I asked myself, is Barton nearby? Am I still being chased? Then the scene in my mind changed, I was at the hospital. When would the nurse come in with more painkillers? I asked myself.

I became aware of how cold it was in the ICU room. My family stood around my bed wrapped in blankets. I could see their breath as they spoke to me. It felt like a meat locker and indeed in a way, it was. However, the cold was soothing me; I didn't know I'd been burning up with a fever of 103 degrees.

I was told that later that morning, my father, brother and uncle drove to my office to begin putting the pieces back together. Though it was painful, my father thought it was important to jump right in immediately before everyone started feeling too sorry for themselves or me. My mother and sister remained, but I drifted in and out of consciousness after the nurse brought more painkillers and administered them to me.

I think it was a combination of the drugs and my fever that made me hallucinate, not really knowing if I was dreaming or awake. At first it was frightening, small images of things coming at me from out of nowhere, growing larger as they came into close focus and then disappearing before they crashed into me. But behind them all were images of those I loved and that made all the difference in the world.

On Friday, July 30, Kenny, Brian and Uncle Bob were all greeted at the All-Tech offices by an armed guard.

"You can't come in here," he told them.

"Like hell I can't," Kenny said. "My son was shot in there…"

"I'm sorry, but I still can't let you in," the guard cut in.

"My name is on the lease and I'll be damned if you'll keep us out."

The guard was silent for a second, allowing the grieving father his anger.

"Sir, with all due respect, I'm sorry, but I can't let you in."

"Look, we can either do this the easy way or the hard way. Which is it going to be?" Kenny said as he shot the man a very harsh look.

Kenny was six-foot-four and weighed 245 pounds, and though he was in his fifties, he was still an imposing figure.

"I think you'd better leave that old man alone right now," Brian added as Bob nodded in agreement.

Though hesitant, the guard stepped aside.

At first, the only thing they could move were their eyes and heads. Brian and Kenny's feet were nailed to the floor. The carnage they saw in the All-Tech offices was unbelievable. A one-sided war had been fought and the casualties had been heavy.

Barton had fired thirty-nine bullets that day with astonishing accuracy. Wielding a semi-automatic pistol in each hand like a character in a comic book, the bad guy only missed three of his targets and hit not a single window. In little more than fifteen minutes, though it had seemed like hours to his victims, twenty-two people had been shot. Half of them were hit in the back, others in the head or torso.

The walls, desks and some computers looked like a giant Jackson Pollack drip and splatter abstract painting, with one glaring difference: it was all one color, blood red. Some of the computers were still on. The scene was eerie, silent except for the undertone of several computer fans running.

All about the room, large circles of blood two to three feet in diameter were soaked into the carpet. The three men slowly began to move through the battlefield into a back office where two men were standing. One of them, All-Tech's Vice President, turned to Kenny and said in a strong New Jersey accent, "Hello. You must be Mr. Noonan."

Kenny jabbed back at the man, "It's Doo-nan! Not Noo-nan! The same last name as the one who runs the place!"

"I'm terribly sorry Mr. Doonan," he replied in surprise.

"What are you doing here?" Kenny blurted.

"Sir, I'm from All-Tech corporate headquarters. I'm here to decide what to do with this office."

"What do you mean, *do*?" Kenny said, noticeably upset.

"I have to decide whether or not to re-open this office or just close it down sir."

"That's not your decision to make!" Kenny said. "Five people died here yesterday and right now my son is in the hospital, hanging onto his life by a thread. He may be the sixth. As far as I'm concerned, this was the act of a terrorist – the purest evil imaginable. We will not be deterred by evil. A terrorist will not run us off. We most certainly will be reopening. This is now a holy place. Do you understand what I'm saying?"

"Yes sir. Perfectly."

"Now then, you can either help me get this place going again, or I will get someone in here who will!" Kenny added. "Is that plain enough English for you?"

"I'm here to help," Mr. Ogust replied.

"Good."

Turning to the other man, Kenny said, "And who are you?"

"I'm Mr. Shipman, the property manager," the man said in a quiet tone.

"What can you do for me?" Kenny asked.

"I can get you carpet," Shipman replied eagerly.

"Great. Do it."

Kenny, Brian and Bob next walked into the office where Brent, Kathy and Scott had been shot. They all grimaced as they opened the door and saw all the blood on the walls, desks and carpet. A circular stain about twenty inches in diameter had collected next to the printer. To the right, they saw one black polished dress shoe. Kenny picked it up.

"Looks like Brent's," Brian said. After a few minutes of silence, Kenny turned and started towards the door. Slowly, he traced the bloody footprints out of the office, through the conference room and into the hallway. He leaned up against the wall, bracing himself with one hand, visibly shaken, but he pressed on and up to the third floor. After questioning people in several offices, he found Serena's office, where Brent had eventually collapsed. He was trying to reconstruct the events that Brent had suffered through, as if that might take some of the burden off his son.

First, he talked with Serena, then Russell and eventually the others. Lynda had put Brent's things into a plastic bag and she gave it to Kenny. Inside were one black dress shoe, a tie, a belt, a pair of pants and a blue dress shirt.

Twenty-four hours after being shot, Brent was on a life support system. He and a nurse named Ruth had devised a way for him to communicate. One blink meant no and two meant yes, or I agree. Ruth remarked that he was already more alert. The magic first twenty-four hours that Dr. Harvey spoke about had passed; a good start.

"I'm going to un-do these straps Brent. Let's see if you can move you arms or hands," Ruth said.

Brent began by trying to wiggle his fingers, then to move his hand slightly and finally to raise his right arm a little.

"Do you think you can write?" she asked.

Brent blinked twice.

Ruth slid a pen between his fingers, pulled a tray over in front of him and placed a piece of paper on the tray.

"Have at it, Hemingway," she said.

The first thing I wanted to ask or to write was "Where is Mark Barton?" The moment I thought of it my heart rate started to race and I became clammy. He could be anywhere. Maybe he was looking for me, knowing I'd been taken to the hospital. Wouldn't be difficult for him to finish the job he'd started. Ruth sensed my trepidation and said, "What is it Brent? Write it down. Write it down."

I could barely hold the pen. My hand was trembling, but I managed to scribble, "didtheyfindtheguywhodidthis?" Of course, it was unintelligible. I tried a second time trying to make slow, large letters like a child in his first writing exercise. It wasn't working. I desperately wanted to know if they'd caught Barton and I wanted to be able to write, if for no other reason than it would show immediate progress, no matter how trivial.

Then I gave it one more try, a shorter version...Man? Guywhodidthis? Ruth understood. Do you mean Barton? She asked. I blinked twice.

"Yes," she said. "They caught up to him but he killed himself."

I didn't believe her. I knew she was only trying to calm me down, knowing that if I knew he was alive, I would be panicked, helpless. I sighed and tried to swallow, but couldn't.

The media frenzy hit the hospital almost immediately. Brent had only been in the hospital for a day and reporters were already swarming all over the place hounding nurses, parents and friends. One particularly irritating woman, a newscaster from Brent's hometown of Wichita, had gained admittance to the emergency room by claiming to be Brent's sister.

As Brent continued to come in and out of consciousness, he heard his mother arguing with Ruth about all the reporters.

"They won't leave us alone and I don't want them getting in to see Brent. That's for sure."

The rest of that Friday evening, family members shared turns staying with Brent. There were always one or two of them by his side, regardless of the time.

Each time Brent woke up, he scribbled the same message, "Guywhodidthis?" And each time he was given the same answer by his father, mother, brother, uncle, sister or a nurse: "He's dead. He killed himself." Brent wasn't buying it, though.

Though the doctors agreed Brent had passed the critical forty-eight-hour period well, they were still worried. That afternoon, Dr. Harvey came in to check up on Brent and to speak with his family.

"How are you doing?" he asked Sue.

"I'm scared," she said looking up at him with fear in her eyes.

"Why are you scared?" he asked in a concerned voice.

"Well, he got through the forty-eight hours like you said and he's healing so fast. I guess I'm just afraid something is going to happen to set him back. I'm still scared he won't make it," she said, wiping tears from her cheeks.

Dr. Harvey knew that her instincts were right. He lowered his head and then slowly raising it said, "I'm scared too."

At 3 a.m. on Saturday a nurse yelled, "Oh my God! The electricity is out in the ICU!"

Though the emergency generator kicked in and the lights went back on, Brent's respirator didn't. Ruth ran down the hall looking for a portable unit. Brent was heaving and sucking like a fish out of water, straining to get air.

One of the nurses remained, trying to calm him

"Hang on honey. She'll be back in a second."

Brent looked up to her like a lost child, scared but relieved to know someone was there. Within seconds, Ruth was back scrambling up to the bed with a handheld unit. She placed the rubber cup over Brent's mouth, ran the elastic strap around the back of his head and began rhythmically squeezing the bag, forcing air into his lungs. She repeated this for several minutes until finally there was a surge, the sound of electricity coming back on filled the room and the electric respirator kicked back on.

Wouldn't that be something? If I'd been shot five times, but survived, only to die in the hospital because of a blown fuse, Brent thought.

Brent's condition slowly began to stabilize through Saturday and into Sunday, but the same question continued to come up, "Guywhodidthis?"

"Brent, we've told you a hundred times, honey; Barton killed himself. Really he did. I wouldn't tell you that if it wasn't true," Sue said.

Brent still didn't believe it. Between his periods of sleep and his waking moments, he wasn't sure which, Brent would jerk and have spasms when something passed his field of view. He was on hyper-alert, thinking every object or person might be Barton. He called it high anxiety.

When he was awake, he tried to rationalize that it wasn't true, that Barton wasn't coming.

He would be running from the police for sure, not trying to kill me, Brent thought.

But it didn't matter.

Emotions are buried deep and chemicals like adrenaline and endorphins that flood into our systems bring heightened emotions when we feel we're in danger. Logic has nothing to do with it.

On Sunday some doctors came in to see Brent. They asked if he wanted the tube taken out of his nose and throat. Brent nodded vigorously.

It was horrible. The pain was bad, not nearly as bad as my wounds, just a different kind. My throat was as dry as Death Valley in August. I felt like a cactus had been run down my esophagus. In addition, it felt like I was constantly swallowing something that wouldn't quite go down.

The tech guy told me just to relax while he took it out. He slipped on a pair of surgical gloves and pinched the plastic hose between his thumb and forefinger and wrapped his other hand completely around it. Then he began to pull. At first I gagged, and then I began to choke. It felt like a large chunk of meat was caught in my air way and I began to panic. I shook my head back and forth. No. No. Stop.

The tech said it was no problem. This was a common thing. He would try later when I was more relaxed. Yeah, and that'll be real soon, I thought sarcastically.

Then Dr. Ferrier came in and asked if I wanted the massage units taken off my legs. Again, I nodded thinking, I'm sure not the judge of whether they should be or shouldn't be removed, but they're uncomfortable. I mean, even a massage, when it lasts three days, can get a little old.

The truth be known, I felt bad for letting them down on the tube thing, but I thought I was going to choke to death. It scared the hell out of me. Next time however, I'd make it happen.

Dr. Ferrier returned Monday night with the same tech as before. Together, they were able to extract the breathing tube. It was painful and it made Brent want to vomit, but it finally came out after a long slow tug. Brent said it felt like the tech was pulling a garden rake up out of his chest and esophagus. Even with the tube out, after a day or two, he still wasn't allowed water. He'd been getting fluids intravenously and was only allowed to suck on a wet sponge sporadically. Though he pleaded for water, the only relief he got were ice chips and the wet sponges. He was getting plenty of fluids intravenously, but his mind told him he was desperately thirsty.

Later that morning Brent's father came to visit. Brent could see there was a definite bounce in his step, as if he was very happy.

In great sweeping strides, Kenny came to the side of Brent's bed, a grin from ear to ear. In his hands, he held the thick Sunday issue of the *Atlanta Journal-Constitution*.

Brent looked confused. Kenny pulled off the front section of the paper and held it up for Brent to see. The entire page was covered with photos from the shooting with an oversize headline that read, "The Day Atlanta Can't Forget." Kenny quickly turned to page eight, pointed to the paper and said, "That bastard won't have to wait to get to hell. They already burned him." Brent, even more confused, looked to his father with wondering eyes. Kenny began to read:

"Four days after the shootings, on August 2, the Cobb County morgue released Barton's body.

"A hearse, hired by his family in South Carolina, carried it south thirty-seven miles down through Atlanta, past the airport and into the rolling hills of Fayette County.

"It left the interstate and continued nine miles more down Georgia 74, through farmland and intermittent housing developments.

"At Peachtree City, the hearse pulled into the parking lot of a pine shrouded, red brick building with a white smokestack discreetly rising from the rear: Metro Crematory, the sign read, where Barton was cremated."

"Now do you believe me?" Kenny said as he tossed the newspaper on the bed. "I've never lied to you, now have I?"

"Do you think we could get a little coffee in here, son?"

By Tuesday the days were becoming routine: wake up in pain, try to make a fist with each hand, raise my arms as high as I can, move my legs side to side. Here comes Ruth with the pain pills. Here comes the respiration tech. There goes another vial of my blood for testing. Soon, they're going to have as much of my blood as the carpet at All-Tech – but still no water.

"Doctor, how long do you think I'll be here?"

"Well, at least two months and then we can make a better determination," Dr. Harvey said.

"Good Lord! Two months?" I told him. "What the heck am I going to do here for two months? I can't stay here that long, I'll go nuts."

Though my wounds were very raw and inflamed, I no longer had a fever. That was enough for me, though I did have to admit there was a four inch open wound on my side. They'd left it open to drain so there would be no infection, but there was just no way I was going to stay in bed for two months. I called out for my father that night and told Ruth to get him down to my room as quickly as possible. Later on, I realized I must've scared the hell out of him. He came in, in a panic.

"What is it son? Are you okay?" he asked frantically.

"I'm fine Dad," I quietly whispered. "Just get my clothes."

"Why, Son?"

"Cause we are getting the hell out of here!"

He looked at me as if he'd just seen an alien. "What in the world are you talking about? You can't leave here. You can't even walk," he said. Then he began to laugh. I frowned for a moment, disappointed that he hadn't taken me seriously, and then I began to laugh as well, which was a big mistake. I felt like I was being drawn and quartered, but Dad was caught up, even knowing I shouldn't laugh.

You know how that is when something strikes you funny, you can hardly stop. I clutched at my side and tried to suppress the laughs. Dad put his hand over his mouth to try to stop laughing. Really, though, I didn't think it was all that funny.

Shortly thereafter, they moved me out of the intensive care unit and into room 447.

The colors were spectacular. Red and yellow roses, giant azaleas, red and white carnations, hyacinths, honeysuckle, magnolias and gardenias filled the room. The pungent smells not only permeated room 447; the lovely fragrances drifted into other rooms, as well.

There were flowers in vases on the side table, windowsill, the two chairs for visitors, in the bathroom, all over the floor and eventually, spilling into the entryway. Each flower arrangement came with a card offering support to Brent and his family. Some were from friends, others from family, and many even from strangers.

Headlines running not only in the *Journal*, but also in national magazines, spewed out accounts of the tragedy constantly. Conjecture, speculation and theory ran rampant. The most onerous reports attributed Barton's killing spree to his failures at day trading, a thought that angered Brent to no end.

One article said, "Speculation on a motive has centered on Barton's work as a day trader, investors who dabble in risky moment-by-moment changes in the stock market, which dropped sharply Thursday.

More balanced, yet still suspicious of trading losses, was the report by *Atlanta Journal-Constitution* staff writers Jay Croft and Alan Judd when they wrote,

"Key aspects of Barton's crimes remain a mystery. Although he seemed to be motivated by his day trading losses, which totaled about $217,000, nothing explains why his frustration turned into violence. Nor can much be determined about Barton's movements his final day: where he spent the three hours before the shootings began; how he escaped from Buckhead despite a massive police presence; and where he went before he emerged in Cobb county four hours later."

chapter twelve

Agonizing Questions

As the buzz about the Atlanta workplace massacre played on the media and in the newspapers, the entire nation wanted to know the same thing that Brent would later spend much time and effort searching for answers to – why? How could a father take the lives of his own children? How could he kill his friends and colleagues? Everyone involved at Momentum and All-Tech all agreed Barton had been genuinely well liked. No one had ever had an argument or even a disagreement with him. He came to work in a jovial mood each day and left with the same attitude. He spoke often about his family and how much he adored them, talking of his love for his wife, his pride in his daughter and his many outings with his son and the Boy Scouts.

However, while Barton insured that the entire story might never be known, he did leave behind some clues, among them hints from his own mind.

In an attempt to shelter Brent from the media, the name on the medical chart at the end of his bed read: John Harvey. Despite the identity change, for days flowers and greeting cards piled up in Brent's room. Finally, as the gifts continued, Brent turned to his parents.

"I've been thinking about all these flowers and gifts, but also of my friends that did not survive. I really appreciate all the flowers and cards people have been sending, but nine people have been buried. I would rather have their families get these flowers. Maybe you could arrange to tell the press so that they could tell people to send their flowers to the cemeteries or the families of the victims. Can you do that for me?"

"Certainly, Brent. That's a lovely thought. We'll take care of it."

The next day a single vase with two magnolias and several yellow roses sat on the table next to the bed. All the others were picked up and distributed to the gravesites.

However, within a day or two, the room again was overflowing with new flowers. The outpouring of support was truly astounding.

Brent was still in a lot of pain and intravenous lines remained his only source of nourishment. Now the doctors concentrated on ensuring he wouldn't have major complications. They were especially concerned about the possibility of staph infections, which in some cases can cause death. There were already formidable problems: nerve damage, severely damaged vital organs, the potential for pneumonia from fluid build-up in his lungs, blood clots and a host of other dire possibilities.

Large gaping wounds still remained in Brent's arms; his arms and his side were packed with gauze. His left arm and hand were in a permanent clinch because of all the nerve damage he'd sustained.

Once a day a nurse came in and carefully pulled the heavily soaked gauze pads from his wounds. They were always soaked in blood and some disgusting yellowish ooze. Each time she replaced the stained coverings with fresh white ones and gently stroked his brow. "You're definitely getting better," she insisted.

Brent's father, Kenny, and his brother, Brian, had been supervising the restoration of the All-Tech office each day between visits to the hospital. The old carpeting had been pulled up and the floors sanitized. New padding and carpeting had been installed. The old bullet riddled furniture had been replaced with new, the holes in the walls spackled. The painting was complete and motivational posters adorned the walls only four days after the rampage. One poster simply said, "Courage," another "Faith" and yet another, "Opportunity," simple reminders of the heights the human spirit may reach for and sometimes attain.

One by one, some clients trickled back into the All-Tech office. Though still exhibiting their shock and horror they came to show their support and to attempt to start the healing process.

On Monday morning, August 2, the same day Barton was cremated, those present in the office formed a circle as they prepared to meet with crisis counselors, who had been brought in to lead talks and facilitate the healing process. This continued day after day.

Discussions centered on individual stories of narrow escape, gruesome killing and chaos and the continued nightmares and fears the survivors were facing.

Dr. Harvey entered Brent's room one Tuesday morning.

"Brent, you seem to be the subject of a media frenzy," he said with a smile on his face, as if Brent would be flattered.

"Yes, I know. One reporter tried to get in here by telling the staff she was my sister," Brent replied, shaking his head.

"Well, I can continue to have security hold them off or if you're up to it, you can give them an interview. I can tell you this for sure though; they won't go away until they get a story."

I was very tired and sore, but mostly I was afraid of what questions would be asked. My dad had given me some of the stories about that day's events, but those were mainly about what was known through police reports and eyewitnesses. Reporters would want to know why. Perhaps it was a good idea to talk to them. Otherwise, they would continue speculating and blaming Barton's day trading habits and perhaps me, for the insanity. Some of the articles were already portraying day traders as a bunch of crazed gamblers who sat in dark cubicles manically trading stocks, losing money hand over fist, and ruining entire families with a single key stroke or mouse click. None of which, of course, was true. I could already see the headlines: "Mark Barton's family seeks $10 million in damages from Atlanta brokerage firms in wrongful death suit."

"I do know one reporter who would do a good and fair job," Dr. Harvey said. "If you want to tell your story, he's the person who will give you a fair hearing and let you tell it your way."

Brent decided to grant the interview. He felt the world needed to know that Mark didn't snap because of day trading, but because of his twisted personality. By this time Brent had become aware that Mark Barton must have had far more complicated problems than anything they had known about at All-Tech.

At this point, Brent did not know much more than the rest of the public or the other victims of Barton's psychopathic tendencies. As far as he was concerned, until Barton pointed the two guns at him, Brent considered him a friend.

No, he didn't hate the man, though he didn't know why not. Certainly, Brent thought, he had every right to. It just seemed that hating the man would be a lot of wasted energy. What would be gained now? Not a damn thing.

But he was scared. "Yes, I know Barton is dead and can no longer have an affect on me; nevertheless, it is as if Barton was reaching out of the grave," he told family. In addition to his injuries, post-traumatic stress caused Brent pain and agony. Brent often twitched when someone walked into the room, or when a bird flew by his window. Any sudden sound caused stress. Perhaps the combination of stress and the pain killers were causing Brent's nightmares, scenes where he seemed to run in place, never getting further than an arm's reach from some unidentified attacker. He woke up drenched in sweat, breathing heavily; each time the nightmare was the same and each time it seemed so real. Brent carried these memories with him most of the day despite his best efforts to suppress them.

Then there were the panic attacks. He didn't want to worry his family with all of it, but the panic attacks were the worst. They came out of nowhere and not because Brent was thinking of Barton. They started with a vague feeling of fear, attached to nothing in particular, just free-floating hyperactive anxiety, as the doctors called it.

When a panic attack began, without warning, Brent got clammy. The walls in the room began to close in on him. His heart began racing, despite the numbing effect of the drugs, and he simply felt scared to death about nothing in particular. As soon as Brent got that flutter in his stomach, he steeled himself for the event, telling himself it was all emotion, irrational emotion flooding his system with chemicals. These chemicals caused the panic, not his thoughts. He tried to override them with logic, telling himself there was nothing to be afraid of and eventually the demons would subside and go away.

Mark Picard from NBC came to see Brent. His mannerisms were an immediate indication of his character, that of a gentle and honest man. He moved slowly, spoke slowly, smiled and asked if he could pull up a chair.

"Brent, if it's okay, I'm going to ask you some pointed questions," he said in a soothing tone.

"Go ahead, shoot," Brent said, immediately catching the irony of his response. The two smiled uncomfortably.

Because Brent was still so weak, the interview didn't last long. Brent, unshaven, frail and still in a great deal of pain, talked in slurs, occasionally not making any sense. He showed the reporter his staples and gauze inserts. He showed him the scars down the front of his chest. He told Picard that Dr. Harvey had given him the large teddy bear that he clutched to squeeze whenever he thought he was going to cough or sneeze, to help ease the pain.

"I'm not a psychiatrist, but it seems like you've got a lot of misplaced guilt. None of this was your fault. The man was a monster, just another madman. He could've just as easily been in Duluth as Atlanta. There are plenty more like him out there. Hey, the fact that the man killed his own children is a testament to that, don't you think?" Picard offered.

"What? What do you mean he killed his own kids? When? How?"

"I guess you haven't been reading the papers or magazines. I have a copy of the *Journal* here in my briefcase. You can read it if you like when you feel up to it. It's sad though. I've gotta warn you. He killed his wife too. It's all in there."

"My God!"

Each new revelation provided a larger shock than the previous. It was horrific enough that Barton killed nine people, but to murder his own wife and kids was unthinkable. It was beyond comprehension. Though I didn't want to read about it, I was compelled. So, when Picard left, I picked up the paper.

The *Atlanta Journal-Constitution*:
"On Thursday night, the 29, after police discovered the bodies

of Leigh Ann Barton and her two children, a mourning friend of Mychelle Barton sat alone on the sloping grass, bare feet poking beneath the yellow police tape, eyes on an open door 150 feet away.

'I'm just trying to sneak a peek so I can see my best friend,' she says of Barton's daughter. 'I just saw them take a bag out. It was a big bag. It must have been her mother.'

'I wish it hadn't happened. I'm mad 'cause now I can't go to the Girl Scouts with her,' she says. She pauses. 'I'm probably going to buy some flowers. I wish they would give me something of hers – one of her toys or something. I wish she wasn't even there. I wish she were spending the night with me. It's so stupid.' She wonders, 'Maybe I could take her cat. Is the cat dead too?'"

Brent laid the newspaper on the table as the tears welled up in his eyes.

Counselors came to see Brent. Questions like, "Tell me about the shooting?" "How do you feel?" "Are you upset?" seemed painfully obvious. Brent couldn't explain the horrific nightmares or visions to himself, let alone a stranger. He soon learned to pretend to be asleep when they came to visit.

I was going through a series of ups and downs with the counselors. They were here too early and were ineffectual. Questions like, "Tell me about the shooting, how do you feel, are you upset" were ludicrous. I wanted an ear, someone to listen to me. I didn't want to be analyzed. I wasn't crazy. I certainly didn't want to relive the shooting. Just listen, don't look at me like a case study.

Though his emotional recovery was moving like a glacier, Brent's physical improvement was nothing short of astounding. Within nine days of the tragedy, Brent was out of bed and walking, albeit painfully, but standing and taking some steps. He'd spent most of his time sitting in a rocking chair or lying on his back for nine days and now the nurses and doctors had nicknamed him "The Miracle Man."

On Friday, August 6, Brent's uncle was in the hospital room and was stunned when Brent insisted on going for a walk.

"You can't walk, Brent. You have three different IVs going and you're plugged up with gauze in two different places with open wounds. What if you pull open staples or stitches?" Bob said.

"I'm going to go with or without you. Which is it going to be? Will you help me or not?"

"Yes," Bob replied, knowing Brent as he did. Brent slowly shuffled his legs to the side of the bed. Brent's uncle, Bob, put his arm around Brent and underneath his left arm to help swing Brent down. The second Brent's feet touched the cold linoleum floor and his uncle began to bear some of his weight, the pressure under Brent's arm was like a bolt of lightning surging through him. He winced and groaned but took a deep breath and stood up. Together the two men slowly made their way down the hall. Brent's goal was to make it to Meredith's room. She had been admitted at the same time as Brent. One of her major arteries had been severed and she almost bled to death. They never made it. They traveled all of fifteen steps and then Brent was too weak to continue. Nevertheless, Brent considered it a success. His uncle thought it was a monumental achievement.

Each day thereafter brought more progress–physically–but emotionally Brent's psyche was still bandaged from head to toe.

One day, nurses pulled out the IVs in Brent's arms but left the one near his heart so that they could continue to administer drugs. His arms both felt numb for the most part. Brent now began to use his arms and, for the first time in almost two weeks, he was allowed solid food. His new diet consisted of Graham crackers, Gatorade and

Jell-O.

Though he was managing to eat a little, his body wasn't processing the food properly. At first doctors thought he might be constipated, though eventually Brent did have a bowel movement that proved his plumbing was working. The news drew a round of applause from his family.

More get well wishes adorned his room at this point: Brent got an autographed basketball from Bobby Knight and a letter from Indiana University President Myles Brand. He received letters from football coach Lou Holtz and Kansas Governor Bill Graves. Hundreds of others were piled so extensively throughout the room that they had to move the stacks of get well wishes to create a path from the door to his bed and the bathroom.

The nurses and his family pinned banners on the walls with slogans like, "Celebrate Life," "Get Well," "God Bless You," each signed by children, adults and famous figures, as well as ordinary people he never met. A member of the Air Force Thunderbirds aerobatic team personally delivered an autographed poster signed by each of the pilots.

Though friends and family continued to visit, Brent's Uncle Bob became a daily fixture, along with his roommate, Brian Schlossberg. Putting his job aside, he came in for several hours each afternoon and brought the daily news clippings, which were already being assembled into a scrapbook.

In addition, fellow day traders and clients came by, keeping Brent apprised of how the market and the business was doing, always assuring Brent that though tragedy had struck better times were coming.

Governor Roy Barnes came to see him. However, even with all the attention and the great work of the hospital staff, Brent fought depression. He was riddled with guilt and anxiety, blaming himself for what had happened. He should have seen that Barton was crazy. He should have kept a gun in his desk. At times he told himself he should have jumped on Barton's back when he'd opened that door and seen Barton facing the other way raising his guns once again. He couldn't stop thinking of and reliving the tragedy.

One day after Brent confessed his continuing guilt to his dad, Kenny said consolingly, "Brent. If I was seven feet tall and weighed 300 pounds, I would'a been a star in the NBA – but I'm not."

That same day a kind and gentle man, the CEO of the hospital, came to visit Brent. He was the type that you immediately confide in. Though he had just introduced himself and pulled up a chair, Brent found himself confessing how his guilt plagued him.

The man shook his head, empathizing. "Get those thoughts out of your head right now. That's what all victims go through at first. After you begin to feel better your thoughts will be clearer and you'll see the truth of it all. The man was a monster, pure and simple. You know, Brent, there are bad people in this world."

"But…" Brent shook his head.

"But nothing," the man said, "let me tell you a strange story."

For the next thirty minutes, the man related how several years before, he'd been the CEO of a large chemical company and he'd come to know a chemist by the name of Mark Barton. He explained how Barton had been fired and then later returned to the plant when it was closed to break in and steal confidential files, formulas and client lists.

He continued to explain how Barton went to jail but was freed under an agreement that he would return everything he'd stolen.

"I'm the one who should feel guilty, not you. I let the bastard off the hook. If he'd spent a few years in jail, this wouldn't have happened. He probably would never have become a day trader. Who knows? Yesterday is gone. All we have to do is work on today and tomorrow." He got up and walked towards the door. "When you accept that, you'll finally recover from this tragedy, Brent. Trust me, you're going to be just fine," he said with a knowing smile.

Nevertheless, when night fell and the clock on the wall across from his bed seemed to stand still, Brent's mind returned to Barton and his fear multiplied. Brent wasn't ready to accept the hospital CEO's advice. He continued to seek reasons to berate himself and to blame himself. *Why didn't I fight him, why did I run?* was the recurrent question. There was never an answer. *What would a stronger, braver individual have done differently?* The questions and guilt deepened Brent's depression. He fought to accept what happened and move on.

To fight his emotional battles Brent tried exercise. With each passing day, he became a little stronger walking or taking "laps" around the floor, each day another lap, all without the help of a walker.

In the meantime, the story of the Atlanta workplace violence was not going away. The story of murder at the office was still the number one story along with the demise of the stock market.

Every day articles focused on the world of day trading; how day traders were a rogue new breed of gambler, using computers in small dark rooms, trading in a rapid-fire frenzy in stressful environments. The stress, they all theorized, was what drove Barton to become a fiend.

Brent searched for all he could learn about Barton and read all the articles speculating about the evils of day trading. He wanted to set the record straight and tell his side. He decided he would give another interview to NBC's Katie Couric.

Couric began by asking, "How did it feel to be shot five times? Does it still hurt? How long will you have to remain in the hospital? Why did he target you? Was there anything in his demeanor that tipped you off?"

I did my best to answer her, though I was exhausted and in a great deal of pain.

As Katie continued the interview I knew what she was thinking, what went unasked. What they really wanted to ask was, "Why did he choose you? Did you do something to make him mad? People don't just shoot friends for no reason."

Off camera, she added something powerful. She said, "The facts of this tragedy reach a level of perfidy beyond anything I have ever heard about. Brent, if he had lived, it would have been impossible for Barton to atone for his crimes or expect absolution."

When Couric and the crew left, I was exhausted mentally and physically.

Though he still had seriously depressive times, Brent's energy and optimism about life were slowly awakening. On August 8, 1999, Brent celebrated his twenty-sixth birthday with his family in room 447 of the Northside Hospital. The celebration was simple – a celebration of life.

When you've seen the icy gaze of the grim reaper, smelled your own death on his hot tongue, really, really known what it feels like to be dying, then you realize how cherished a smile is, a hug, a breath of fresh air, a loved one, the day itself, even if only one more.

I was not who I had been. I was now on an odyssey of resurrection, of resolution. Every tiny thing in my new life would be treasured. I would give thanks every night for all that had transpired that day, for one more chance to smell a flower, to see a child smile and giggle, to hear the voice of one of my family members.

Brent was struggling to be positive. Realizing how grateful he was to be alive was a good start, but his emotional recovery would be a roller coaster ride.

A week later, Kenny and Sue helped Brent into a wheelchair and pushed him out of the hospital in which he was being treated, across the street and into St. Joseph's hospital where Scott and Kathy were recovering. Those visits were both joyful and sad. Scott looked horrible. He'd lost thirty pounds. His face was gray and gaunt, his hair faded and dull. He seemed so frail. Despite his outward appearance, he told Brent he was recovering and would be leaving the hospital soon.

When the two finished comparing war wounds, Brent wheeled himself down the hall to Kathy's room. As he approached, knowing how serious her wounds had been, his stomach began to churn. He was anxious to see that she was alive, but nervous about her condition and what she might say, especially since he couldn't stop blaming himself for what had happened to her.

When Brent opened the door to her room he saw dark, thick sunglasses covering her eyes. For a moment, he breathed a sigh of relief, thinking, as he came close to the bed that, on the surface, she looked healthy and not nearly as fragile as Scott.

Yet Kathy's condition was even worse than he'd imagined. Though Brent knew she'd been struck in the temple, he didn't know it took both her eyes. She was, as she soon told him, permanently blind. Brent was heartbroken.

I felt so guilty. My condition was going to improve but Kathy would never see again. On top of that, she would later endure six different surgeries, mostly for cosmetic reconstruction on her face. She was kind enough to tell me it wasn't my fault and she was resolved not to let it ruin her life. She would remain strong in the face of adversity. My heart ached for her.

On August 10, Scott and Kathy left the hospital. However, the five-inch-wide hole in Brent's side was still open to let infection escape from his body and that meant that he couldn't go home. But every day in the hospital might bring a new infection, though he showered with anti-bacterial soap three times a day.

Then, while monitoring his blood work, Dr. Ken Braunstein discovered that Brent's platelet count (the part of the blood that forms clots to prevent bleeding) had soared. Normal levels are in the 150,000 to 300,000 range. Brent's had risen in the last two days to 700,000 and soon had reached 1.5 million. Though his wounds were healing nicely and he was beginning to feel better, he would have to remain in the hospital until his levels were normal. Every morning nurses injected Brent with blood thinners in an effort to stave off a clot, or worse, a stroke. It wasn't working. By the end of the week, his platelet levels had reached nearly two million.

"These are alarming levels, Brent," Dr. Braunstein explained. *So much for scaring the patient,* Brent thought.

"We do have an option that may help, though," he continued. "It's a chemotherapy drug."

"What are the side effects?" Brent asked.

"Nausea, vomiting, cramps, among others."

Not wanting to try this drug, because of the side effects, Brent discussed the treatment with his parents. They agreed that he should pass on the treatment. He was getting better, finally able to eat solid food. They didn't want to take the chance now that he would vomit and tear open all his stitches.

Brent lay awake most of the night to the sound of the clock ticking agonizingly slowly and praying. He prayed:

I asked God to heal me, physically and emotionally. I asked for divine intervention to bring my platelet level down to normal so that I could go

Photo courtesy of Brent Doonan

Brent Doonan, a middle child, was born in 1973, in Great Bend, Kansas. Along with his brother and sister, Brent grew up in a happy family. His parents supported and encouraged Brent to follow his dreams.

A natural athlete and student, Brent was an All-American Wrestler and State Wrestling Champion. A National Honor Society member, Brent graduated from Indiana University with a Bachelor of Science degree.

Photo courtesy of Brent Doonan

Photo courtesy of Brent Doonan

In his mid-twenties, Brent opened All-Tech Investment Group of Atlanta, Georgia with his partner, Scott Manspeaker.

Digital photo services courtesy of Al Kruper, AK Photo, Fanwood, NJ AKphoto@aol.com

Harvey Houtkin, the Founder and President of All-Tech Investment Group, is shown at his office in Montvale, New Jersey.

Photos courtesy of Brent Doonan

All-Tech Investment Group, Atlanta, Georgia, used the latest in computer technology to keep its day traders in the midst of the action on a moment-by-moment basis

Mark Barton, a former chemist, made a quick connection at All-Tech. His explosive high risk investment strategies quickly earned him the nickname "The Rocket" amongst his fellow day traders.

Mark Barton is shown in an undated familiy photo along with his wife, Leigh Ann, daughter Mychelle Elizabeth and son, Matthew.

Police officers crouch behind their van in the Buckhead section of Atlanta during what became known as "The Atlanta Massacre."

Still armed to fight a small war, Mark Barton was cornered at a local gas station by police.

Police officials remove the body of one of the three victims, a woman and two children, at the home of Mark Barton.

Catcher Eddie Perez, of the Atlanta Braves, bows his head during a moment of silence for the victims of the previous day's shootings in Atlanta.

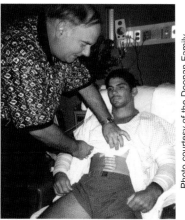

Trauma surgeon Dr. John Harvey examines Brent's wounds during rounds a few days after his surgery.

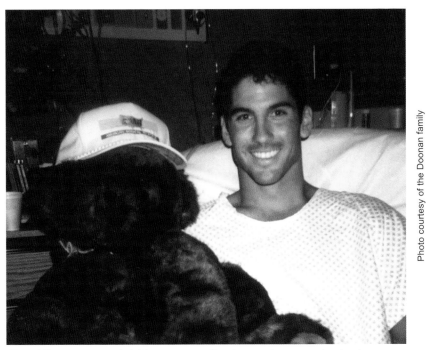

Brent Doonan was told to squeeze the bear whenever he had an urge to sneeze or cough, in order to prevent any strain on his stiches.

Boy scouts carry the flag draped coffin of Matthew, Mark Barton's son, from the White Columns Chapel in Lithia, GA, following services for Matthew and his sister, Mychelle.

Thousands of well wish-
ers sent Brent flowers,
notes and cards.

All photos shown on this page
courtesy of the Doonan family

Georgia governor Roy Barnes visits Brent Doonan at the Atlanta hospital
where Brent was treated.

Brent Doonan's mother, Sue, stood by
her son every step of the way as he
fought to recover.

Brent inherited his "Can-do"
attitude from his father,
Kenny.

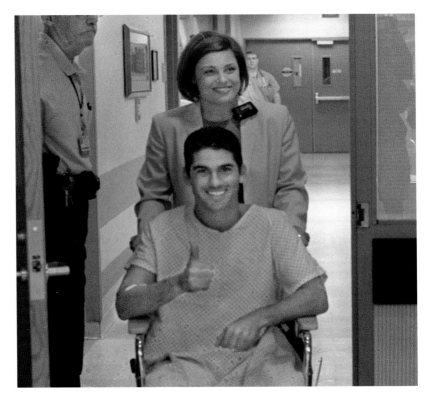

Brent Doonan left the hospital just over two weeks after being admitted, near death, as the result of five bullet wounds he received at the hands of Mark Barton.

Six years after that terrible day in Atlanta, the future looks bright for Brent Doonan, pictured here with his wife, Sarah, and his son, Jaxson.

home and recover. I also asked Him to take the burden of guilt off my shoulders.

A friend had once told me that for many years he worried about money, not having enough to make ends meet. Then he began praying. He knew that God was infinitely strong, could bear the weight of the world on his shoulders, so my friend asked Him to assume the burden of worrying about money. That way, my friend could spend his time being productive instead of worrying. It worked. He said he could literally feel the worry fleeing his mind.

I asked God for the same favor. Lord please take this guilt from my shoulders. It is all that I think about day and night. I'm consumed with it and I'm confused by it.

The following morning a nurse came to draw Brent's blood for a medical test. Several hours later, she returned to announce in a buoyant mood, "Brent, your platelet level is going down, not dramatically, but down." Dr. Braunstein told him that if this improvement continued, Brent could leave in a few days.

At 3:00 p.m. on August 12, a nurse wheeled Brent down to the first floor. Bandages still covered the open wounds on his arms and a hospital gown covered the one on his side. He was told there would be three television stations asking him questions for no more than five minutes. Brent had agreed to one final press conference before he went home.

As the doors opened into the room, flashbulbs began popping from every direction and Brent was asked to walk up to the podium to answer questions. As he looked around he saw there were at least thirty reporters with pens and pads ready. Some had tape recorders and there were several news cameras running. Brent was nervous, but took a deep breath and began to speak.

"I want to thank all the great people of Atlanta and the nation for their incredible support, flowers, letters and phone calls. I truly feel that thousands of people made this miracle possible.

"As for the why of it, I don't think we'll ever know. Mark Barton was sick, very sick. He managed to hide his illness from his neighbors, co-workers, family and friends.

"I don't believe this had anything to do with me, my company or the business of day trading. There are plenty of people day trading who live normal lives. They work hard, they go to church and they help in their communities. Yes, it can be stressful, but what job isn't when you think about it? And no, I don't hate the man. I don't feel anything about him except confusion. I feel sorry for his family and those that thought they knew him. I feel sorry for all of my colleagues and the families of those we've lost. Nine people died on July 29. God chose to save others and me. I do not know why. Now, I just want to go home for some r and r. I'm leaving the hospital with a few less organs than I came with. But I feel great today and I'm ready to get on with my life."

On Friday, August 13, 1999, two weeks after the shooting, Brent Doonan walked out of Northside Hospital with his mother, father, uncle and sister. He decided he would leave Atlanta and fly back to Wichita with his parents. However, his release was bittersweet. Though he could walk slowly, a full physical recovery would take months. Questions would plague him for years. The emotional scars he bore because of Mark Barton's violent rampage would last a lifetime.

chapter thirteen

Entering a Murderer's Mind

During and after his recovery, many agonizing questions kept revolving in Brent Doonan's mind concerning Mark Barton's past and personality. Brent kept asking himself, *What had made Mark Barton snap? Was his mental imbalance more deeply seated?*

At the same time, similar questions were being debated by professionals and the public for whom the Atlanta massacre had stirred fears and questions about workplace violence.

There is evidence, in the early history of Mark Barton's life, that the psychopathic tendencies he had were present long before Barton lost vast amounts of money day trading, but had gone undetected.

In *Small Criminals Among Us*, Gad Czudner, Ph.D., identifies the three main skills that are essential in the development of young children. They are: social intelligence, which implies manners, customs or cultural habits; emotional intelligence, the ability to communicate with emotions; and moral intelligence, the child's ability to show consideration for others, to have respect and to show sympathy and empathy. Furthermore, Dr. Czudner states that, "criminality is a developmental process which begins in early childhood" and often results from the lack of development of social, emotional and moral intelligence.

Although there is little documentation about the early history of Mark Barton, it is clear that he grew up with a very strict father, who took on the role of the harsh disciplinarian of the house. According to Dr. Czudner, "parents using conditional love, whether father or mother, produce a very insecure child…the child feels loveable if he meets his parents' expectations, unloved if he does not," and "this inconsistency can lead to development of a neurotic, disturbed child." According to this theory, Barton's strict upbringing could have caused his young mind to develop improperly.

During Barton's middle childhood and into his teenage years he engaged in criminal activity, by robbing a convenience store on two separate occasions. More specifically, as pointed to by Dr. Czudner, it is the peculiar motivation of the young criminal which leads him or her to steal and feel no guilt afterwards. "These budding criminals never show empathy or guilt about how much distress they have caused their victims. In fact, they usually show quite a bit of excitement about their endeavors and often brag to their peers about their stealing." In Barton's case, he bragged to his psychologist about his enjoyment and exhilaration in the process of theft: casing possible targets, finding out where the money is kept and plotting how to get away with it.

Not only did his acts of theft indicate that Barton was a budding young criminal, but they exposed multiple other characteristics of young criminals, in addition to connecting similarities between Barton's juvenile and adult crimes. Barton's psychologist reported him to have "fancied himself a master criminal." According to Dr. Czudner, one of the similarities between juvenile offenders and adult criminals is that both are "intoxicated by power and control." Young Barton's infatuation with the idea of being a successful thief mirrored his adult behavior, as he took the lives of his family and innocent people at All-Tech and Momentum Securities, perhaps to gain some sort of control. In addition, his juvenile fascination with theft and power set the stage for his future thresholds and expectations for experiencing excitement and power. As with most criminals, the stakes got larger and larger.

To approach the truth, it is necessary to address the earliest influences on the development of Mark Barton's mind. Barton's actions shocked the public because of his seeming normality in his upbringing, his public persona and his familial involvement. According to the field of psychopathology, psychopaths usually show signs of this disorder at a young age. Mark Barton had many common characteristics of a budding psychopath: as an adolescent he was developing a criminal mind through robbing convenience stores, experimenting heavily with drugs and feeling like an outcast from society. As revealed in the Psychopathy Check List-Revised, "juvenile delinquency" and "early behavioral problems" were both evidenced in Barton's early years. Furthermore, Barton's anti-social tendencies as a teenager and his possible rage at being rejected by society at a young age point to his possible continued psychopathic development.

There are many different kinds of psychosis, but the criminal minds of psychotics adhere to certain criteria. A psychologist at the forefront of psychopathology, Robert D. Hare, after twenty-five years of research published the Psychopathy Check List-Revised, as found in the *Manual for the Hare Psychology Checklist*, also known as the PCL-R, a highly reliable and respected method used in the diagnosis of psychopathology. The PCL-R is a classification system that is used by mental health professionals to identify psychopaths. It includes a twenty-point behavioral and personality assessment, a guided interview and a background review. The twenty characteristics defined by Hare's PCL-R, 1991, cover "interpersonal characteristics," such as "glibness," "superficial charm," "manipulative," "lack of empathy" and the "chronic and versatile antisocial lifestyle," including "need for stimulation/prone to boredom," "parasitic lifestyle," "impulsivity," "juvenile delinquency" and "revocation of conditional release."

Based on the applicability of these characteristics to Mark Barton's behavior, beginning in adolescence and gradually escalating to the shootings at Momentum and All-Tech, a strong argument can be made for declaring Barton a psychopath. Although all analysis of Barton must be done in retrospect, the few facts that are known about his life seem to point to this type of deep psychological disturbance.

After losing his job at TLC, Barton broke into his former company and stole files. His composure and lack of guilt whenever he spoke to the authorities pointed towards a key thread in all of Mark Barton's criminal acts, as "the range of a psychopath's activities depends upon his intelligence and his opportunities," according to Dr. Eric Berne in *A Layman's Guide to Psychiatry and Psychoanalysis*. Throughout his criminal career, Mark Barton, a chemist and an extremely intelligent man, evaded the authorities and accepted no responsibility for his rage toward the people in his life. In the interviews and depositions of Mark Barton, the first documented testimony giving insight into his personality and mind occurred after the murders of his first wife and her mother, and later during his deposition at the insurance company. Barton's other testimony with a mental health professional occurred after he was accused of sexual abuse. Here his psychopathic qualities were again substantiated.

Through his various interviews with authorities, showcasing his vehement displays of self-justification and the pain he caused virtually every person he came into contact with, family and friends, Barton seems to have evidenced the traits Dr. Hare describes in his book *Without Conscience:* "Psychopaths are social predators who charm, manipulate and ruthlessly plow their way through life, leaving a broad trail of broken hearts, shattered expectations and empty wallets. Completely lacking in conscience and feelings for others, they selfishly take what they want and do as they please, violating social norms and expectations without the slightest sense of guilt or regret."

It can be argued that Mark Barton either charmed his way into people's hearts, as in the case of both his wives, or falsely misled his acquaintances to believe that he was trustworthy and stable, as he did with his many work associates throughout his deviant employment history, only to end up destroying the lives of practically everyone around him.

Mark Barton's psychosis heightened just one year before the shootings at All-Tech and Momentum Securities, when his behavior became recognizably characteristic of psychopaths. One poignant indication of psychopathic behavior, animal abuse, was exhibited by Mark Barton in 1998. It was reported that Mark Barton shot his eight-year-old daughter's kitten. Barton then proceeded to take his daughter on a search for the pet he had killed. This happened months before the shooting at All-Tech and Momentum Securities.

Animal cruelty or the killing of animals is included in the paradigm of what the FBI calls the "homicidal triad." The homicidal triad was developed by the FBI to identify characteristics of violent and homicidal individuals, particularly serial killers, and to identify potential future criminals. The criteria included in this "triad" are experimentation with fire, bedwetting at an inappropriate age and animal cruelty or cruelty to other children. The FBI, in addition to many psychologists and mental health professionals, specifically cite incidents of animal cruelty as a precursor to future acts of violence. An individual who kills or tortures animals, either as a child or adult, is seen as "rehearsing" to kill humans. Psychopathic individuals "may kill or torture animals, because to them, the animals symbolically represent people," reported an FBI Special Agent.

According to a study conducted by Northeastern University and Massachusetts SPCA, individuals who hurt animals were five times more likely to commit violent crimes against humans. Mark Barton was included in a list of mass murderers including Jeffrey Dahmer, Albert DeSalvo, the "Boston Strangler," Ted Bundy, the "Deliberate Stranger," David Berkowitz, "the Son of Sam," Patrick Sherrill, who shot fourteen people in a post office and others, all of whom had killed or tortured animals.

In an article entitled *The Possible Motives of Atlanta Day-Trading Mass Murderer, Mark O. Barton* by Aubrey Immelman, released by the Unit for the Study of Personality in Politics (USPP) two days after the shootings at All-Tech and Momentum Securities, based on psychopathological literature, Mark Barton fit the profile of a "sadistic borderline personality" or an "explosive psychopath." Individuals with this type of disorder appear to function normally on an everyday scale, "but lack the necessary psychological strength and cohesion to maintain control in all situations, periodically erupting with precipitous and vindictive behaviors." These outbursts, also called "adult tantrums" by experts in the field of psychopathology, are "characterized by uncontrollable rage and fearsome attacks upon others," and often, as in the case of Barton, "occur against members of the psychopath's own family." The difference between "adult tantrums" and the tantrums of a child lies in the reason behind the emotional outburst. Unlike a child who throws a tantrum to try to get what they want, an "adult tantrum" serves as more of an emotional release of a "pent-up feeling of humiliation and degradation." Is this evidence conclusive enough to assume that Barton's murderous "adult tantrum" was caused by his significant day trading losses?

According to Immelman, "Whether justified or not, certain persons come to symbolize, for explosive psychopaths, the sense of frustration and hopelessness that sparks their explosive reactions," and psychopaths often feel compelled to destroy these "symbolic figures." Often these "symbolic figures" come to represent their own feelings of betrayal, frustration and failure, and when faced continually and repeatedly with these emotions, "their limited controls may be quickly overrun by deeply felt and undischarged resentments." Often these feelings are provoked by "the mere presence of symbolic individuals." The psychopath feels that such reminders "must be obliterated."

Frequently, when explosive psychopaths confront these feelings, they are "provoked into a panic of blind rage" and "the resulting violence is a desperate lashing-out against symbols rather than reality." Perhaps a bad stock market day, in addition to the stresses of day trading, wasn't, as most people had assumed, the cause of Barton's rage. The nature of Barton's suicide note in correlation with the methodology of his murders supports this idea.

Barton wrote: "I killed Leigh Ann because she was one of the main reasons for my demise, as I plan to kill the others…kill as many of the people that greedily sought my destruction." In the suicide note he left behind, Mark Barton identified his victims, his family and work colleagues, as those who caused his "destruction" and "demise." In addition, Barton's emotionally ingenuous and inarticulate reasons point to a characteristic of "sadistic borderline" psychopaths. As Immelman purported in her article, "Unable to verbalize what they feel and why, feeling out maneuvered and humiliated, the psychopaths respond," by "removing the irritation."

Other than his family, Barton seemed to choose his victims at his workplace at random, another characteristic of "sadistic" or "explosive psychopaths." "Because these explosive psychopaths may be provoked by otherwise innocuous interactions, their victims often seem rather incidental and arbitrarily selected," Immelman wrote.

As mentioned earlier, psychopaths often feel emotionally weak, inferior or victimized and thus either lash out to release these pent-up emotions or take on a set of external standards that overcompensate for their lack of control, such as religious zealots. Often psychopaths indulge in behaviors without taking into account the possible consequences, as they are emotionally selfish and inadequate. Mark Barton was known to be rigidly controlling with his first wife and throughout his life exhibited extreme, fanatical religious beliefs and subscribed to distorted religious doctrines. Barton's flagrant affair with Leigh Ann and his obsession with day trading point to his warped personality and inability to handle average responsibilities. He gambled with life constantly by throwing the dice with no concerns for the risks he took.

A *Time* article, "A Portrait of a Killer," reported in depth on Barton's unstable and often self-centered behavior. The author reports that in May of 1993, when Barton began having an affair with Leigh Ann Lang, he "bought a new wardrobe and began keeping up a tan." When Barton's first wife, Debra, grew suspicious, Barton's reaction points to his unstable mentality: "The key to the whole thing was I started going to the tanning bed, and she didn't like that…she was jealous…all throughout the relationship…because I was in outside sales. She found her own dog's hair on me at one time…and she asked me if it was another lady's hair…I just denied it."

Hare's PCL-R, as earlier discussed, provides a list of characteristics of a psychopath. Upon examination of Barton's behavior and recorded statements regarding his relationship with his first wife, sev-

eral of these characteristics seem particularly applicable to him. For
instance, Barton's rather light-hearted comment that his wife didn't
like it when he went tanning displays a talent for "glibness/superficial
charm," as listed in the PCL-R. In addition, Barton could be manipulative, turning into something of a con artist in order to promote
his own interests, and he seems to have displayed characteristics that
Hare calls "grandiose sense of self worth," "lack of remorse or guilt,"
"callous lack of empathy" and "failure to accept responsibility for [his]
own actions." Common in psychopaths, each of these traits points to
Barton's self-centered approach to his relationship with his first wife,
and his equivocation that, although he was having an affair, he was not
to blame for the problems in the relationship with his wife. He
emphasized his wife's jealousy and faulty logic concerning his affair
with Leigh Ann, seeming to hint that the affair was somehow a result
of these shortcomings in his wife, rather than acknowledging that he
might be doing wrong through his own unfaithful behavior. Barton
slickly freed himself of blame through twisted logic, so that his admissions of the affair were devoid of both guilt and empathy. All of this
points strongly to psychopathic tendencies.

Barton displayed many notable characteristics of a psychopath,
but some of his behaviors and attitudes also pointed to the possibility
that he suffered from borderline personality disorder. His disjointed
explanation of the disintegration of his relationship with his first wife
provides an example of the skewed rationale often employed by those
with borderline personality disorder. He identified his change in self-
image—his new tanning and dressing habits—as the cause of his
wife's disapproval, but failed to make a connection between these
changes and his own instability, particularly in regard to his personal
image. Barton rationalized his unfaithful behavior in such a way as to
allow him to blame his wife for their problems, claiming that she was
jealous of his job situation and insinuating that he was in some way

superior to her. He denied his wife's accusations of cheating, but his denial contained more condemnation of his wife's faulty reasoning than avowal of his own innocence. Barton showed a total lack of stable or justifiable behavior by having an affair and blaming his unfaithfulness on his wife. This points to his inability to maintain stable interpersonal relationships, self-image and behavior, a trait characteristic of individuals with borderline personality disorder.

As the media and the public attempted to understand the motivations of Mark Barton, they raised the suspicion that Mark Barton had a serious emotional disorder that came more and more into view.

Was Mark O. Barton a psychopath dressed in middle-class American males' clothing? And if so, why and how did he pick his victims? What was Mark Barton thinking? How did his violent inclinations go undetected for so long?

Further evidence in support of the possibility that Mark Barton had borderline personality disorder was revealed in his suicide note. The suicide note disclosed his mental instabilities in the months leading up to his murderous rage at All-Tech and Momentum Securities. Borderline personality disorder (BPD), as defined by the National Institute of Mental Health, "is a serious mental illness characterized by pervasive instability in moods, interpersonal relationships, self image and behavior."

According to the National Institute of Mental Health, "people with borderline personality disorder often have highly unstable patters of social relationships. While they can develop intense but stormy attachments, their attitudes towards family, friends, and loved ones may suddenly shift from idealization (great admiration and love) to devaluation (intense anger and dislike)." Both of Barton's marriages were marked by his emotional instabilities and idiosyncrasies. As reported in *Time*, Barton's affair with Leigh Ann started in May of 1993 and by June of 1993, Barton reportedly told some of Leigh Ann's friends at dinner one night that "he had never loved anyone more than Leigh Ann and he would be free to marry her by the first of October." At this point Barton was still married to Debra, and had tried to take out a life insurance policy on Debra a month earlier. A few days after his profession of love for Leigh Ann, Debra and her mother were found murdered in Alabama. A little over seven months after Debra's murder Leigh Ann moved in with Barton and his two children. Five years later Leigh Ann and his two children would be the next to fall out of favor with Barton.

"People with borderline personality disorder exhibit other impulsive behaviors, such as excessive spending, binge eating and risky sex," The National Institute of Mental Health states At the time of his death, Barton, after spending the entire $600,000 from his first wife's life insurance policy was also up to total of $217,000 in debt to Momentum Securities and All-Tech. Furthermore, Barton used day trading as a form of gambling, always sustaining extreme losses or making substantial gains; his volatile spending habits and monetary decisions were alarming.

The possibility that Mark Barton suffered from borderline personality disorder is further supported by theories revealed in the second part of Immelman's article, *The Possible Motives of Atlanta Day-Trading Mass Murder, Mark O. Barton*. Mark Barton's anxiety and fear surfaced in possible response to the state of his life. In his suicide note Barton explained, "I have been dying since October," and related that some nights he was "so terrified that I couldn't be that afraid while awake. It has taken its toll...I have come to have no hope." According to the article, Barton's admissions in his suicide note point to the possibility that in the "days or weeks prior to his killing spree, he may have developed acute panic attacks," and in this highly anxious state, borderline personalities' "inner controls disintegrate," as their emotions and behavior becomes chaotic. This emotional chaos may escalate to the point of "a brief psychotic disorder," that usually goes away in a few hours or no more than a day or two. In the case of Barton, these nightly chaotic episodes might have driven him to murder his family.

The article also points to evidence in Barton's suicide note that supports that his admissions to having a sort of psychotic breakdown could "be presented as an acute delusional episode, characterized by projection, in which Barton disowned his undesirable, sadistic personal traits and motives and attributed them to others." This is supported in his reference to his father's fears being passed down to him and from him to his son, his mention of his wife, whom he blames for his "demise," and others, "who greedily sought my destruction."

In the end, the report states, individuals with sadistic borderline personality disorders, when "'faced with repeated failures and frustrations, their fragile controls may be overwhelmed by undischarged and deeply felt angers and resentments…may surge unrestrained to the surface, spilling into wild and delusional rages.'"

Linda Lerner, attorney for All-Tech Investment Group, told CNN, "I don't know that you can necessarily tie his [Barton's] trading to those killings."

Bill Campbell, the Mayor of Atlanta, stated, "Quite honestly, I don't know if we'll ever know what the true motives of Mr. Barton were."

A CNN headline expressed the general consternation, "Shooter lost $105,000 in a month, but motive still a mystery."

Newsweek and *Time Magazine* ran stories illustrating the tumultuous years in the life of Mark Barton leading up to the murders to offer insight into the developing mentality of a mass murderer, in an attempt to glean some idea of his motive.

Mark Barton's motives became a topic of heated debate, becoming the center of a media frenzy and unanswered questions in the public. Why had he committed such atrocious acts? Was it the pressures of day trading and continual losses that made him snap? Perhaps he was deranged from an early age? Or was Mark Barton a mere demographic, a new breed of men, the failed breadwinners, victims of and angered by a society that equates a man's worth to his financial stability.

As reporters in print and media and the general public searched for the source of the demons that drove Barton to murder, some media began focusing on the psychological and socially relevant motives for the brutal assault that left thirteen dead in its wake. In a story released August 8, 1999 in *Time Magazine*, "A Portrait of a Killer," covering the years of Mark Barton's life preceding his killing spree. *Time* reported that Barton's daughter at the age of two and a half years old, "told a day-care worker that her father had sexually molested her." In such cases a custody hearing ensues, though, given Barton's daughter's age, "it was difficult for state attorneys to build a solid case around her against Barton or prevent him from keeping custody of the kids."

According to one *Atlanta Journal-Constitution* article, Douglas County District Attorney David McDade recounted the catastrophe, delving into the reasons for the tragedy and into Barton's past, seeking professional evaluation of them. The psychologist, whose name was not mentioned, "said it was his opinion that Mr. Barton was capable of homicidal acts and thoughts. Ideations is the word I think he used," said McDade.

He found out that mental evaluations of Barton took place and were reported to a social worker at the Douglas Department of Family and Children Services. The psychologist did not include his suspicions of Barton's murderous capabilities in his written report and "his only written observations about Barton were that he appeared, 'perhaps understandably, irritated by the insistent suspicion of authority figures and by these new allegations of possible sexual abuse.'" The psychologist's notes continued, " 'He appeared somewhat controlling, power oriented and very suspicious…He appears to have been irritated by living in a household with a woman he considered much brighter than he and a woman around whom he felt he had to be 'perfect.'"

Time also reported that McDade, who reviewed the 1994 custody hearing, could not stop going over the clues and insights about Barton's state of mind. "'It was disturbing enough to have a trained psychologist and a competent prosecutor reporting these things back to us,' and 'It's absolutely chilling to think about now.'" According to the aforementioned article in *The Atlanta Journal-Constitution*, Cathy Bitterman, the social worker involved in the case, after McDade, was quoted as saying "'David, David, David, we knew it…Do you remember what the doctor said?'"

So how did this revealing psychological evaluation fall between the cracks? Why didn't authorities keep Barton under surveillance? How did Barton get away with possible child abuse and why was the case dropped? Most importantly, why were Barton and the safety of his family not kept under close watch?

According to *The Atlanta Journal-Constitution*, Joyce Goldberg, Communications Director for the Department of Human Resources, stated there was no other option but for Bitterman to "close the case." The psychologist's evaluations were inconclusively incriminating, because the psychologist "never put his suspicions in writing," and after his evaluation of Barton's children, "sexual abuse was ruled out…there was no evidence in support of it." Goldberg intimated the problems with the psychologist's suspicions, "'he did not go on the record on that…It was one of those heart-to-heart kinds of things. You know, 'I find nothing to substantiate the sexual abuse, but I'll tell you what I feel.'" With no evidence of physical abuse in the psychologist's statement, the allegations against Barton were dubious and child protection services had to close the case. Furthermore, without the psychologist's suspicions in writing, even with the knowledge that Barton was capable of murder, the agency could not sustain surveillance and involvement in the lives of Barton's children.

The investigation by the Department of Family and Child Services and a psychologist exposed the violent tendencies of Barton years before the shootings at All-Tech and Momentum Securities. After the shootings, an early deposition, covered by *Time* in "A Portrait of a Killer," offered additional clues to a perplexed public about the "mystery of Mark Barton." Hints regarding Barton's real capability for violence and murder had been accumulating for a considerable time, from the investigations behind the sexual abuse charges to the deposition following the murder of his first wife to the confessional note Barton left on his coffee table before committing the worst workplace massacre in history. *Time* examined all of these pieces of evidence thoroughly in order to get inside the mind and understand the rationale of a mass murderer.

Months before the murder of Debra Spivey, his first wife, and her mother, Mark Barton had taken out a life insurance policy on his wife and afterwards he tried to collect the total payout of $600,000. The insurance company was hesitant to grant Barton the money, as police had considered Barton a suspect in the murders of his first wife and her mother in Alabama. The insurance company "balked, subjecting him to six hours of questioning," in which Mark Barton narrated "his life in sober and calculated tones."

In the insurance company deposition, Barton spoke "candidly about the rootlessness of his life": his failed relationship with his first wife, his affair with Leigh Ann and his scattered and questionable employment history. Perhaps the deposition may have offered insight into the time bomb that was Mark Barton's mind, a force that would cause him to explode at Momentum and All-Tech.

An article in *Newsweek* offered some additional details in the mystery that was the life and mind of Mark Barton, in an attempt to draw a clearer picture of his switch from a seemingly average man to a murderer.

"Barton's cyberspace 'profile' as an America Online subscriber was, in retrospect, slightly ominous," *Newsweek* claimed. A year before the killings at All-Tech and Momentum Securities, Barton's AOL account profile listed his hobbies as "day to day stock trading," and his personal quote was "a dollar earned is a dollar saved." However, this description greatly changed by the next year. "He no longer listed himself as married, and his hobbies included, 'Guns, Day Trading'" and sadly enough, "his personal quote was from the Clint Eastwood shoot-'em-up *Sudden Impact*: 'Go ahead, make my day.'"

At this point, perhaps growing desperate, as reflected by the distressing changes in his AOL account, Barton seems to have made one final attempt to gain some semblance of reason and control in his life. He turned to religion. He began to attend services and get some counseling through the Jehovah's Witnesses. A minister told *Newsweek* that Barton explained his inability to stop gambling on stocks, even after his wife left him over the money he had lost; an obsession the minister termed "a fever he had." Barton also related to the minister his night terrors, and "feared he had inherited some kind of undefined mental imbalances from his father." Barton also tried to find solace in the bible, specifically from Revelation 21:4: "and there shall be no death, neither sorrow, nor crying, neither shall there be anymore pain."

Although little is known about Barton's history with the Jehovah's Witnesses, despite his allusions to the sect in his suicide note, it is known that he was not a baptized follower. As well as trying to find out about his newfound religious interest in which the dysfunctional aspects of his personality took on new forms, media outlets searched for clues in Barton's domestic and financial life hoping somehow to ascertain his motives. Every piece of information about his life was important, but perhaps nothing gave better insight into his motives than the disjointed reasonings left behind in his suicide note. The letter, typed and printed out on personalized paper, was left in a plastic folder on the coffee table in his apartment. In it Barton expressed his twisted rationale for his actions. The content of this note was painstakingly scanned for insights into his motives and mind.

The note began, "To Whom It May Concern," a salutation often used in business letters when the audience is unknown or, as *Newsweek* chillingly pointed out in the "Rage of the American Male," "He wrote us a letter," "us" meaning the world.

In the article entitled "A Portrait of a Killer," *Time* points to the "tantalizing enigmas" left behind in Barton's suicide note. As Barton got into his message, he flatly directed the reader to the body of his wife in the master bedroom closet and openly admitted to killing his wife and two children, while denying any involvement in the murder of his first wife and mother-in-law, despite the similarities in the way both crimes were committed.

After this, Barton relayed the methods by which he murdered his wife and children, establishing a frightening contradiction through his intentions in the note and the reality of the murder scene. In structurally straightforward, simple sentences Barton explained, "There was little pain. All of them were dead in less than five minutes. I hit them with a hammer in their sleep and then put them face down in the bathtub to make sure they did not wake up in pain." His words juxtaposed the brutality with which he killed his children and the care that he took to dress them in their P.J.'s and put them into bed, placing their favorite toys around them. *Time* concludes that in Mark Barton's last attempts at explaining himself in his suicide note, "he scattered clues but no answers."

Expanding on this further, *Newsweek* ran an article entitled, "Rage of the American Male," that speculated that the murders have the propensity to "reveal something meaningful about our society... we wonder, what does it mean about the struggles of American men?"

Following the description in the letter of his murderous deeds, Barton apologized, questioned his actions and gave answers to those questions:"Why did I? I have been dying since October. I wake up at night so afraid, so terrified that I couldn't be that afraid while awake." In October, Barton's wife moved out. Barton went on later in the note with specific reasons for killing his wife and children. "I killed Leigh Ann because she was one of the main reasons for my demise, as I plan to kill the others," and as for the children, "I killed the children to exchange them for five minutes of pain for a lifetime of pain. I forced myself to do it to keep them from suffering so much later on. No mother, no father, no relatives."

The note continued with an admission of his murderous methodology, his mental hauntings and embedded religious allusions, among other tortuous enigmatic admissions.

In an attempt to break down Barton's blunt admissions, *Newsweek* explained Barton's attack on his family and his colleagues as a transference of sorts, "When the sources of our agonies are not visible, we invent enemies - typically the people closest at hand." *Newsweek* offers that Barton ignored his real enemy, "a culture that feeds the fears of many American men... a culture that holds up a frightening mirror."

"It has taken its toll. I have come to hate this life in this system of things. I have come to have no hope," Barton wrote.

Particularly concerned with these lines, *Newsweek* applied Barton's words to a larger context, as a reflection of the state of modern man. The unhappy comment, *Newsweek* pointed out, "could have been written by many ordinary men in America, who sense that some vague shifting 'system' has let them down." Furthermore, men like Barton were deprived of the chance their fathers had during World War II, "the chance to ground their manhood on utility, dedication and loyalty....beyond mere earning power." Accordingly, with this shift in gender specific values, today's men are "measured by bicep and SUV size, by image and celebrity...valued only for their stock-market portfolio." In this light, Mark Barton fit the modern man bill, "a Dockers-and-polo-shirted figure seated alone in his suburban home, wired to the Internet so many hours a day no one else could make a phone call."

In another line he explains his hauntings as possibly inherited from his father, "The fears of the father are transferred to the son...It was from my father to me and from me to my son...I had to take him with me." In a type of Orestian blood grudge, Barton might have murdered his son to break the cycle. In "Rage of the American Male," *Newsweek* concluded, "Barton's demons were masculine demons," as, "To be a man has always been to receive and pass on a patrimony of skills and a place within a system." Furthermore, "many men suspect that all they have inherited are their fathers' fears - of being found wanting, incapable, not needed," while not having "inherited the tools to deal with those fears."

It is important to point out that besides the investigations behind the sexual abuse charges, the deposition following the murder of Barton's first wife and the suicide note he left on his coffee table on July 29, 1999, little is known about Barton. Each of these pieces of evidence have been thoroughly scanned by media outlets, victims of his rage and the world, in order to try to understand, "Why?"

The evidence that Barton's actions were psychopathic and/or

characteristic of sadistic borderline personality disorder appears conclusive: Mark O. Barton's demons were classifiably characteristic of
a mental and emotional imbalance, disorder or psychosis masked
behind a veneer of normalcy dressed in khakis and a polo shirt.

"Psychopaths have little difficulty infiltrating the domains of
business, politics, law enforcement, government, academia and other
social structures. It is the egocentric, cold-blooded and remorseless
psychopaths who blend into all aspects of society and have such
devastating impacts on people around them who send chills down
the spines of law enforcement officers." Dr. Hare's statement from an
article in *Psychiatric Times* offers a chilling insight behind the picture
of Mark Barton on the front pages of newspapers across America
after the Atlanta Massacre, which smiles back in eternal defiance.

chapter fourteen

Day Trading:
Ups and Downs

On Wednesday, July 28, 1999, the United States Stock Market saw major declines. The Dow Jones fell over 180 points, 2 percent, and most importantly for day traders, the NASDAQ fell 3 percent, and in the previous two weeks had fallen by a total of 7 percent. Before Wednesday, July 28, one day prior to the mass killing by Barton, the dot com stocks, whose values had soared in the last year, had lost up to half their value in the preceding months (BBC). The decline of the market would be the backdrop to the tragic events that would unfold on Thursday, July 29, 1999 and would mark the beginning of many hardships for day traders who, up until this point, had been riding the wave of the stock market swell.

Call it bad timing or the bitter irony of life, but Mark Barton's shooting spree forever changed the reputation of day trading. Day trading became associated with the ups and downs intrinsic to the stock market in its fast paced world and people began to associate day trading with stress that could drive traders to gambling and murder.

Day trading's new bad reputation was publicized throughout the media blitz covering Barton's rampage. This bad publicity, coupled with the decline of the stock market, negatively stigmatized the practice of day trading and foretold its impending decline. Public attitude towards day trading shifted and it was regarded by most as the bad seed of stock market investments. In turn, the former "get rich now" attitude open to everyone fell under the scrutiny of the Securities and Exchange Commission (SEC), resulting in regulations of day trading techniques and its investors.

Before the Atlanta shootings, day trading was the new kid on the block, who became the most popular kid overnight. In the mid-nineties day trading caught the attention of the media world, and many financial outlets began focusing on the self professed computer savvy black sheep of the stock market scene, day traders.

The beginning of day trading was extremely symbolic of its inherent qualities and supporters. Day trading arose from the access made available through the use of the internet in order to trade stocks. Consequently, throughout the nineties, the rise of the internet and the success of the dot com companies became the bread and butter of day traders who mostly focused their attentions on the NASDAQ market, which was also computer based. Unlike the quotidian scene of brokers yelling and shouting on the New York Stock Exchange floor, day traders sat quietly in front of their computers and executed sales at the click of a mouse. This new method of trading stocks and the phenoms who began to make millions through the process ushered in the success of day trading, to the disapproval of staunch Wall Street prescriptivists.

In order to understand day trading's fall from grace in the media, it is necessary to examine its rise and the truth behind the day trading craze that endured until Mark Barton ruined its image.

As early as November of 1996, an article entitled "For Day Traders, an Hour is Long Term" by Suzanne Woolley, appeared in the Finance section of *Business Week*. The article explained the new trading phenomenon that was sweeping the nation: "Thousands of people from all walks of life are joining the ranks of stock-market day traders, who move in and out of stocks on a daily basis, rarely holding positions overnight. Some firms are capitalizing on the craze by offering schools for day trader wannabes."

There were essential differences between this new form of trading and the traditional way in which stocks were traded. According to the *Business Week* article, traditionally, investors hoped to make a profit after a stock had risen "scores of points," over the course of years, whereas "day traders' horizons may be the next two hours—or the next twenty seconds. And they think in terms of trying to make a quarter or eighth of a point."

Essentially, day traders buy and sell stocks throughout the day and as the stock rises and falls, they sell and buy, with the hope of making profits from small fluctuations in price. Most day traders only trade with high volume and well known stocks, as opposed to low volume stocks. Day traders either work from home, if they have the necessary equipment, computer, cash and extremely fast internet connections, while others pay a fee to trade out of day trading firms, like All-Tech and Momentum Securities.

Despite these general characteristics, the *Business Week* article establishes that day trading also had its own inherent differences from traditional trading. First, some day traders "focus on NASDAQ stocks and trade through NASDAQ's Small Order Execution System (SOES)," and some included in this group are known as "SOES bandits, who watch the bid and ask prices of NASDAQ market makers—the firms that stand ready to buy or sell a particular stock at a particular price." While other day traders "sign on with firms geared to short-term trading in New York Stock Exchange-listed stocks, and they trade on the NYSE's SuperDOT system." Both groups use computers to keep a vigilant watch on market fluctuations and to execute their sales. Secondly, most day traders usually need "Fifty thousand to one hundred thousand in cash or marketable securities" in order to "get started." Day traders also "use margin so they can get the buying power of twice that amount—and in some cases even more leverage than that."

Finally, the article asked the question many were curious about: Is day trading a lucrative career? The end of the article provided insights but not a final answer. "Some day traders have lucrative careers, but a big payoff is far from a sure thing." The truth was that from the beginning, hopeful investors should have evaluated the risks as well as the possible gains, but of course the lure of quick, big money tantalized many.

Two years later, the article "Young Traders Make Waves" appeared in the *Jacksonville Business Journal*. Jeff Ostrowski reported the rise of "a new generation of 20-something day traders shaving profits from small fluctuations in NASDAQ stocks," citing "about half a dozen day-trading firms have sprung up in South Florida in the past couple of years." By this time, day trading was in full swing, and the growth of day trading firms in Southern Florida was characteristic of such growth in other cities.

Then on July 19, 1999, less than two weeks before the shootings at All-Tech and Momentum Securities, *Time Digital* did an enormous spread on day trading.

The opening article in the *Time Digital* spread was entitled "A New American Pastime: What happens when Internet Populism meets Wall Street Good-times?" The article extolled the power of day trading as the combination of business and the internet, as "in just a few short years online vines have climbed and twined themselves around nearly every business success story." In a statement that would soon prove to be a dramatic irony *Time Digital* claimed, "Day trading is the true intersection of this Internet empowerment and Wall Street good-times, a digital populism that, for the moment anyway, seems to be the mouse with the golden click." *Time Digital* went on to identify the prodigious success of day trading as "America's new pastime," as the United States of America "was rapidly becoming a nation of quote-happy day-traders, with politics replaced by the Dow and sports crowded out by the S&P 500."

In another *Time Digital* day trading spread by Nathaniel Wice, "Everything You Need to Know About E-Trading," the author listed the best sites to help even those "equipped with the lowliest, net-connected PC." Wice went on to point out what was central to the day trading phenomenon: that even with an unsophisticated PC, an individual can track stocks and "sip from the burbling brook of gossip" for free on the web, "even if most of these tools were not designed for hobbyists. But that's part of what makes it so much fun."

This playful and humorous attitude with which the media addressed day trading continued in the largest article in the *Time Digital* day trading spread. The title read "Confessions of a Day Trader, A Bid and a Prayer: Financial parasite, short-attention-span savant and modern-day market maker—meet day trader Joey Anuff," by Joey Anuff. In connection with the headline there was a picture of a bespectacled middle-aged man in his pajamas surrounded by computers and the necessary accoutrements for a typical late night day trading vigilante; the picture is meant to be humorous. However, if one superimposed Barton's face into the picture, it would no longer be funny; it would be ominous and chilling.

Anuff's cynically and humorously charged article takes the reader through the mind of a day trader, the intermittent pitfalls and successes of day traders, the trader's move to become a serious day trader and the future of day trading.

Anuff starts out by stating that originally, his "money was in mutual funds," but "...I thought I could do better. And like so many who stumbled into an online brokerage account during the bullish latter months of 1998, I almost couldn't help being right."

The decision of many individuals to become day traders, like Brent Doonan and Anuff, was a Pollyanna venture. Before day trading, the possibility of big gains on the stock market was reserved for those fortunate enough either to have a competent broker or own lucrative stocks. The prospect of becoming rich from day trading was exciting and new. Everyday Americans became involved in the big money gains of the stock market, seeking the possibility of quick profits, sometimes in the course of one day, whereas experienced investors in the past often waited for stocks to mature over the course of years. Anuff continues, "Like most of today's digital day traders, I didn't spend ten years on the floor of the American Stock Exchange. Indeed, I'd never purchased a single stock until a little over a year ago...all across the nation, people of limited means and intelligence are getting rich quick by buying and selling companies like Yahoo and eBay and Amazon. Why not me?"

The allure of day trading extended beyond excitement, as many individuals like Joey Anuff turned to day trading because they felt stymied and delayed by their brokers, who act as the middlemen between their clients' requests and the execution of buys and sells of the clients' accounts. "When I experimented with rapidly moving in and out of stocks," Anuff explained, "there was no broker mediated system that would even answer the phone in the time it took me to make a round trip through the market."

In order to be a serious day trader, one must have three prerequisites, according to Anuff: "a small brick of cash with which to trade, bottomless cynicism, which is critical for assessing the folly of one's fellow traders…and an incredibly wired gig. The more amped the technology on your desktop, the better you're able to know precisely what's happening in the market at any given second." Keeping this in mind, most day traders did not have the necessary technology to set themselves up successfully in day trading, since it required a very fast internet connection, which at the time existed as either a DSL line or a cable modem. Many day trader hopefuls turned to day trading firms such as Momentum Securities and All-Tech, which had all the necessary equipment and guidance to ensure optimum market access and performance.

Given the opportunity, why wouldn't everyone want to day trade, make quick money, and lots of it? As Anuff points out, "There are endless losers in this game too, of course. And there are times when I've counted myself among them." This is a key point that was rarely touched on during the day trading hype. Some that failed in day trading lost a lot, while others had enormous wins. The risk involved in any investment, which should have been considered common knowledge, even in the realm of day trading, seemed to get thrown by the wayside in all the excitement of the new internet trading venture.

Many individuals who became involved with day trading were under the false impression that there was only money to be made, not to be lost. Also, in day trading, there are a lot of responsibilities resting on the individual, coupled with the requirements of knowledge of the internet and the stock market, both of which are out of the control of day traders. These traders are in charge of their own monetary decisions, which in some cases created alarming or at least chancy situations. Some people are not equipped to handle the burden. As a result, some of those who decided to go into day trading were unable to handle the pressures and did not recognize the risks

included in this type of quick-decision stock market trade or investment.

"It was a choice that cost me ten thousand dollars," Anuff relates
of one particularly bad loss, and then goes on to say, "As it was, I
made back most of my loss…within two weeks, and to date I've
managed to make as much as a day trader as I do at my day job. But
put to a choice, I'd keep my day job." Anuff, like many other day
traders, trade on the side, while others quit their day jobs. It is a personal decision, but not one without consequences.

A result of day trading's popularity, highlighted by the spotlight
the media had positioned over it, was queasiness among experts. But
few foresaw the impending doom that would befall the stock market, in addition to many day trading firms.

Nevertheless, by the late nineties, some media outlets were
already suggesting that with the click of a button entire life savings
could be lost. From there it was argued that day trading was akin to
gambling, with more losers than winners. Others felt this was the
nature of the stock market, which is metaphorically symbolic of the
ups and downs inherent in life. Many people were about to learn
day trading wasn't all about luck, intuition or what some day trading firms promised in their advertisements.

A little over a month after the shootings at All-Tech and
Momentum Securities, Arthur Levitt, Chairman of the U.S.
Securities and Exchange Commission, stood before the Senate
Permanent Subcommittee on Investigations Committee on
Governmental Affairs and spoke at length about day trading, specif-
ically about the SEC's concerns regarding day trading.

In his opening statement, Chairman Levitt explained that day
trading is "neither illegal nor is it unethical. But it is highly risky."
Furthermore, the real issue raised by the chairman was not day trading's status on the investment totem pole; rather it was the concern

raised by the public's "false belief" that day trading is a "surefire strategy to make them rich. And, when individuals are swayed by misleading advertising, the Commission has a duty to act."

The "misleading advertising" was a direct reference to the marketing strategies of some day trading firms, which were under attack for falsely conveying the surety of success in what was deemed a highly risky practice, with few reaping substantial profits. Suddenly, failed investors were stepping forward into the spotlight focused on day trading firms, like All-Tech, pointing their fingers, voicing their grievances and seeking retribution. The fate of day trading seemed to unfold like a Greek tragedy; the hordes of investors who couldn't wait to get involved with day trading opportunities were now the forces that claimed misuse and sought its demise.

Chairman Levitt opined that day trading's seeming hugeness was the result of the new attention directed towards it and not the actual number of investors. With an estimated 7,000 day traders as compared to approximately 80 million individuals that own stock and more than five million investors using the internet for brokerage services, "the Commission does not believe that day trading currently presents systemic problems for our markets." Even with his admittance and clarification of its limited reach, Arthur Levitt spent the majority of his time at the podium explaining the risks inherent to day trading and its participants in addition to the SEC's regulation of its practices.

What followed was an explanation of the new trading phenomenon to the Subcommittee, in terms of its risky investing principles which do not adhere to standard trading philosophies, which discriminate against rapid buys and sells that do not take into consideration long term effects and the company in question's history. Also, the risk and volatility of executing fast paced transactions in securities raises the issue of a potential investor's knowledge of the degree of risk he or she is taking on. Day trading raised considerable concerns due to some of the firms involved. In particular it was expressed that a firm that taught day trading techniques might potentially mislead clients. The voicing of these concerns exposed the need for full disclosure to investors of the possible risks.

Would the committee have met had the shootings in All-Tech and Momentum Securities not occurred? Perhaps not, but Chairman Levitt raised important questions and concerns similar to those voiced by some in national media. Now it was suggested that day trading firms had to be monitored more carefully and new rules concerning their practices had to be put into effect.

A little over a year after the shootings at All-Tech and Momentum Securities, the NASD under the United States Securities and Exchange Commission proposed the addition of two important new rules regarding the Approval Procedures for day trading accounts.

This amendment would "require a firm that is 'promoting a day-trading strategy,' directly or indirectly, to deliver a specified risk disclosure statement to a non-institutional customer prior to opening an account for the customer." In addition to requiring that the firm uphold the SEC's mandatory supplication of a "risk disclosure statement," to the investor, this new rule would require the firm to either approve the customer's account for day trading or the firm would have to obtain a written agreement from the customer stating that the customer does not intend to use the account for day trading activities. In addition, the firm would be required to "exercise reasonable diligence to ascertain the essential facts about the customer," performing a financial background check that would include his or her financial situation, tax status, prior investment and trading experience and investment objectives. Thus, unsuitable investors who are financially unqualified for day trading are kept from making unsuitable monetary decisions; such practices would hopefully weed out deranged investors like Mark Barton.

About two months after Arthur Levitt first focused the SEC's attention onto day trading, All-Tech Investment Group wasn't the only day trading firm being sued, as lawsuits became the means through which day trading firms, guilty and innocent, were being punished. Day trading firms became looked upon as a contemptible and odious breed of business which had swindled the retirement funds of countless unsuspecting investors, among other crimes.

Lawsuits would soon be launched against even ethical day trading firms. In Brent's case the profession that had provided so much hope to the ambitious twenty-something go-getter, would continue to be the source of new painful events that would not let him forget the calamity. Brent and many others he knew and cared about had endured much at the hands of Mark Barton.

In addition, since Mark Barton had become synonymous, in the media's eye, with the disastrous effects day trading could cause, new stories about him kept cropping up, further damaging companies such as All-Tech and Brent's future.

Brent could not put the man and his personal demons or the day of the catastrophe out of his mind. Every day he was forced to relive his own and others' trauma and tragedy.

chapter fifteen

Painful Aftermaths

On Brent's first day out of the hospital a man in a dark suit appeared at the front door of his parents' house, rang the bell and said to Sue, who opened the door, "Are you Brent Doonan's mother?"

"Yes I am," she said, wondering who he was.

"Good. Consider your son served," the man said as he handed her an envelope, turned and walked away.

"Served?" she repeated in a shocked voice, ripping open the envelope. At the top of the sheet of paper inside in large bold letters it read, "Summons." She read that the wife of one of the All-Tech victims was suing for damages.

"Oh my God," Sue said aloud, and then after walking inside and into Brent's room she slumped down into a chair and read the documents aloud.

The suit included five defendants: Brent Doonan and Scott Manspeaker by way of their LLC, the office's leasing company, the building security company and All-Tech's corporate offices. Brent remembered thinking, jokingly at the time, when he was in the ICU, that the only bad thing that hadn't happened was being sued by Barton's relatives for wrongful death. Now, even that didn't seem unlikely.

The lawsuit asserted that the shooting was foreseeable. It alleged that the defendants knew or should have known that day trading was stressful, that a person who loses a great deal of money may be capable of committing harm and acting irrationally.

Brent's struggle to recover and return to a normal life took another blow. Even if he eventually was vindicated, it would cost him a fortune to retain an attorney and defend what could be a series of lawsuits. His stress index soared, so doctors placed him on further doses of an anti-anxiety drug; it seemed to do absolutely no good.

Brent worried day and night about the other victims, more law suits and the future. Kenny tried to console his son by telling Brent this was just another example of greedy attorneys trying to cash in on people's misery. The two discussed blame, guilt, who really was at fault, the tragedy that occurred, the catastrophe and the result that no one could have predicted. *What had really made it happen?* Brent's dark thoughts never relented. *Could I have done something more? Was it my fault?* Just as he had been beginning to recover his hope and optimism, more sorrow plagued him.

He argued with himself repeatedly. First, it was his fault. Then, he would decide that society had gone too far in its quest to blame someone, anyone, for life's tragedies. It seemed everyone had an excuse. No one ever took responsibilities for their own actions anymore, he reasoned. But then didn't that include him as well? Perhaps he should have screened his traders more carefully. Perhaps a psychological profile would have been helpful, but few small companies required that.

Maybe the wife of the victim was right and just in her suit. Agonizing questions went round and round in his head.

Filled with guilt and doubt, Brent tried to refocus. He told himself he would have to fight to get better so as not to be beaten down. To give in would mean that Barton had won. He had to concentrate on getting back his health.

Nevertheless, Brent's recovery was slow going. He ached from head to toe and was worn out just from climbing a flight of stairs. A couple of weeks after he'd come home, some counselors from his religion class, Father Dan and Father Sherlock, came by to pray with him.

The two men comforted Brent. One person gave Brent a copy of the bestseller *When Bad Things Happen to Good People* by Harold S. Kushner. Brent also received a copy of the serenity prayer.

"God grant me the serenity to accept the things I cannot change, courage to change the things I can and the wisdom to know the difference."

"Brent, you must try to live through this day only. Don't try to tackle all of life's problems at once," Father Dan said. "Focus on strengthening your mind and your resolve as much as your body. Adjust to what is and don't try to adjust everything to your own desires. Be unafraid; especially do not be afraid to enjoy what is beautiful and right with the world. You are alive. You have a loving family and many dear friends. Count yourself lucky, but above all, hang onto your faith like you held onto your life and you will never loose your way."

After the two men's visit, Brent felt his heart lifting. Many times in moments of doubt he repeated to himself their words of comfort and the prayer he came to know so well.

At night, Brent was packed between a half dozen pillows to help him cope with soreness and pain and he could only sleep on one side. During the day, he had to shower three times, with the help of his mother, since he couldn't reach his open wound. The five-inch-long, three-inch-wide gash had to be soaped and rinsed with warm water to keep it free from infection.

When that was complete, the wound had to be filled with saline soaked gauze and then that had to be taped over.

When Brent wasn't sleeping or showering, he was meeting with doctors who monitored his blood work and general health as well as the incision. During his first visit with a local surgeon, Brent was lying on an examining table when the doctor said, "We have some build-up under this one. Nurse, can you bring me a scalpel?"

"Huh? What do you mean a scalpel?" Brent asked anxiously.

"Sorry Brent. There is quite a bit of build-up clotting under the wound. I have to release it."

"Without anesthetic?"

"You won't feel a thing," the doctor promised. Brent began to get clammy as he saw the gleaming razor in the doctor's hand, but it had to be done. The surgeon carefully pressed the knife to Brent's wound and drew it across the open flesh and carefully made an incision in Brent's stomach. The physician was right. It looked horrifying, but Brent felt nothing. It didn't hurt, but watching the blood and fluid ooze out made him queasy.

It was a very bizarre feeling to actually watch someone cut your stomach; to see the discharge of fluid, yet have no pain medication. Fortunately, it did not cause agony. Before we left his office, the doctor showed us how to pack that wound as well. Again, the wound was left open to heal and again we had to pack a gauze strip directly into the wound before taping it closed. On the way home we joked about packing the strip right into my stomach as I said, "I hope my stomach doesn't eat the thing!" And two weeks later, my mother thought it did.

I had been resting in bed when my mother came in and said that we needed to repack the strip in my stomach. For a few seconds she left the room to get the supplies. Since we had joked about my stomach "eating" the strip of gauze, I figured that she would believe the scenario. So I gave it a try.

I carefully pulled back the tape that was holding the strip in place and grabbed the gauze strip. Since the strip was so small, I wrapped it in a little ball and tossed it in the waste basket. Next, I carefully resealed the wound with the tape and it looked as if the wound had been untouched. Finally, I rolled to my side and pretended to have fallen back to sleep.

When my mother returned I pulled my shirt up and pretended to be weaving in and out of sleep, as if I were not following what she was doing. As usual, she tore the tape back and threw it in the wastebasket. Then she squealed.

"Oh my God, the strip is gone!"

I opened my eyes as if I were alarmed "What do you mean the strip is gone?" I asked with a look of amazement on my face.

"It's gone," she said with a concerned look upon her face, "your stomach ate it!"

As soon as she uttered those words, I could not hold my laughter back any longer. I burst out laughing.

"I'll get you for that one," she vowed as she began laughing, also.

In addition to all the medical scrutiny, Brent was still the center of media attention. The media called incessantly. Eventually his family asked if they could make a deal. If Brent did one long interview for everyone, would they give him some room to recover without their constant prying eyes? No deal.

Both night and day the media continued to call. The horrifying story of Mark Barton and his murders of so many continued to raise questions in the public's minds about the dangers of workplace violence.

Brent spoke weekly with Scott, Meredith and Kathy. Scott was recovering far more quickly than the others. Meredith was getting better day by day, but Kathy's plight pained Brent. The sight upon which she depended in her line of work had been taken and the last vision she had was that of a maniac shooting her co-workers.

During the days that followed Brent spoke with friends he hadn't heard from in years. And to further keep his mind busy, he wrote cards and letters and started a scrapbook of newspaper and magazine articles as well as some of the more poignant letters he was receiving.

He tried to focus his thoughts on positive ideas, faith, encouragement and trust in a productive future. But thoughts of Mark Barton always came to plague him. Sometimes they would be nightmares, other times they would be bloody visions; visions so real they scared him into panic attacks. In one Barton was standing at the end of Brent's bed pointing a gun at him. Brent often tried to stay awake until the late hours of the morning in an effort to keep from dreaming. Eventually though, out of exhaustion, he would doze off and Barton would return. One time, Brent dreamed that as Barton pointed a gun at him, he tossed Brent a baseball bat to defend himself as Barton laughed and Brent instinctively reached to catch it. But, of course, there was no bat, only the horrific image of Barton from which Brent finally awoke soaked in a cold sweat.

On September 26, Brent returned to Atlanta. It had been two months since the tragedy and Brent was eager to get back to the office, to go to work. It was hot, as it had been that day two months before, so Brent wore a short sleeved shirt and covered the bullet holes in his arms with small patches.

The drive from the airport to the office was tense, as one by one the buildings and streets where the carnage occurred came back into view. Though Brent was reluctant to return, afraid of the flood of visions he might have, he knew that he had to get back to work and help Scott.

That afternoon, he had lunch in a small café in Buckhead. Next to him on the counter was a copy of the day's *Atlanta Journal-Constitution*. It had been eight weeks and still the headlines were shouting at him, "The Day Atlanta Can't Forget," in ninety-six point type.

God, please help me to forget, he prayed to himself.

He debated whether to read the article, which was a full five pages long, complete with graphic and poignant photographs.

Since the first page contained a basic overview of what had occurred, I turned to the second and third pages. At the top of the page were pictures of those who had lost their lives followed by those who had survived. My picture was there along with a paragraph about All-Tech. It was the one a reporter took when I left the hospital. I was beaming and giving a big thumbs up gesture with my right hand.

The paper had done a phenomenal job of writing the story; I thought only a few minor things were incorrect. But overall, it must have been very difficult to piece together that day's events.

As I looked again at the pictures of those who had perished, tears sprang to my eyes. Then, when I turned to the fourth page and read the details of how Mark had slaughtered his wife and his own children, I felt sick to my stomach.

Later that afternoon, Brent arrived in the parking lot next to Building Eight and the All-Tech offices. He sat in his car for a full thirty minutes staring at the building through the window. His mind flooded with the scenes of the massacre. Finally, Brent took a deep breath, opened the car door and walked slowly to the building's front door. With each step, his heart rate increased until it was pounding as he reached for the door handle.

Inside, the office looked unchanged; the carpet, though new, was the same color as the original, as was the color of paint on the walls. The trading floor looked the same, with the exception that there were only half as many traders as there had been originally.

One by one, the traders turned their attention from their monitors to Brent. Eventually, they all stopped what they were doing. Many came up to Brent and began to shake his hand and hug him. They wanted to know how the surgery went, how he felt and how he'd managed to escape.

Scott had hired a new assistant. They talked about business, about the stock market and about the media attention. Nothing was said about the lawsuit though. It was decided that Brent would work half days at first, until he felt strong enough to work full days. Then he excused himself and walked out of the conference room and slowly down that hallway that had seemed a mile long when he had been trying to find safety that horrible day in July.

He was going to the third floor to see Lynda, Serena, Russell and the others. He wanted to see the room again where his life had been saved, possibly by the angel he believed so fervently he and the others had seen. He wanted to personally thank each of those who had ministered to him.

Brent began to retrace his steps down that hall. He wanted to go back along the same exact route he had taken that day when Barton was chasing him. Brent only reached the half-way mark. Suddenly, the walls began to close in and the hallway started to feel much narrower. He stopped, held himself up against the wall with his shoulder and took a deep breath. Once again, in his mind's eye, he saw the woman who'd been shot in the back of the head. He shivered as the sight came to him of her hair matted with wet blood and the matter of her brain.

Brent began to have another panic attack. He turned, about to find his way back to All-Tech, but caught himself. He stopped and closed his eyes. He took a deep breath and turned around repeating to himself the serenity prayer.

Then he took another deep breath and once again began to make his way to his destination.

When Brent reached Serena's office it was locked. There was now a buzzer on the outside that had to be pushed to alert those inside that someone wanted to come in. There was also a peephole installed in the door. When Lynda opened the door, Brent stepped inside.

"Oh my Lord! Look everybody! Look at who's here! It's Brent!" Lynda yelled. Everyone came running out of the back offices to greet and hug him. They congratulated him on his recovery and returning to work. Then they all joined hands, stood in a circle and took a moment for a silent prayer of thanks. That afternoon when Brent left he was exhausted.

Brent's second day in the office began right at the opening bell. Though he'd planned to stay only until noon, he spent most of the day talking with old clients on the phone.

The first few weeks were the most difficult. Being in the office brought on a state of anxiety. It often culminated in Brent heaving up any food he'd consumed. Any quick movements startled him; people passing by his office door, a bird flying by the window, the noise of a machine, even the unexpected ringing of a phone were all causes for alarm. His stomach was constantly agitated by the stress and he began taking antacid pills by the handful.

Though everything seemed normal, All-Tech was, in fact, struggling. They had lost nearly half of their business.

Each day, the mood at All-Tech got gloomier and bleaker. Phones that used to ring non-stop now rang only a handful of times the entire day. Those who had once considered day trading a panacea now treated it like the plague. Negative publicity and the market's spiraling death throe were taking their toll daily.

In time, Meredith returned to the office, providing a short-lived renewed sense of optimism. Like Brent, she wasn't going to let Barton win. Meanwhile, Kathy was fighting the toughest battle of all. Struggling to learn how to function in a world without light, she did not return to work.

Month after month the markets declined, a slide that in hindsight was the worst ever in history, mostly precipitated by the dot com bust. Everyone who had made money, from the gardeners to the Wall Street boys, was now losing it. Attempts to teach traders at All-Tech how to "short" stocks, in order to make money as the stocks plummeted, were in vain. Most of them were just not comfortable with the process. Day traders just kept buying stocks hoping each day was the bottom. One by one, they were wiped out and there were no new traders to take their places. The wealth effect had been turned inside out. Those who had bought expensive cars, boats and houses based on the values of their portfolios were now forced to sell everything at considerable losses. The pawnshops were doing phenomenally well. To make matters worse, the process had affected everyone in the market, not just day traders. Common mom and pops, lawyers, doctors, retirees: all had taken a beating. Most were fed up with the market or broke; many vowed never to enter it again, in any capacity. Prospects for new clients were nowhere to be found.

To keep from dwelling on the precipitous fall of All-Tech and falling into a deep depression Brent tried to focus on regaining his physical health. Each day during the lunch hour, he climbed the stairs from the second floor to the seventh. Though that might not have been a huge effort for most, it took all the strength Brent could summon. At night, he walked on a treadmill and took walks around the block. Eventually, those walks turned into runs and the runs turned into miles instead of blocks. Within three months, he'd worked up to a tight jog; a full run took another two months.

Then Christmas came with a wonderful surprise. I met a girl named Sarah on a blind date. Though neither of us was looking for a relationship, we hit it off right away.

Five-foot-nine, with long blonde hair and an athletic build, Sarah was stunning. I quickly learned that she was just as beautiful and intelligent on the inside.

She was working at a hospital in Augusta, Georgia and I still lived in Atlanta, with a friend, in the condominium in Buckhead. I spent many evenings talking to Sarah for hours over the phone. On the weekends, I went to Augusta or Sarah came to Atlanta and it wasn't long before our relationship really began to deepen. The five days I worked were pure hell, so I lived for those weekends. By the time Friday came around, I was as giddy as a schoolboy, filled with the anticipation of being with a woman I was falling totally in love with. Each time we were together we found more and more in common. I began to conceive a new future filled with our love.

Sarah was proud to be the bright spot in Brent's life. The stock markets continued to be down. His business was bleeding money daily. No new traders filled the void and by now, the lawsuits were rampant. One by one family members of victims filed suits.

Though he wanted to, Brent's attorney forbade him to call any of the victim's families to offer condolences. It appeared that he didn't care; on the contrary, Brent cared very deeply about these people.

Office morale was now at its lowest ebb. Few investors had the financial means to dabble in the now dark world of day trading and those few who did had another reason not to trade. At least once a week, Brent received a cryptic response from someone over the phone along the lines of, "Yeah, but am I going to get shot over there?" Or, "You aren't going to shoot me are you?"

Though they all understood fear too well, it was inconceivable to Brent, Scott or Meredith that other human beings could make jokes or voice such comments to the victims of such a tragic event. On one telephone call, Brent, growing angrier by the day, finally blurted out, "I was shot five times and I am still in the recovery process. Thanks for being so considerate about the situation." The phone went dead.

The following week Meredith announced that she was leaving to take another job. Her departure made Brent think more and more about Kathy. As time passed, she underwent numerous reconstructive surgeries and he visited her often, though always at a loss for words.

Thoughts of selling the business were dismissed. The once thriving All-Tech that had been worth seven million dollars now had no value. But Brent's personal life was his one source of renewal.

Meanwhile my relationship with Sarah blossomed. I adored her. We understood one another in so many ways. I don't know what I would have done if she had not been in my life at this point. My slow recovery and pain, the lawsuits, the nasty calls, the bills piling up…it all looked dismal, but she was always there for me. When I was with her, I never thought about my problems.

When she had free time, she jogged or walked with me around the trail that circled our office complex. It was the perfect spot to get away from all the noise of Piedmont Road. Behind the building were graceful tall trees, chirping birds and the occasional rustle of leaves.

One day, in this tranquil setting we were the only ones in sight. As Sarah and I were walking down the path, a gentle breeze came up and we

both heard a voice say, "Brent." It was a soft voice, but quite distinct. I turned
abruptly to see who was calling me and one was there. Sarah had turned as
well.

"Did you hear that?" I asked her.

"Yes. Someone called your name."

We gazed at each other; there was no one around us for fifty yards in
every direction. Not wanting her to think I was crazy, I didn't express what
I thought might be occurring, but I had my own ideas. My first thought was
that it was the spirit of one of the victims. There was no doubt in either of
our minds, that someone or thing had called my name, but who and what
for?

Brent and Scott knew they should get out of the business, but
they continued to wage a valiant fight. Later they would look back
and feel it was too protracted. They fought with the home office for
financial assistance and none was forthcoming. They fought with
attorneys in hundreds of hours of depositions, continually repeating
the same stories until both were exhausted. The depositions brought
back again and again the horrific memories of that terrible day
when Mark Barton exploded.

In everything Brent did, whether it was in high school, on the
wrestling team, or in his college studies, once he started something
he finished it; he never quit. Now he felt like a failure. However, he
knew it was time to close All-Tech. He and Scott had fought the
good fight, but it was over.

Brent's emotional demons compounded his feelings of failure.
He had recovered remarkably well physically, but he remained
exhausted emotionally. The only time he felt any relief from the
memories was when he was with Sarah. They had long ago stopped
rehashing the negatives of that day and were moving in a new direction together. One night at Brent's, Sarah brought up the comfort-

ing voice they'd heard in the park. Brent told her he thought it was one of the victims. Sarah said, "No, I think it was an angel and I think we will be hearing from him again."

It would be a few months until her premonition came true and once again, as in the Buckhead office where Russell and his friends had seen an angel, the voice would come at another life-threatening moment.

chapter sixteen

A Changed Life

O n August 5, 2000, Brent's family threw an enormous birthday party at a country club in Wichita for him and his mother; they shared birthdays. The previous birthday had been a dismal event in Brent's hospital room, so the family decided to make this a special celebration. They were going to celebrate two birthdays, but more importantly, they would all be celebrating life.

Throughout the early part of the evening guests continued to arrive. Friends from all around the country had made the journey, including the mother of Brent's girlfriend, who came from Augusta.

It was an awesome party. There must have been a hundred people there. My mother and the club had decorated the area to the hilt complete with large round paper lanterns hanging everywhere, a formal stage, podium and professional sound system. A ten-piece band played while the guests danced on a polished hardwood floor. Each table sat six people, with crisp white linen tablecloths, candles and silver place settings. In the center of each table was a magnificent floral arrangement. The night was perfect. The only gift I had asked for was a digital camera and when Sarah gave it to me, I thanked her, but shrugged it off. I must have looked quite ungracious, but the truth is, I had her engagement ring in my pocket and I was scared to death I'd lose it, or that she wouldn't accept it, so my mind was on that. We had never discussed getting engaged.

By nine o'clock, all the guests had arrived. The candles had been blown out and the crowd had sung the last line of happy birthday, when Brent walked up to a friend and handed him his new digital camera.

"Tony, get ready to put this thing to good use," Brent said. Then he stepped up on the stage, stood in front of the small band, pulled the microphone off its stand and said in front of a hundred friends, "First, I want to give thanks to God for carrying me through my ordeal. Had it not been for His loving hands, I would have certainly perished that day one year ago.

"Next, I want to thank my family for being there day in and day out on the most trying days of my life. I also want to thank Derek, who flew to Atlanta and ran our office while Scott, Meredith, Kathy and I were in the hospital.

"Now, I want to thank one other very special person. I know she is very shy, but I told her before the party that she had to meet everyone here, because you are all the people I love."

Brent looked across the expanse of people standing around the dance floor and saw Sarah at the very back; she was blushing and held one hand over her mouth, petrified that Brent would bring her up on stage.

"Sarah, would you please come up and join me? I want you to meet my friends," he said. At first, she held back, and then several of the people standing around her gently nudged her and told her it was okay. Slowly, she walked to the podium.

"Friends, this is Sarah. Sarah, these are my friends and family."

Brent spent the next five minutes telling the story of how they'd met. Sarah blushed throughout.

"I want you all to know that Sarah is just as beautiful on the inside as she obviously is on the outside."

A loud cheer accompanied by whistling went through the crowd. Then Brent reached into his pocket, withdrew a small white box with a ribbon around it and dropped to one knee. He was so nervous he could barely hold the box without trembling.

"Sarah, there is one birthday present for which I haven't asked. Obviously, this is the most important one of them all. Will you marry me?"

Sarah was speechless. She looked around at the crowd, which was also still, then blushed and turned back to stare intently into Brent's eyes, as if she were searching his soul. Brent's heart started racing, as he thought *she's going to say no, she's taking too long.* He hadn't even discussed an engagement before tonight, let alone the proposal, which he now was making, in front of hundreds of people.

"Yes. Yes, of course I will. I love you Brent," she said and the party went crazy. People started cheering, throwing napkins in the air and the band struck up the wedding march as Brent rose to his feet, gently put both arms around Sarah, and kissed her deeply.

In the fall of 2000, Brent finally walked away from the day trading business, turning to a new business venture with a former client. Together they formed a solid management team. His former client would be president while an executive from a Fortune 500 company would be the CEO. Brent would contribute as the Chief Financial Officer while two other associates would be Chief Information Officer and Human Resources Director.

The underlying concept was to form an online real estate firm, at the time something unique. All the team needed was money; a big investor, perhaps several.

In the meantime, Brent put everything he had left from his venture in the stock market, or had in savings, into the new venture. He even borrowed against his car. Some of the money went to set up a convertible note that would be repaid or could be converted to stock in the new business. The remainder of the money was used as a down payment on an office. These funds were to be placed in an escrow account and were not to be touched without his consent.

Unfortunately, the venture went sour. All the funds Brent had placed with the company, including the money in the escrow account, simply vanished in an astoundingly short period of time.

Shortly after signing a promissory note with Brent to repay all the money, his partner filed for bankruptcy.

It was April and Brent had lost more money and once again he had been deceived by a person he'd trusted. It was another bitter life lesson. He'd given up a good job in Chicago to pursue the day trading business with Scott, survived a maniac's rampage, gotten out of the day trading business and then lost nearly everything within three short months to a man who openly admitted to misusing funds. At the age of twenty-six, he was disillusioned by his failures. Part of him said he should just suck it up and go on with his life, another part wanted to focus on the mistakes he had made. He went through rounds of questioning his ability and his gullibility. Yet he did not want to become embittered and jaundiced toward others. This was not the person his father and mother had raised him to be. Once again, blind trust had caused more pain.

Although I survived tragedy, I now found myself fighting anger, wallowing in the what-ifs. I was floundering and no amount of love and guidance from Sarah could help.

I revisited the mistakes my life. How could I not have recognized Mark Barton was a psychopath? How dumb of me to trust my new partner, little more than a stranger, with the life savings I had left. That's when, lying in bed staring at the ceiling trying to go to sleep, I heard a soft voice say, "Brent."

Once again I prayed for guidance. I asked God to help me handle this new disappointment and to let me get on with my life. I prayed for insight until I fell to sleep.

The next morning Brent awoke with a renewed spirit he hadn't felt in months. He knew now he had to take charge of his own mind. He decided to quit crying over spilt milk and to get on with his life. He was after all, nearly the luckiest man alive. He'd survived near death, financial ruin and humiliation and he'd found Sarah. There were many other people in the world with much larger problems than he had, he kept reminding himself.

And so, on a warm day in early April, he and Sarah gathered their belongings, packed their bags and moved to Kansas. He was finally going home.

Brent and Sarah were married on May 4, 2001 in a beautiful ceremony with more than five hundred guests in attendance.

After temporarily moving in with Brent's parents, Brent went to work for a restaurant franchise while Sarah got a job as a Cardiovascular Invasive Specialist at a local hospital. In July, they moved into a new home along with their hundred pound American bulldog, Katy.

By the end of 2001, there were no more day traders; there were scarcely any investors. In addition to the worst market cycle in history, corporate greed and scandals wiped out thousands upon thousands of people's retirement plans. Homes were lost, lives too.

The lawsuits filed against Brent and Scott were slowly, one by one, being dismissed. Brent and Scott were not held responsible for the tragedy that had happened. The truth would ultimately prevail that the distorted mind of Mark Barton was the sole cause of the Atlanta massacre.

chapter seventeen

Sorrow and Miracles

Brent's new insights into himself and the life he wanted to live caused him to go back over the day he and so many others encountered the rage of Mark Barton.

As I reflect on that hot day in July when tragedy struck, I cannot help but wonder why my life was spared when so many others were not, why I live with so few problems while others endure so much. Perhaps it's all about learning lessons in a Karmic world. Maybe it's pure luck. Perhaps God has a plan for all of us. Here are some of the things that happened that day that cause me to ponder my own fortunate outcome. Were they chance or miracles?

As shots rang out, I was initially struck twice. Some of the other victims were shot in the head and directly in the heart.

The shot in my abdomen missed my heart by one millimeter (about an eighth of an inch), before curving and exiting out my back, just a fraction of an inch from my spine.

The bullets Barton used were hollow point "cop killers" which nearly always spell certain death because of the large exit wounds they create. However, Barton was too close when he shot me. The bullets went through me before they had a chance to expand.

After sustaining the initial shots, I remained alert enough to analyze the situation and had the presence of mind to head for the exits. At that point Barton, standing on the other side of the now open door had another chance to finish me off, but he choose to shoot someone else, giving me the time to flee.

As I lurched through the doorway, I bumped him just enough to knock him off balance. He did manage to fire three more shots at me, but none of them proved fatal.

Purely by luck, I managed to take the right escape route; going the other way would most likely have spelled death.

Was it chance that the elevator arrived in time to save me, as Barton stood pointing his guns at me while the door slammed shut?

Was it chance that I found the only office on the entire third floor whose doors were unlocked at the time of my flight?

After I fell into Serena's office, she ran to the kitchen to get some paper towels, the only thing that could possibly stop the bleeding. Ironically, the office had been out of paper towels for several weeks and Serena had just stopped by the store that morning on the way to work to buy more. By chance, she bought twice as many as she usually did, because she didn't want to run out again.

I lost nearly all of the blood in my body during my escape and I lay on the floor for more than an hour. The doctors could offer no explanation as to why I survived. Most didn't think such a thing was possible.

Serena had the presence of mind to ask me if I was allergic to any-thing—morphine, which she promptly relayed to the paramedics. Surely, they would have administered it, had she not asked.

How about Dr. Harvey the trauma surgeon? It was his day off that day, but a friend, an EMT, asked him if he wanted to go for a ride in the ambulance that afternoon, the one that brought him to Buckhead on an emergency call. Paramedics are great people and very skilled, but they aren't trauma surgeons.

Though you could argue that all of these were chance or lucky coincidences, other things seem more miraculous to me. First, when Lynda placed her hands on me in the office building, she said, "God spoke through the touch, that it was going to be okay." She said, "I never doubted it after that, that you would live. I had already been told."

Then Serena saw what she described as a Christ-like figure beside me as she watched and held the paper towels to my chest. She said she could feel his hands on top of hers. At that point she looked to Russell who said he'd seen something similar though different, a spirit holding my head in his hands. Then he described the same sensation as Serena's. That is when the blood flow stopped. That is when they heard a voice softly say, "Brent."

I believe it was divine intervention. I had been kept alive for a reason and it wasn't the last time I was spared. There is one final story about the last time I heard the soft voice.

It was March 3, 2001, before Sarah and I were married. We were going to take a trip from Atlanta to Wichita for our engagement party. Since I am a pilot, I decided it would be fun to fly us there, though the weather was blustery and rain threatened. Low clouds stacked from 500 to 15,000 feet. The plane, a single engine Piper, was not pressurized so we would be forced to fly in the middle of the clouds for about half of the six-hour trip.

Sarah doesn't particularly like to fly in small planes, particularly in cloud cover. I explained that it would only be a slight mist and that the trip would be completely safe, probably safer than driving twenty hours. Sarah suggested taking an airline, but in the end she relented.

We climbed into the plane Saturday morning and as predicted the rain quietly hit our windshield as we rolled down the runway.

To reassure her even more, I took extra time to check the engine and spent longer on the engine run-up phase making sure that everything was working properly.

Seconds after lifting off we were into the clouds, relying on instruments to navigate. The only sounds were our breathing, the engine droning on and the tattoo of rain on the window.

When we reached 8,000 feet, I leveled the plane off and leaned the engine for cruise speed, again, checking all the gauges. Again, I reassured Sarah, who still seemed tense, clenching her hands into fists.

Eventually, she relaxed as we talked about the upcoming engagement party and I continued to check the engine settings, fuel levels and the outside air temperature. I focused mostly on the air temperature as icing leads to most of the flight accidents that occur in the winter. As we made our way across Georgia and Alabama, the temperature stayed between forty-five and fifty-five degrees. Though concerned about icing, I saw the temperature was well above freezing, which meant there should be no problem.

We had been in the air for a little over an hour when I heard the engine sputter a bit. Glancing to the manifold pressure gauge, I noticed the indication fluctuating between 2200 and 2300 – no problem. Temperature was now at fifty-three degrees, also no problem.

Still, I didn't like the sputtering sound. Perhaps there was something wrong with the engine, I thought to myself. I grabbed the throttle and pushed in until the manifold pressure rose up to 2400. Everything was fine for a few moments until we dropped suddenly as the pressure dropped.

"What was that?" Sarah wanted to know as she gripped her cushion tightly.

"I don't know," I said.

In the 300 hours I'd logged in flight hours in that plane, I had never picked up any substantial amount of ice or had carburetor icing in the engine.

Those facts coupled with the air temperature led me to rule out icing. Instead, I focused my attention on the possibility of a much larger problem, perhaps a mechanical breakdown. I redialed the air traffic controllers.

"I'm losing manifold pressure and I want to start down," I said in a relaxed voice.

He replied, "Yes, sir. No problem. Descend and maintain 4,000 feet."

With that I began directing the plane into a slow descent. Suddenly, the engine sputtered and missed badly again. This time the manifold pressure dropped to 1,500 and the plane began to shake. Sarah called out, "Oh my God."

Now my own heart started racing and my hands began to get clammy. I knew, however, that I had to maintain a calm demeanor to keep Sarah from going into a full-blown panic and to bring the plane safely down. The rain was coming down heavier now and the clouds were taking on a much more ominous dark gray color. My GPS told me that we were 200 miles away from our refueling stop and I didn't know exactly where we were. I began to worry.

Turning to Sarah I said, "Find the approach plates for Alabama, we're going to land right now."

She turned to the back seat and began frantically pulling out papers.

Calling the controller again, I told him we needed to land, "We're having trouble." Just then the small plane shuddered badly.

"Where exactly am I?" I asked him.

"You're about ten miles southeast of Huntsville International. Is that where you want to go?"

"If that's the closet airport, yes!" I replied emphatically, not really knowing if we would make it or not.

"Okay, descend and maintain 3,000, turn right to a heading of 270. I'm going to take you around for the three-six right approach."

"Down to three and right 270." I responded.

"Sir, would you like to declare an emergency?" he asked.

"No, not at this time."

Passing through 5,000 and then through 4,000 feet, the plane shook even more violently as the manifold pressure dropped to the low teens and then shot back up. Each time the engine missed and dropped in manifold pressure, I jerked the throttle back and forth as a way to keep the engine running. Sarah was petrified and began to pray.

We were losing altitude rapidly as I struggled to keep the plane's airspeed up and avoid stalling in the thick cloud coverage. It was like a white out, nothing but thick clouds blocking our view of the ground.

"Sarah, get the Huntsville approach plate out and look up the ILS 36 approach." By chance, that is one of the first things I had been teaching her about flying just a week before.

"Here it is," she said as she folded back the chart for me to read.

"Perfect. Now just hold the map so I can see it."

Though I was trying my best the plane was shaking so badly, I couldn't focus on the tiny print on the map. And, the controller was giving me missed approach instructions, but I knew now that if I missed the approach we would crash. There was no visibility to climb after a missed approach and the engine barely had enough to keep us maintaining a 500-foot-per-minute descent. Climbing out of there would be out of the question.

"Okay, calm down," I said to myself. *"You have one shot at this."* I was scared to death, but I knew not to dwell on that. For a second, I turned my head toward Sarah and quickly glanced at the map for the approach frequency. This time, I saw the numbers clearly and immediately dialed them into my radio. By chance, I had dialed the frequency just in time. We were straight south of the runway; the instrument gauges were telling me that I needed to turn toward the airport immediately, which I did.

In the meantime, the air traffic controller had instructed me to contact the control tower. In doing so, it was clear to the controller that I was heading directly towards the runway.

After checking in with the control tower personnel, the voice of the controller snapped at me, saying, "Sir, you are not cleared for the approach."

"What do you mean I'm not cleared for the approach?" I thought. Didn't the other controller tell her that I was having problems? This was life or death. I was going to land this damn plane somewhere and right now; a clearance was immaterial at this point.

"Ma'am, I'm having engine trouble. I am putting this plane on the ground. Do you see me lined up for approach?" I asked in a quivering voice.

"Yes sir. You are lined up and you're cleared for approach."

As the rain spattered heavily on the window, I kept focused on the gauges with my hands firmly on the controls. I was at 400 feet above the ground and still could not see through the clouds. I was also petrified, as was Sarah, but there was no time to dwell on it. I kept revving the throttle trying to muscle the engine up. By now the plane was shaking so hard I couldn't read the dials.

Tears were streaming down Sarah's cheeks.

"We're going to die, aren't we, Brent?"

"No sweetie. We are not going to die."

Then, about a quarter mile out, the clouds parted slightly and just in time I saw the runway. Once again, the engine coughed and sputtered as the plane heaved back and forth. We slowly descended and were now ten feet, five, and then touchdown! Our landing was nearly perfect, as the engine nearly shut off halfway down the runway.

As soon as we stopped, I called out, "We made it, Peach. Everything is okay." A feeling of relief washed over my entire body as I took off my seatbelt and turned, melting into Sarah's arms. Never had we hugged each other so tightly. Then I pulled back slightly and looked into her face, which was streaked with tears and said, "I love you."

For the next few moments we sat there in a sort of daze, just trying to breathe deeply. I thanked God for keeping us alive.

"I'll go find someone to help us. You stay here," I told her, but she didn't respond and I knew that she wasn't only scared, she was angry. I didn't blame her.

Sarah remained next to the plane while I walked to the maintenance hangar, returning moments later with a couple of mechanics who looked the plane over and started it back up a couple times. After fiddling with a few things, one of the mechanics reported his prognosis: "Sir, I think you've got a bad case of carburetor icing. I don't know how you got that thing on the ground."

"There's no way," I replied. "It's fifty-five degrees out."

"Yes sir. But that's what we are thinking. I would bet on it," he added.

I needed a second opinion so I called my good friend and flight instructor and asked for his opinion. "On a scale of one to ten, what are the chances of icing?"

He replied in a voice that spoke of his disappointment at my mistake, "I'd say a nine or a ten."

"What?"

I couldn't believe it. I had kept a very careful eye on the temperature gauge and had convinced myself that the problem had nothing to do with icing. But I was wrong.

"Sarah. It was my fault. It was icing and if I'd recognized it, I could have taken care of it."

She didn't reply, but instead sat in the plane and cried for the next fifteen minutes. There was only one thing to do. Buy her an airline ticket and then fly the plane on myself. I didn't want to leave it there and have to come back later and retrieve it. The problem was she didn't want to fly with me and she didn't want me flying alone.

"Peach, the plane is safe. It was me. This time if anything happens, I know what to do."

Even before the words were out of my mouth I knew it was a feeble attempt, but I did know in my mind and heart that there would be no fur-

ther problems and eventually, a half hour later I convinced her. Well, perhaps convinced isn't the right word, but she did agree to fly the rest of the way with me.

After getting off for refueling, we got back into the plane, taxied to the end of the runway, and then took off. This time, I took even more time to check the entire engine before lift off. Everything was running beautifully. Flight conditions hadn't changed in the nearly two hours we were on the ground, so we were faced with low cloud coverage again. Climbing to cruising altitude once again, I leveled off and after about fifteen minutes, I checked the manifold pressure again. It was plummeting. Once again, the plane began to shake violently. Sarah began to cry again.

"Well, let's see if they were right. If it's not the carburetor like they said, we're in trouble," I said. Not exactly comforting words, but the truth. Then it happened. As the wing tips began to sway back and forth and the plane continued to shake, I heard it, "Brent." It was that familiar soft voice I'd heard twice before. Sarah had heard it too. She instinctively jerked her head around to look behind her. But of course, there was no one there.

Without saying a word, I reached for the carburetor heat lever and gently pulled it to the on position. For awhile, the engine coughed and sputtered. After a few minutes the engine once again began running smoothly. The mechanics were right. As the heat burns off the ice, the resulting water runs through the engine, which makes it run rougher than normal.

Sarah leaned over, put her arm around me and kissed me. Wiping the tears from her face she simply said, "Brent."

chapter eighteen

Victims
and Survivors

Thirteen people survived Mark Barton's explosive anger; twelve were laid to eternal rest. The shootings of July 29, 1999, have seared the minds of the victims and their families, who, left in the wake of Mark Barton's destruction, must heal their wounds and bury their loved ones.

Riding the elevator and walking into their offices that morning in July, nine people had no idea what lay in wait for them that day, but their families would remember what they left behind. Thirteen people would be spared their lives, but their scars would last a life-time; the body does not forget.

The *Atlanta Journal-Constitution* ran an article on Friday, July 30, 1999, a day after the shootings at Momentum Securities and All-Tech Investment, entitled, "Our 'Terrible Tragedy,'" one of the first newspaper stories covering the shootings and detailing the wounded and the dead. A little under a month later on September

26, 1999, another article ran in *The Atlanta Journal-Constitution* entitled, "The Day Atlanta Can't Forget," which extensively covered the
day of shootings with a comprehensive timeline of Barton's rampage
and those he left wounded, dying or dead. CNN, two days after the
shootings, on July 31, 1999, released a report, "Memories of those
who died: They loved travel, fly-fishing," which gave background on
seven of the victims killed by Mark Barton's bullets. The accounts of
the victims that follow are based on these sources and Brent
Doonan's experience.

At around 2:20 p.m. on July 29, 1999, Mark Barton walked into
Momentum Securities, located on the third floor of Two Securities
Center, at 3500 Piedmont Road NE. Barton waited for a half an
hour for Momentum's manager, Justin Hoehn, before he opened
fire on the office, shooting, with a nickel-plated Colt .45 in his right
hand and a black Glock 9mm in his left, down the line of work stations. Four were killed and many others were wounded.

Kevin Dial, thirty-eight years old, was an office manager at
Momentum Securities and the first to be shot by Mark Barton, who
uttered the last words Dial would ever hear, "It's a bad trading day
and it's about to get worse." Kevin Dial was shot twice at point-
blank range, and reportedly, he was shot at such a close range the
gunpowder covered the skin surrounding the entrance wound on
his back. One of the bullets punctured his heart and left lung, and
after losing large quantities of blood, Dial died.

Kevin Dial, a native of Texas, was the son of the former NFL
player Buddy Dial, who played for the Pittsburgh Steelers and was
also a wide receiver for the Dallas Cowboys. A year earlier, Kevin
Dial had been diagnosed with an inoperable brain tumor. He was a
brain tumor survivor and reportedly, "one of the happiest guys,"
according to a co-worker.

After shooting at several traders along the back wall, Mark Barton turned his attention to Scott Webb, thirty years old. From inside an office along the back wall Webb shouted, "What the hell is going on around here?" With that, Barton turned and fired, sending a bullet through the back of his chair, through his right lung and into his chest.

Scott Webb, a former stock broker and college tennis champion, had recently moved from Chesterfield, Missouri, and become a day trader. Reportedly, Webb collected fortunes from fortune cookies and, in the words of a former neighbor, "he was such a nice young man and always had the time for a beautiful smile."

Barton next pointed his gun at Russell J. Brown, forty-two years old. Reportedly, Brown was from Cumming, Georgia, and began day trading after he had left law school to care for his ill father and brother. Russell Brown applied his mathematical acumen to his day trading career, which was cut short by three bullets from Mark Barton's gun.

The last at Momentum to be killed by the bullets of Mark Barton was Edward Quinn, fifty-eight years old. Quinn might have survived, had he not turned when the bullet went through his neck; it exited his body and came through the back of his neck, severing the jugular vein and an artery before leaving the left side of his body.

A retiree of the United Parcel Service, where he had been an executive for many years, Quinn, a devout family man, had welcomed his first grandchild a couple of weeks before he died. Quinn had just started day trading and reportedly had a goal to travel around the world and play golf on all the best courses.

In addition to the four dead victims of Mark Barton's rampage, many other Momentum employees were wounded, while others were lucky enough to run and hide.

After first shooting Kevin Dial, Barton shot down the line of work stations, first wounding Andrew Zaprzala, forty-three years old, and then thirty-one-year-old James Jordan. Jordan was shot once and as he ran for the door Barton shot him again in the arm. Once in the hallway, James Jordan saw Justin Hoehn, who had just returned to the office and placed a call to 911.

Inside the office, Barton's rampage continued, as many were wounded. Bradley Schoemehl, twenty-four years old, was shot twice; one bullet went through his back, while the other went into his shoulder. Marci Brookings, twenty-nine years old, was shot in the shoulder at her reception desk while Barton finished off the room, and was trying to get into a closed room off the back wall where two employees had hidden. Before leaving, Barton fired another shot into Scott Webb, who was slumped in his chair. Then he shot Bradley Schoemehl again, in the forearm. Schoemehl was lying on the floor, pretending to be dead, alongside Andrew Zaprzala, who was doing the same. With that, Mark Barton exited the building to continue his lethal rampage.

After crossing Piedmont Road, a little after 3:00 p.m., Barton entered Piedmont Center, which housed All-Tech Investment Group, at 3525 Piedmont Road NE.

Shortly after Brent Doonan made eye contact with Mark Barton and let him into the conference room, Barton's bullets made contact with Brent's body. After removing two handguns from underneath his shirt Barton fired two shots into Brent, one into his chest and one in the arm. Then Barton shot Kathy Van Camp, thirty-eight years old, in the temple, and Scott Manspeaker, co-manager of All-Tech, twenty-seven years old, in the chest and in the arm. After firing these shots, Barton stepped out of the manager's office with his hands behind his back before he once again pulled out the .45 and the 9mm and began shooting up the trading floor.

The first bullet whizzed by Nell Jones's head, smashing into her computer monitor as she managed to dash towards the front door. Jamshid Havash, forty-five years old, was sitting at a table just outside the manager's office, and before he could get away Barton shot him in the back, killing him instantly.

Havash, whose home had been seriously battered by a tornado in 1998, left behind his wife and children in their native country of Iran, where they remained, when he was shot and killed. Barton then turned right towards the work stations in the middle of the room, where people were taking cover under desks while some escaped through a side door.

Allen Tenenbaum, forty-eight years old, had tried to crouch behind his work station but was shot in the back and killed. Tenenbaum was president of Congregation OrVe Shalom and owned a Great Savings grocery in downtown Atlanta. Tenenbaum had been planning his first trip to Israel for the upcoming year.

Dean Delawalla, fifty-two years old, was running towards the door when Barton's bullet hit him in the middle of the back, traveling up into his throat and out his left eye. As his body fell, Barton shot him again, insuring that Delawalla was dead. A former attorney and businessman, Delawalla gave up his law practice a year earlier in order to day trade. He was a devout Muslim and had been planning on taking his daughter and her friends to Chuck E. Cheese over the weekend for her fourth birthday.

Moving back to the front of the room, Barton shot twice at Joseph Dessert, sixty years old, who was standing at his work station at a table near the front door. One bullet hit him in the right shoulder and another struck him in his upper chest, killing him. Dessert, a real estate broker, was new to day trading. He had nearly missed being killed that day, as he returned to work from meeting with a friend shortly before Barton entered the All-Tech office.

Vadewattee Muralidhara, forty-four, was shot in the head point
-blank in the hallway after coming out of the women's room. The
mother of two was a newcomer to Atlanta and day trading. She was
killed instantly.

Those that Mark Barton did not kill in All-Tech, he severely
wounded. Harry Higginbotham, sixty years old, was shot in the
head, Fred Herder, fifty-four years old, was shot in the back. Yuzef
Liberzon was also shot in the head. Sang Yoon, thirty-three, was shot
in the arm, Charles Williams, fifty-five years old, was shot in the
chest, and Meredith Winitt, twenty-two years old, was struck by a
bullet in the back.

It had taken the police nearly an hour to discover that there
were two different shooting locations, and it took even longer for
paramedics to arrive at the scene. For some they arrived in time, for
others it was too late. Aware that they were fighting the clock, the
paramedics had set up a triage: they would try to save the savable
and leave the dead or about to die. Victims were classified as emergent, urgent or non-urgent. The emergent and non-urgent were
told to wait while the EMTs applied thick gauze pads first to stop
the bleeding. Some were then administered morphine for the pain
and started IV drips with fluids. Some people struggled to stay alive;
others were being placed on gurneys and rushed outside to waiting
ambulances.

After being treated at the hospital, all the victims wounded that
day at Momentum Securities and All-Tech Investment Group survived, and after being released from the hospital, recuperated in their
homes. For some it took longer than others, but the emotional scars
left behind by the experiences of that day would be a force all involved
in the massacre of July 29, 1999, whether directly or indirectly, would
have to deal with for the rest of their lives. In the aftermath, some
moved away, some returned to day trading and some did not.

According to *The Atlanta-Journal Constitution* in an article entitled, "For some survivors of shootings, the wounds are long lasting," released on February 24, 2002, by Jim Auchmutey, the path of recovery has led some of the victims away from day trading.

Reportedly, Yuzef Liberzon suffered permanent brain damage after being shot in the head by Barton at All-Tech. He had to relearn English and his native Russian. Harry Higginbotham, who also worked as a day trader and was shot in the head, began working as a pilot. Meredith Winitt, who was shot in the back at All-Tech, had a lengthy recovery and now works in a bank. Sang Yoon opened a dry cleaners' after being shot in the arm by Barton at All-Tech. Charles Williams, shot in the chest at All-Tech, has since retired.

Those that did not return to day trading tried to move beyond the tragedy of that day, but for Fred Herder, it seems life was too much. Herder had been shot in the back, but recovered and returned to day trading, reported *The Atlanta Journal-Constitution* on February 24, 2002 in "Death of a Day Trader." Sadly, less than two and a half years after Barton's murderous rampage, Fred Herder committed suicide on November 29, 2002.

Herder's was the only tragic death among the survivors since the brutal shootings in July, but his suicide raised awareness that maybe, for some, being left to live in the wake of something so traumatic was not a gift. People like Brent Doonan, among other survivors of the shootings in Atlanta on that humid July day, had to deal with the mental aftermath, which manifested itself as post-traumatic stress disorder.

According to the National Center for Post-Traumatic Stress Disorder, "Most people who are exposed to a traumatic, stressful event experience some of the symptoms of Post-Traumatic Stress Disorder (PTSD) in the days and weeks following exposure," to either experiencing or "witnessing life threatening events."

An individual who has experienced a traumatic event, according to the National Center for Post-Traumatic Stress Disorder, goes through a series of "reactions to the events that may be categorized into different phases."

First, in the impact phase, survivors react to the "impact of a disaster," and try to "protect their own lives and the lives of others." Some, like Brent, after the event, might feel "people may judge their actions during the disaster as not having fulfilled their own or others' expectations of themselves." Others may "respond in a way that is disorganized and stunned." The National Center for PTSD cites some identified stressors that might occur during the impact phase: threat to life and encounter with death, feelings of helplessness and powerlessness, loss, dislocation, feeling responsible, inescapable horror and human malevolence.

Second, is the immediate post-disaster phase, also called recoil and rescue. During this phase, "there is recoil from the impact and the initial rescue activities commence." Although the rescue phase may delay some of the emotional reactions, and emotional reactions are highly subjective, most people during this phase exhibit certain emotional reactions which the National Center for PTSD identify as including: numbness, denial or shock, flashbacks and nightmares, grief reactions to loss, anger, despair, sadness and hopelessness. Also, the ebullience of having been rescued or having survived the disaster is hard to process and accept while the "destruction the disaster has wrought" is still fresh.

The last phase identified by the National Center for PTSD is the recovery phase, which is "a prolonged period of adjustment or return to equilibrium that the community and individuals must go through." The intensity and duration of this phase is determined by the level of destruction created by the disaster. In the wake of rescue and extensive media coverage, often "other needs emerge that are both existential and psychological" for the individual who experienced the disaster. Emotional reactions may be repressed by the individual, and can also manifest as physical maladies such as, "sleep disturbance, indigestion, and fatigue, or they may present as social effects such as relationship or work difficulties."

Brent Doonan dealt with a host of post-traumatic stress disorder symptoms including: denial, nightmares, panic attacks and guilt. Especially after returning to All-Tech, with the tragedy still quite fresh, the first couple of weeks were the most difficult. For Brent, being in the office elicited feelings of acute anxiety as he connected the place with the events of July 29.

As is common in people who suffer from PTSD, some physical symptoms are characterized by digestive maladies, such as nausea, vomiting and upset stomach. Brent vomited every morning upon entering the scene of his trauma and took scores of antacids to calm his nervous stomach throughout the day. He was startled by quick movements, even if they were non-threatening, as is characteristic of PTSD, and the National Center for PTSD reports, "psycho-physiological alterations associated with PTSD include hyper arousal of the sympathetic nervous system, increased sensitivity of the startle reflex, and sleep abnormalities." In *Healing Journeys: How Trauma Survivors Learn to Live*, Linda Daniels states that, "Along with memorabilia, trauma sites, crime scenes, cemeteries and other settings associated with the ordeals often evoke strong feelings and memories. For those who are going through a period of denial, these settings may bring them face to face with acknowledgement that the event really happened. For others, such sights are emotional triggers and may set off spasm or grief." For Brent Doonan, the crime scene was his office. The place that had once been a source of excitement and productivity became a location associated with death and pain. Brent's hypersensitivity after the trauma could have been particularly acute because he had to confront the reality of what happened every day, just by going to work.

However, Brent Doonan was not the only survivor of the events of July 29 to experience Post-Traumatic Stress Disorder. Fred Herder had been shot in the back at All-Tech during Barton's rampage in 1999. Barton's bullet had been too close to his spine to have been removed. Approximately two and half years later, Herder took his own life. Fred Herder had experienced a traumatic event and his suicide can be connected with PTSD. According to the National Center for PTSD, "a large body of research indicates that there is a correlation between PTSD and suicide....some studies suggest suicide risk is higher due to the symptoms of PTSD...in contrast, other researchers have found that conditions that co-occur with PTSD, such as depression, may be more predictive of suicide." Dr. Linda Daniels, in *Healing Journeys*, devotes an entire chapter to trauma and suicide, in which she states, "Traumatic events, with their varying intensities of cognitive, behavioral and emotional aftereffects, may unfortunately lead some survivors to seriously contemplate and plan suicide." Arguably enough the events that Fred Herder experienced on July 29 could have impacted him in ways that led to a later development of PTSD, which can be extremely detrimental to a person's mental and physical health when left unrecognized and untreated.

Certain therapeutic approaches commonly used to treat PTSD, as described by the National Center for PTSD include, cognitive-behavioral therapy, medication, psychotherapy and group treatment. In the case of the victims of Mark Barton's rampage, those who returned to day trading and those who did not were forced to some-how come to terms with the experience. At All-Tech, those who had returned to the office, after the disaster, went through group therapy. They formed a circle and talked with crisis counselors who had been brought in to lead the talks in order to facilitate the healing process.

The discussions centered on the tragic and surreal events of July 29, 1999, in addition to individual stories of narrow escape, gruesome killing and chaos.

On September 26, 1999, in "Moving Beyond July 29," the *Atlanta Journal-Constitution* reported that it took "sixteen days to hold all the funerals for the nine people who died in Mark Barton's July 29 shooting spree." Nonetheless, the emotional and physical aftermath of Barton's rampage would last beyond sixteen days and would unfold over time for both his victims who survived and the families of those who did not.

"Dealing with trauma is not a time-limited endeavor, but an ongoing process," Dr. Daniels states in *Healing Journeys*. This would hold true for Brent Doonan and the other survivors as the stressors of the trauma revisited them as they fought to go on with their lives.

In recent years the deepening crisis of workplace violence has spread to many professional areas and places of employment, including post offices, hospitals and court houses. Such explosive outbreaks have led health professionals, the media and the public to speculate as to the underlying causes.

According to the United States Department of Justice, in a report released by the Bureau of Justice Statistics, *Violence in the Workplace*, "Workplace violence accounted for eighteen percent of all violent crime during the seven year period...about 900 work-related homicides occurred annually" with "more than eighty percent of all workplace homicides...committed with a firearm."

In addition to these startling statistics, the evidence in this report shows a new profile of a perpetrator at large, a white middle-aged male armed with ammo, shooting up his co-workers; the Mark Bartons of the world.

Statistics illustrate that males made up "more than four-fifths of all workplace crime," and in terms of race, "whites made up eighty-four percent of the population and were the offenders in fifty-five percent of all workplace victimizations." Furthermore, in the seven-year span concerned in the survey, "persons age thirty or older, when compared to younger persons, were perceived to have committed the highest percentage (forty-three percent) of crimes occurring at work." The weapon of choice for workplace perpetrators was some kind of firearm, as "shooting accounted for more than eighty percent of all workplace homicides." In terms of the time frame when workplace violence occurred most frequently, "more workplace crimes occurred between noon and six p.m. than in any other six-hour period of the day." Lastly, workplace homicides were further reported to be largely committed by current or former colleagues or associates as, "coworkers or former co-workers committed a higher percentage of homicide in the workplace when compared to customers or clients (seven percent versus four percent of all workplace homicides, respectively)."

These demographics shocked the steady ground upon which most thought their places of employment rested. Could the events of July 29, 1999 in Atlanta foretell of a new, dangerous world, where one has to assume a defensive and questioning stance as to which of his or her co-workers might bear guns and ammo instead of bringing briefcases and reports? Barton's murderous rampage has been repeated at other times in workplace violence history. Should people start wearing bulletproof vests to work under their business suits or uniforms?

"Homicide is the third-leading cause of fatal occupational injury in the United States...there were six hundred and thirty-nine workplace homicides in 2001 in the United States, out of a total of eight thousand, seven hundred and eighty-six fatal work injuries," reported the Bureau of Labor Statistics Census of fatal Occupational

Injuries.

In the last few years we have seen workplace violence spill over into areas we once thought were stable examples of democracy at work.

On February 5, 2001 William Baker carried a golf bag loaded with guns into the Navistar engine plant in Melrose Park, Illinois. Baker had been fired from his job at the Navistar plant. However, Baker returned for revenge, shooting and killing four employees and wounding four others. After his murderous rampage, William Baker fatally shot himself.

So far, 2003 was one of the deadliest years in the past decade for workplace violence. On July 8, at the Lockheed Martin plant near Meridian, Mississippi, an employee armed with a semiautomatic rifle and a shotgun shot randomly at workers, killing six and injuring eight. The gunman, Doug Williams, an assembler at the plant, then shot and killed himself. On July 23, at a Century Twenty-One real estate office in San Antonio, Texas, an employee, armed with a .357 magnum, shot to death two co-workers and critically injured one, before he intentionally drove his car into a concrete barrier, killing himself. On August 27, a laid-off employee entered Windy City Core Supply, Inc. in Chicago, Illinois, armed with a Walther PPK.380 semi-automatic pistol and shot six people to death. The perpetrator was then shot and killed by the police. These tragic incidents are included among too many other shooting sprees in the workplace in 2003.

In addition to the industries, companies and businesses which witnessed shooting rampages of their employees, the United States Justice System also became a victim of workplace violence.

On Friday, March 11, 2005, Brian Nicholas, brought up on charges of the rape and captivity of his girlfriend, was scheduled to appear at the Fulton County Courthouse in downtown Atlanta.

Before entering the courtroom, Nicholas attacked the deputy sheriff, overpowered her and took her gun and then turned the gun on the courtroom. He killed the judge and the clerk while holding the rest of the court room hostage before he managed to escape, killing another deputy sheriff on his way out of the courthouse, after having wounded several others throughout the murderous rampage. After a strange fugitive encounter in which he held a woman hostage in her apartment, Nicholas eventually gave himself up to authorities.

Has violence in the workplace become an all-too-familiar scenario across America? And are the perpetrators of these workplace shootings, like Mark Barton, symbolic of a new type of psychopath, the disturbed employee? As these questions continually turn up with each new incident of brutal shootings in the workplace, the families of those left dead and those who have been injured struggle with the emotional and physical pain that remains.

epilogue

During Brent's struggle to recover his will to live positively, he has spent much time searching for answers as to what it was that made Mark Barton commit such atrocities: killing his first wife and mother-in-law (in all likelihood), killing his second wife and his two children, his own flesh and blood and then going on a rampage murdering another nine innocent people.

The notes and other clues Barton left behind seemed to Brent to indicate Barton felt he'd become a failure. At first, he grew angry, then deeply depressed and ultimately very afraid, perhaps paranoid, suffering a psychotic breakdown. Perhaps, as some have said, he heard the voices of demons or perhaps the demon was him. Whatever it was, Barton himself had reached the point of hopelessness. He never learned that regardless of what life has in store for each of us, there is always hope.

Unfortunately for Mark Barton and tragically for others he victimized, he blamed his failures and loss of hope on everyone but
himself. He even made references as to how his father caused his distorted state of mind, claiming, "The fears of the father are transferred
to the son." Brent felt, ultimately, it could be theorized that Barton
killed his family, friends and strangers, because they were symbols to
him of his inadequacies.

All of these questions and theories drove Brent Doonan in his
search for answers. He hadn't known about Barton's first wife until
his research led him to uncover the threads of that tragedy. In the
aftermath of the heartbreaking calamity that had befallen him and
many others, he was desperate to find the answers. For months, he
combed through hundreds of newspaper and magazine articles
searching for clues. He contacted Barton's mother, an old high
school friend of Barton's, acquaintances and others who had known
the man.

Then one day Brent's phone rang. It was Barton's first wife
Debra Spivey's father. He related how his daughter had met Barton
and how he had liked him at first, but how his sentiments quickly
changed, the more he knew of the man. However evil Mark was,
though Debra's father said he now wanted to close the entire tragic
event from his mind and focus solely on the good things he remembered about his daughter. Brent understood.

Brent's investigation of the underlying reasons for Mark
Barton's catastrophic rage took Brent down many roads. He did not
get all the answers he was looking for relative to Barton's true motivation. However, Brent did change his view of his own life dramatically and did come to feel he had insight into why he was spared
twice — so far.

On that hot summer day in July 1999, I came face to face with a psychopathic killer, a man who I thought was my friend up until the second he pulled out two handguns and opened fire. In a fraction of a second I went from being a young, successful entrepreneur in control of my world to a wounded person who lay bleeding on a conference room floor, clinging to life.

In that instant my world came crashing down.

I no longer cared about the new condominium I was going to buy or the sport utility vehicle and Harley Davidson motorcycle that I already owned. As I looked down the barrels of the two deadly pistols, I knew every possession that I owned suddenly meant nothing.

My life meant everything.

After being shot, I found myself engaged in the hardest battle of my life. I struggled as I have never struggled; I fought as I have never fought. Only my prayers and the will to live carried me through that difficult time. I believe it was a combination of the two. Though perhaps it was a miracle.

As time has passed since that dreadful day, I have often been asked what it is like to be shot, how the bullets felt as they tore through my body, and what went through my mind as I lay dying on that conference room floor surrounded by strangers.

It was one of my goals to answer some of these questions in this book as accurately as possible. More important than trying to answer what it was like to get shot, however, is replying to the questions of how I have coped with moving beyond that day, how I now view life and how mine has changed.

As a result of that day I have aged both in years and in knowledge. At times, I have tried to completely erase July 29, 1999 from my memory. If only I could forget about it altogether, I reasoned, I would never have to relive that terrifying event. My clients would return and my business would remain open. For the rest of time the evidence of or history of the man I knew as Mark Barton would remain hidden in the annals of a police report, collecting dust in an abandoned warehouse.

The truth is, I will never forget that day. If I could, I would not want to. To forget that day is to forget all the events that led up to it and all the good things that have since followed.

In the process of opening and operating the brokerage firm, I learned a lot about people and a great deal about running a business. I enjoyed working and growing with Scott and I cherish the time I spent with Kathy and Meredith, however short. All told, I loved what I was doing and in the end, my regrets are few.

I am left with many fond memories, most of which outweigh the savage ones created by Mark Barton. I was left to pick up the pieces and move on with my life, to learn from the tragic event which Mark Barton caused while trying to focus on the positives which have come as a result. Today I have realized all one can do is live, live for the days that are good and try to react positively to those that are not.

I now realize that every person has his or her problems, every family, their issues. I understand that everyone will go through difficult times in their lives, for difficulties are a part of life itself. It is how we deal with these difficulties that ultimately sets each of us apart. And I am still learning the ways to do this.

In working through the tragedy, I cannot ignore that my life has changed. Each day when I step out of the shower or when I take off my shirt, I think of Mark Barton. I notice the scars, which remain on both my arms, across my abdomen and along my side. I see the bullet holes and the chest tube wounds, all of which form a grim reminder of my encounter with death and the ways that it will forever change my life. At these times, I am also reminded of how I should live; actually, how we should all live.

The scars that Mark Barton and others like him leave behind on victims and on society are truly incalculable. Depressive reminders of these crazed persons can eat away at one's soul. They can be open wounds, painful reminders of events in the past. They can also be small scars, subtle reminders of the day when one faced absolute devastation and won. The choice is yours.

In essence, almost everyone in his or her lifetime will be forced to choose between being a victim or a survivor. The survivor comes to realize that when life comes crashing down, as it sometimes will, we must gather the strength we have left to rebuild the broken parts.

I chose to be a survivor. To me, it is the only way to live, the only way to move beyond life's difficulties.

Nevertheless I grapple with why I lived while others died. I used to ask myself that question every day. Luck? God's choice? A will to live? Maybe all three. I've learned through my personal experience and from what I see in the world around me that no matter what life hands you, you have to love the possibilities for civility regardless of how harsh the circumstances, otherwise you exist in either a state of numbness or fury. There is no middle ground.

We all live in a time of great potential harm and we must learn to acquire the graces that the love of others affords us. This is what allows us to live a life of anticipation as opposed to one of deprivation. My wife, my son, my family and my friends encourage an otherwise restless soul to be at peace. I never forget to hug those I love every day, because I can never be sure that they will be with me tomorrow, or that I will be with them.

There is an intersection where character and hope blend, but it can only be seen from a higher altitude; I believe, through a will to live. The everyday isn't perfect. It confines some and leads others astray. What I've learned is that the weight of everyday life is a burden I want to carry. Life is like a good story broken into chapters. The tragic chapter in my life was just that, a part of the whole. It has its place in my overall story, but only a place; it isn't "the" story of Brent Doonan. For in that, I hope many more chapters are to follow.

I've also learned that the will to live isn't something you learn; we all have it in varying degrees. It's hardwired into our being. Today, I strive not to worry myself with the small stuff. I have learned that when your life is nearly taken away, you need to step back and decide what is really important. In the grand scheme of things, the small stuff will soon be forgotten. It is on the life-changing events that we should dwell.

I take the time to do things that make me happy, because once a day is gone, it's gone forever. I enjoy spending time with my son, learning to see the world through the eyes of a two-year-old, and listening to the pure untainted laughter of a child brings me great joy. I love spending quality time with my wife, riding my motorcycle and hanging out with friends.

I count my blessings each day for I know that tomorrow can all be swept away. I realize that every day I live on this earth is a gift from God; that each day lived is a blessing.

And I realize that nobody is perfect. No matter how hard we try, we all make mistakes. To me, therein lies the secret of life. To face the challenges that come our way, to react the best we can and to realize that there are times when we will fail. Though, it is in failing that we often learn the most.

When I reflect on what happened that catastrophic day in Atlanta, I used to ask myself who really failed. Was it the day trading firms or the building managers, the security company or the property owners? All were sued immediately following the shooting.

Now I have come to realize, in one way or another, all of us were victims of a senseless tragedy. However, there was only one person who failed himself, his loved ones and his fellow human beings. He failed in two marriages and in two brokerage firms. He failed when he most likely snuffed out the lives of his first wife and mother-in-law in 1993, though he was never arrested for the crimes. He failed when he took the life of his second wife and when he took the lives of his two children. Mark Barton failed when he wounded and killed innocent people who had done nothing to him and he even failed by taking his own life.

But society failed too. Each time we let a child grow up to be an outcast of society and each time we do not find psychological help for those who need it, we fail. I firmly believe that it is the responsibility of each of us to make a difference in the world. Maybe it is in the way we raise our children.

Perhaps it is in the way we treat others. Either way, each of us bears the responsibility of preventing the next Mark Barton.

It has been six short years since I came face to face with a deranged gunman and it has taken me equally long to forgive him for carrying out this senseless tragedy. Today I am grateful for God's blessing. I look towards tomorrow in the hopes of making a difference in the world. And I reflect on the past as a reminder that when life breaks we must piece it back together and carry on.

In the final analysis, we all have our tragedies. Mine wasn't unique, though I certainly felt that way at the time. The defining moment for all of us is how we deal with adversity.

The choice, as with all things in life, is ours; to be a victim or to become a survivor. I chose to focus on life, to put aside the anger and frustration and to replace them with hope, forgiveness and thanksgiving. This is what gets me through, along with my prayers.

I now realize that before all of this happened to me, I was trying to control everything in my life. I wanted everything to be perfect and orderly. I did not like resistance. I was headstrong, high-strung, controlling and overpowering. Ultimately I was selfish. Then, shortly after the tragic day Mark Barton snapped, I received the Serenity Prayer as a gift. I reflect on it each morning. Now, I start every day with the same words:

"God grant me the serenity to accept the things I cannot change, courage to change the things I can, and the wisdom to know the difference."

I say it to myself as I dress in the morning and I say it for each of you.

Just for today, I will be happy.

Just for today, I will adjust myself to what is. I will take life as it comes and fit myself to it.

Just for today, I will exercise my soul in three ways: I will do somebody a good turn and not be found out and I will do at least two things I don't want to do.

Just for today, I will be agreeable. I will look as well as I can, dress becomingly, talk softly, act courteously, criticize no one and not find fault.

Just for today I will be unafraid. Especially, I will not be afraid to enjoy what is beautiful and to believe that as I give to the world, the world will give to me. We are simply part of nature anyway. Nature is the sum of creation. From the Big Bang to the whole shebang. It's making snow forts, it's spring moving north at about thirteen miles a day, emotions both savage and blessed, the harvest moon, fat rainbows, the courtship tunes of birds, the sparkle in the eye of a person you love, a new leaf struggling to move the earth skyward in your garden, a shaft of bright warm summer light spilling over my shoulder as I read a good book, a call out of the blue from someone I love, my dogs licking my cheeks, my son giving dad a big hug.

In the end, all we can ask for is a little peace of mind, a measure of fulfillment, the ability to love hard and to be loved; to work hard but also to play hard. Happiness is no longer my only goal. I know that those moments come at random intervals. I've also noticed they seem to happen more often when I'm helping or loving someone and not dwelling on my problems or my tragedies.

This morning, as I look into the mirror, tighten my tie a little, check to see if I caught all the spots on my face while shaving, I pause and walk back into the bedroom to gaze at my beautiful wife Sarah and my baby son. I smile and say to myself, "Thank you God for one more bountiful day." And I start along my new path through life; I walk it one step at a time, one day at a time.

If you liked *Murder at the Office,*
then you'll also like these New Horizon Press,
Real People/Incredible Stories, True Crime Releases:

Deadly Masquerade
A True Story of Illicit Passion, Buried Secrets and Murder
by
Donita Woodruff

Hungering for a second chance and the bustle of the big city, Donita, a young single mother, decides to move her family from a small town back home to Los Angeles. Hurting from previous romantic relationships, Donita is hesitant to start anything new until she meets academy award nominee David Allen—successful, handsome and charming. The two are swept up in a whirl-wind romance. Life seems too good to be true, but even wedding bells can't hide her new husband's secrets. Suddenly, Donita and her children are caught in a world of vicious lies and double lives, where nothing is as it appears.

Mysterious phone calls, a questionable ex-lover and an unsolved murder all begin to unravel in Donita Woodruff's true life account, *Deadly Masquerade.* When the perfect man reveals a sordid double life, Donita has one choice—to take matters into her own hands. Risking it all, she investigates the evidence of a twenty-year-old homicide, only to discover a dangerous game of cover-up that leads right to her front door. Trusting no one in this rogues game', she must hide what she knows to bring the killer to justice and protect her children.

Deadly Masquerade is a suspenseful page-turner full of skeleton-in-the-closet secrets and deadly liaisons, with a twist so bizarre and shocking, it could only be true!

Donita Woodruff has been interviewed extensively by both print, including the Associated Press and the *National Enquirer,* and television-ABC, *NBC, The Montel Williams Show, CNN World News*-media for her role in the capture of fugitive killer Freddie Turner. Her true life tale of survival and triumph led her to write her first book, *Deadly Masquerade.* She lives in California with her two children.

A New Horizon Press True Crime Release:
0-88282-266-7 $24.95 HC

Real People/Incredible Stories

Faces of Evil
Kidnappers, Murderers, Rapists and the Forensic Artist Who Puts Them Behind Bars
by Lois Gibson and Deanie Francis Mills

Every day, Lois Gibson is able to put power, control and a sense of justice back into the hands of victims of violent crime, heinous rapes, kidnappings and murders. Gibson, herself the victim of a violent rape, uses her skills to coax from the memories of victims the most intimate details possible and with the stroke of a pencil, reconstructs the faces of their tormentors. These eerily accurate portraits have been directly responsible for the capture of over 700 vicious criminals for which her skills are noted in the *Guinness Book of Records*.

Faces of Evil is Gibson's riveting story of how she became the world's most successful forensic artist, interwoven with her thirteen most suspense-filled cases. Gisbon takes you with her inside the gritty atmosphere of forensics, putting you behind the scenes of terrifying enigma after enigma and into the victims' mind set as they seek vindication. Follow the nine-year-old girl who sees and helps catch her mother's killer, the pregnant blind woman who identifies and aids in the capture of her rapist and the hero cop whose deathbed description leads police to his killer.

This is a fascinating true crime book like no other; mixing chilling crime scenes with the inspiring story of one woman's passion for justice.

Lois Gibson is a twenty-two-year veteran forensic artist with the Houston, Texas police department. Recently profiled in *People Magazine*, Oprah Winfrey's *"O"* magazine, *Reader's Digest, Dateline NBC* and *Unsolved Mysteries*, she regularly appears on *America's Most Wanted* and is also the holder of the Guinness World Record Certificate in Forensic Art. Gibson has a B.A. in Fine Arts from the University of Texas at Austin and is a Professor at Northwestern University as well as being affiliated with the FBI and U.S. Marshall's Service. She resides in Houston, Texas with her family.

Deanie Francis Mills is a widely published writer whose work appears in *Redbook, Good Housekeeping* and *Parent* and is the author of *Torch* (Penguin Putnam) *Tightrope* (Dutton Signet), *Losers Weepers* (Putnam Berkley) and *Ordeal* (Dutton) She resides in Hermleigh.Texas with her family.

A New Horizon Press True Crime Release:
0-88282-258-6 $24.95

Real People/Incredible Stories

Trail of Blood
A Father, a Son and a Tell-tale Crime Scene Investigation
by Wanda Evans in Collaboration with James Dunn

When Jim Dunn got the heart-stopping call every parent dreads: 'Your son has disappeared," on a Sunday night in 1991 and then saw his son's blood splattered apartment, it set into motion a six-year nightmarish odyssey of desperate searches. Ahead were moments of frantic hope, growing despair and finally acceptance that Scott was dead, despite the fact that his body was not found.

As Dunn worked with Lubbock, Texas police investigators and followed his own leads, mounting evidence pointed to Scott's live-in girlfriend and her new lover. However, Dunn learned there was a seemingly insurmountable problem to getting justice for his son: Texas law insists on a body before prosecuting anyone for murder and Scott's body was nowhere to be found.

Frustrated, Dunn turned to members of the little-known Vidocq Society, highly experienced criminologists and forensic experts who crack the coldest "unsolvable" or "unprovable" cases around the world. Vidocq member Dr. Richard Walter, *a* forensic *pathologist and criminal* profiler, consulted *Scotland* Yard, studied DNA evidence and blood spatter patterns and then pointed out who he deduced had killed Scott and why. The D.A. agreed, but said his hands were tied: Scott's body still had not been found. However, when Walter set forth a unique theory based on the fact that there was enough of Scott's blood in the room to prove murder, the DA brought the case before the grand jury. Six years after his disappearance, Scott's girlfriend Leisha Hamilton and Tim Smith, a love-smitten neighbor, were tried and convicted of Scott's murder.

"A Brilliant and utterly gripping mix of crime-scene investigation and courtroom drama. As good as CSI gets, as far as actual forensics, combined with a family tragedy that awakens compassion for the surviving victims." Connie Fletcher, *Booklist,* March 1, 2005

Wanda Evans, a noted journalist, writer and speaker, has been published in many venues, including *Reader's Digest, Good Housekeeping* and *Southern Living.* A former columnist for the Lubbock Avalanche-Journal, she lives in Lubbock, Texas where she is working on two political biographies.

James Dunn, a former sales and marketing professional and CEO of the software company Comprehensive Marketing, is an active member of the Vidocq Society and Parents of Murdered Children. He is a financial planner, lives in St. Marys, GA, with his wife and continues to hope for the day he can bury his son.

A New Horizon Press True Crime Release:
0-882822-261-6 $24.95

Real People/Incredible Stories

Missing:
The Oregon City Girls
by Linda O'Neal, Philip Tennyson and Rick Watson

The *Oregon City Girls* are missing and time is running out before another little girl disappears...

Ashley Pond was a normal twelve year old until January 9, 2002. Ashley never made it to school that day and never returned home.

Suddenly, a close-knit community is ripped apart by tragedy and gripped with fear. Police and federal agents are tossed into a dizzying search for the missing girl, but with no clues and no witnesses they fear the worst. Nearly two months later, Ashley's friend and classmate Miranda Gaddis also goes missing, taken from the same school bus stop. The horrifying development has the town wondering if a serial kidnapper lurks in their midst. Law officials know a predator is out there and more children are in danger.

When local police and federal agents fail to find the girls, a frustrated Pond family turns to one of their own: Linda O'Neal. O'Neal, step-grand-mother to Ashley and a Private Investigator, is sent on a wild chase after clues and suspects. But after stake-outs and fact-finding, her hunches all lead to one culprit—a suspect police aren't looking at. Now, O'Neal must do whatever it takes to bring the perpetrator to justice and find the truth behind two missing girls.

"A gripping tale."   The Portland Tribune

Linda O'Neal is the step-grandmother of Ashley Pond and was the lead pri-vate investigator during the case. She has taught several courses on criminal and legal procedure at The College of Legal Arts.

Philip Tennyson is a documentary filmmaker and author. He has written two previous books, *Getting Screwed* and *Living to 110*. O'Neal and Tennyson are married and live in the Portland, Oregon area.

Rick Watson has worked in law enforcement for a number of years and is the author of several screenplays. He now lives in the state of Washington.

A New Horizon Press True Crime Release:
0-88282-268-3 $23.95

Real People/Incredible Stories